Uncharted Journey

GLOBAL POLICY BOOKS
FROM THE CARNEGIE ENDOWMENT

Critical Mission: Essays on Democracy Promotion
Thomas Carothers

Democracy Challenged: The Rise of Semi-Authoritarianism
Marina Ottaway

Aiding Democracy Abroad: The Learning Curve
Thomas Carothers

**Open Networks, Closed Regimes: The Impact of the Internet
on Authoritarian Rule**
Shanthi Kalathil and Taylor C. Boas

The Third Force: The Rise of Transnational Civil Society
Ann M. Florini, Editor

Funding Virtue: Civil Society Aid and Democracy Promotion
Marina Ottaway and Thomas Carothers, Editors

Assessing Democracy Assistance: The Case of Romania
Thomas Carothers

To read excerpts and to find more information on these and other publications
from the Carnegie Endowment, visit **www.CarnegieEndowment.org/pubs**.

Uncharted Journey

Promoting Democracy in the Middle East

Thomas Carothers
Marina Ottaway
Editors

CARNEGIE ENDOWMENT FOR INTERNATIONAL PEACE
Washington, D.C.

Carnegie Endowment for International Peace
1779 Massachusetts Avenue, N.W., Washington, D.C. 20036
202-483-7600, Fax 202-483-1840
www.CarnegieEndowment.org

The Carnegie Endowment for International Peace normally does not take institutional positions on public policy issues; the views and recommendations presented in this publication do not necessarily represent the views of the Carnegie Endowment, its officers, staff, or trustees.

To order, contact Carnegie's distributor:
The Brookings Institution Press
Department 029, Washington, D.C. 20042-0029, USA
1-800-275-1447 or 1-202-797-6258
Fax 202-797-2960, Email bibooks@brook.edu

Composition by Stephen McDougal
Printed by United Book Press

Library of Congress Cataloging-in-Publication data
Uncharted journey : promoting democracy in the Middle East / Thomas Carothers and Marina Ottaway, editors.
    p. cm.
"Bibliography on democracy and democracy promotion in the Middle East": p.
    Includes bibliographical references and index.
    ISBN 0-87003-212-7 (hardcover) — ISBN 0-87003-211-9 (pbk.)
    1. Democracy—Middle East. I. Carothers, Thomas, 1956- II. Ottaway, Marina.

JQ1758.A91U53 2005
320.956--dc22   2004024551

10 09 08 07 06 05   1 2 3 4 5   1st Printing 2005

Contents

Foreword

ONE OF AMERICA'S GREAT STRENGTHS is its willingness to take on great challenges, often with boldness and daring. Tugging at the coattails of this strength, however, is a recurrent weakness—as America steps forward into vast new undertakings it sometimes does so without adequate preparation, assuming that its strength and vigor will allow it to find, or even to improvise, the needed answers along the way. Of all the tectonic shifts in U.S. foreign policy emerging from the aftermath of 9/11, none is more potentially transformative than the widespread conviction in the U.S. policy community that America must reverse its longtime support for friendly tyrants in the Middle East and push hard for a democratic transformation of that troubled region. Yet it is not at all clear that the vastness of this new ambition is matched by a commensurate understanding of how to proceed in a region that has never known democracy and in which anti-American sentiments are at a record high.

Not long after 9/11, anticipating this surge of U.S. interest in Middle East democracy, the Carnegie Endowment's Democracy and Rule of Law Project, led by Thomas Carothers and Marina Ottaway, created the Middle East Political Reform Initiative to seek answers to two fundamental questions: How is positive political change in the Middle East most likely to occur, and what can the United States and other interested external actors do to support it? This book, the first ever published on the challenge of promoting democracy in the Middle East, is one of the fruits of that effort. As these pages make clear, the difficulties are daunting. The region's entrenched authoritarian regimes are expert in the art of permitting partial reforms that win accolades abroad but create no real democratization at home. Democratic forces are weak, and political Islamists, who are enjoying an oppositional upsurge, have at best an uncertain commitment to democratic values. The United States is constrained in its search for a prodemocratic role—not only by the fervent anti-Americanism roiling the region but by the stubborn fact that the United States still has significant economic and security interests that impel close cooperation with many of the incumbent, nondemocratic regimes.

Yet *Uncharted Journey* is far from a counsel of despair. Drawing on the various authors' invaluable combination of comparative insights from other regions and deep expertise on Arab politics, the chapters herein point to productive approaches open to American and European actors willing to get involved for the long term, to take seriously the internal regional dynamics at play, and to adjust their expectations to a realistic level. No magic bullets are on offer, just the real stuff of political change, from building constituencies for democratic reform to exerting pressure on key levers of change.

The United States, as well as Europe, will be deeply engaged for many years to come in the struggle to help create a better political future for this critical region. For this daunting journey there is no better guide than this book. It is my sincere pleasure that the Carnegie Endowment is able to make it available at this crucial juncture.

Jessica T. Mathews
President
Carnegie Endowment for International Peace

Introduction

1

The New Democracy Imperative

Thomas Carothers and Marina Ottaway

THE ISSUE OF DEMOCRACY in the Middle East has erupted in Western policy circles. U.S. officials, policy experts, and pundits, very few of whom gave the subject more than a passing thought in decades past, now heatedly and ceaselessly debate how democratic political change might occur in the region and whether the United States can help bring about such change. Similarly, in many European capitals the Middle East's potential democratic evolution is the subject of a rapidly growing number of meetings, conferences, and discussions in both governmental and nongovernmental circles.

This new Western preoccupation with democracy in the Middle East has a clear source. The terrorist attacks against New York and Washington on September 11, 2001, threw into question a long-standing pillar of Western policy thinking in the region—the belief that the political stability offered by friendly Arab authoritarian regimes is a linchpin of Western security interests. In the process of post–September 11 review and reflection, many people in the U.S. and European policy communities reversed their previous outlook and now see the lack of democracy in the Middle East as one of the main causes of the rise of violent, anti-Western Islamic radicalism, and as such, a major security problem. And it follows directly from this conclusion that attempting to promote political reform and democratization in the region should be a policy priority—one of the key methods for eliminating the "roots of terrorism." The new democracy imperative for the Middle East, at least on the part of Western policy makers, is thus driven not by a trend toward reform in the region, but by the West's own security concerns.

To date the U.S. government's efforts to operationalize this newfound policy imperative have been extraordinarily controversial, above all because of the invasion of Iraq. Some of President George W. Bush's key foreign policy advisors believed that ousting Saddam Hussein would not only remove a leader they viewed as a grave threat to regional and indeed global security, but as important, it would also allow the establishment of a democratic government in the heart of the Arab world—a government that would serve as a powerfully positive model to other countries of the region, possibly even creating a regional wave of democracy.

In practice the Iraq intervention has not yet had clearcut positive results on the democracy front, and the prospects for a stable, well-functioning democracy in Iraq remain extremely uncertain. Iraq no longer suffers under Saddam Hussein's despotic rule, but the post-invasion period has been much more difficult than anticipated. There is as much discussion today of whether the unity of Iraq as a nation-state can be maintained as there is of the possibility that it will make a transition to democracy. Moreover, the invasion has inflamed Arab sentiments against the United States, strengthening the hand of Islamic radicals and complicating the life of pro-Western Arab democrats.

Yet the Iraq intervention by no means constitutes the sum total of the new U.S. push for democracy in the Middle East. In the last three years, the U.S government has also initiated a broader, less aggressive range of measures to stimulate and support positive political change throughout the region. U.S. officials have been trying to craft an evolving mix of diplomatic carrots and sticks to encourage friendly and unfriendly regimes to carry out political reforms. The Middle East Partnership Initiative (MEPI) offers support for political, economic, and educational reforms and for improved women's rights in the region. The G-8 "Partnership for Progress and a Common Future" with the countries of the broader Middle East and North Africa (also known as the Broader Middle East and North Africa Initiative) provides a larger diplomatic framework for MEPI and various other related initiatives. The Bush administration has proposed widening free trade between Arab countries and has concluded free trade agreements with Bahrain and Morocco.

For those in the U.S. policy community who were sympathetic to the invasion of Iraq, these sorts of measures are a complement to the military-based regime-change side of the policy; they are the soft side of the new prodemocracy coin. Those who were not sympathetic to the invasion in Iraq, both within the government and in the broader policy community, hope that such measures can develop and cohere into an alternative policy line, a bipartisan, long-term response to the imperative for prodemocratic change in the Middle East. Unfortunately, many Arab policy experts and commentators, often following the lead of their governments, have treated the softer measures as an intrinsic part of the larger, military-oriented policy that they reject outright. They have thus often been hostile to measures that on their own might have commanded their support. Continued or even intensified Arab hostility to the U.S. approach to the Palestinian–Israeli conflict has only fueled that tendency.

Despite the keenly felt urgency of the prodemocracy policy imperative, this broader set of diplomatic and aid measures has gotten under way slowly. It was only in 2003 that U.S. democracy aid programs in the region really began multiplying. It was only in 2004 that senior U.S. officials began to deliver prodemocratic diplomatic messages privately and publicly to Arab counterparts on a somewhat consistent basis. The softer, longer-term side of the U.S. push for democracy in the Middle East is, at best, a work in progress. Its slow advance is in part due to the unfamiliar territory to be traversed and uncertainty about how to proceed. But it is also due to the fact that, as urgent and serious as the prodemocracy imperative appears to many in the U.S. policy community, the stubborn reality remains that the United States has other important security-related and economic interests, such as cooperation on antiterrorism enforcement actions and ensuring secure access to oil. Such interests impel it to maintain close ties with many of the authoritarian regimes in the Middle East and to be wary of the possibility of rapid or unpredictable political change. Given the strength and persistence of these other interests, it is not clear whether the new prodemocracy impulse will result in a fundamental change of the long-standing U.S. support for authoritarian and semiauthoritarian friends in the region or simply end up as an attractive wrapping around a largely unchanged core.

European governments and policy communities are enmeshed in similar policy debates and dilemmas. They feel the same imperative regarding the need to promote political reform in the Middle East, although they are somewhat less inclined than their U.S. counterparts to see a direct causal link between a possible advance of democracy in the Arab world and a decline in radical Islamist terrorism. Moreover, Europe has already been engaged for approximately a decade with much of the region in a broad initiative to stimulate both political and economic reform through the Euro-Mediterranean Partnership (commonly known as the Barcelona Process).

Most European governments have been averse to the military-based regime-change side of the Bush administration's democracy project for the region. Even most of those that decided to participate in the Iraq intervention did so largely on the basis of the security rationale for the action, not the democracy side of it. Their efforts to support Middle East political reform are concentrated on the diplomatic and aid sides of the policy spectrum and emphasize the idea of positive sum partnerships between Arab and European governments. Generally speaking, the northern states of Europe, particularly the Nordic countries, Germany, and Great Britain, are giving somewhat more emphasis to the need for democratic political change in the region, whereas France, Italy, Spain, and the other southern states are more concerned with promoting economic growth that might reduce the flow of immigrants from the region. Like the United States, many European countries have multiple interests and agendas in the Middle East, and although democracy is one of them it has to compete with others. And some of these others, such as the need for a steady supply of Middle East oil, point strongly to the value of close cooperation with some of the nondemocratic regimes of the region.

Nature of the Challenge

Highlighting the vital Western security interests tied to the political future of the Middle East, some policy makers and commentators compare the challenge of promoting Arab democracy with the post–Cold War task of helping advance democracy in the former communist world. Despite what may seem to some the comparable magnitude or gravity of the two challenges, the comparison is misleading; significant differences distinguish the two cases. The wave of attempted democratic transitions that followed the end of the Cold War in the former communist countries took place in a climate in which alternative ideologies to democracy played a limited role. Socialism had lost its appeal. Antidemocratic forms of nationalism still had some life left, but their full impact was only felt in the Balkans. In the Arab world, however, democracy still has to contend with political Islam, or Islamism, a mixture of politico-religious ideas that attract a mass following, have been growing in popularity, and relate uneasily to the ideals of liberal democracy.

In addition, the relationship between the United States and Europe on the one hand and the Arab world on the other is completely different from that which existed between the Western powers and the Soviet Union and its Eastern European allies in the declining days of communism. The Warsaw Pact governments were hostile regimes that many Western governments actively hoped would fall, and the political opposition in those countries, and significant parts of the citizenry, were pro-American. In the Middle East, most of the governments are valued security and economic partners of the West. And significant parts of the political opposition to these governments, and in fact large parts of the citizenry, are anti-American.

Another major difference is the state of political change. In a trend that gathered force across the 1980s, the governments of the Soviet Union and Eastern Europe were buffeted by strong internal pressures for change. By the end of the decade they were collapsing and the region entered a period of profound political transformation, defined not just by the fall of the old systems but by the widespread desire, at least in Eastern Europe, to embrace democracy. The Middle East is in a fundamentally different state. The region has experienced mild liberalizing reforms and internal reform debates over the last fifteen years, at least in some countries. In the last several years this reform debate has intensified, driven both by the Arabs' own reflections on the lessons of September 11 and by the new talk about the need for democracy in the region coming out of Washington and other Western capitals. Yet, despite this heightened reform debate and some modest reform measures, the region remains politically stuck, with entrenched authoritarian or semiauthoritarian governments that are well versed in absorbing political reforms without changing the fundamental elements of power. Arab governments are still unwilling to take serious measures to head off the very worrisome longer-term signs of trouble, such as the rising socioeconomic pressures created by high population growth.

Of course a tremendous variation in the degree of political openness and reform characterizes the Middle East. Several countries, such as Libya, Saudi Arabia, Syria, and Tunisia are highly authoritarian and allow almost no political space. Others, such as Morocco and Lebanon, hold regular elections that are largely free and fair, with diverse political parties taking part and significant amounts of political freedom. Other countries fall in between these two poles, with mixed amounts of political space and reform. Although a spectrum of political liberalization exists, actual democratization remains elusive. Some countries, particularly in the Gulf, are barely beginning to experiment with partially elected legislatures. Even the most advanced reformers have not opened up the main levers of political power to open political competition, levers that are held by either hereditary monarchs or strongman rulers backed by militaries and internal security forces that enjoy political impunity. Although the reform efforts in the region are diverse, they all fail to get at this central democratic deficit.

Critical Juncture

The above analysis highlights an interesting parallel between the state of Western policy toward the Middle East and the situation of Arab political reform—a parallel that frames what is clearly a critical juncture with regard to the possible democratic evolution of the region. The United States and Europe feel a new security imperative to push for political change in the Arab world and have set forth rhetoric announcing a new proreform policy line. Yet governments on both sides of the Atlantic are still struggling to operationalize the new commitment, to connect their new rhetoric to policy deeds. In somewhat similar fashion, in the Middle East debates about political reform have multiplied and taken on a freer, franker character. Yet, as with the new impulse in Western policy, there is a lot more talk about the necessity for change than action to bring it about.

In short, both democracy promotion by outsiders and democratization from the inside have arrived at a critical stage in the Middle East. They are recognized as imperatives, widely explored in discussions and debates, but only partially realized in practice. In both Western policy and Arab political life, moving toward realization of these imperatives is hard both because of powerful vested interests that reinforce the status quo and because of a deeper uncertainty about how to proceed. Whether and how the tensions between the new imperatives and the underlying forces supporting the status quo are resolved is a major issue for the Middle East and for U.S. and European foreign policy for years to come.

Although extensive discussion and debate are necessary for the effort to move forward on these challenging issues, several elements of the current discussions and debates in both Western and Arab circles appear to be complicating the task. One such problematic element is the harsh politicization of the overall subject, principally arising from the war in Iraq. In the United States the question of whether and how to promote democracy in the Middle East has been badly tangled up in the divisive arguments over the legitimacy and wisdom of the war in Iraq. Many European policy experts shy away from explicit references to any democracy agenda, preferring much softer formulations about political reform out of a concern to avoid any association with the Iraq intervention. In the Middle East, the idea of a Western push for democracy in the region, and even the idea of liberal democracy itself, has become somewhat tainted by association with the highly unpopular intervention in Iraq.

Certainly the eventual political outcome in Iraq will have significant effects on politics in the rest of the region. But it is very unlikely that the United States, having experienced much higher human, financial, and diplomatic costs than expected in the Iraq intervention, will pursue military-based regime change in other countries in the region anytime soon. Future U.S. efforts to promote positive political change in the rest of the Middle East will very likely be a mix of diplomatic and aid measures. Thus it would be useful if it were possible to begin to separate the debates over the Iraq intervention from the broader consideration in both Western and Arab policy circles of how best the United States and Europe can be useful partners in supporting positive political change in the region. Yet given continued Arab anger over Iraq, such a separation will be hard to achieve in practice.

A second problematic element of the debates and discussions over democracy promotion and democratization in the region is the lack of available experience and expertise. The Arab world has largely stayed outside the democratic trend that passed through most other regions in the past twenty-five years, which has meant that few Western experts on Arab politics have direct knowledge about democracy promotion methods and few Western experts on democracy promotion have much knowledge of Arab politics. In like fashion, concrete experience with both democratization and external democracy-promotion programs is in relatively short supply in the Arab world. Those lacunae in Western policy circles and Arab political life are starting to be filled as democracy-promotion efforts and political reform initiatives increase, but the supply of expertise is still well short of the demand.

One result of this shortfall is a strong tendency to reinvent the wheel and to ignore lessons from the experience of democracy building in other regions. An example in this regard is the enthusiasm that some U.S. and European democracy promoters have shown for civil society support in the Arab world as a key method of democracy building. The unfulfilled expectations that democracy promoters have experienced in other regions with regard to the hoped-for transformative effect of aiding Western-style advocacy nongovernmental organizations (NGOs) seem not to be taken into account by some of those who rush to embrace the civil society cause in the Middle East.

Another consequence of the shortage of experience and expertise in democracy promotion in the Arab world is that the new community of enthusiasts of such work frequently evidences unrealistic ideas about how much impact outside actors can expect to have when they try to alter the political direction of other societies. Some people appear to believe that if enough people in Washington decide the Middle East needs to become democratic, democratization will happen, just by the force of the American will alone. Yet the most basic, consistent lesson coming out of the experience of democracy promotion in other regions is that external actors, even very determined ones employing significant resources, rarely have a decisive impact on the political direction of other societies.

A third limiting feature of the ongoing debates and discussions over the issue of democracy in the Middle East is a surprising lack of attention to the core question of what a path to democracy might actually consist of in specific Arab countries. Although both Western and Arab policy experts and commentators say much about the need for democracy in the region, they are surprisingly vague about how they expect it to come about. They emphasize reform led from the top, and the implicit model is a process of gradual reform that takes a country from authoritarian rule through liberalization to democracy without any sharp junctions along the way. Yet in the parts of the world that have experienced democratization in the past twenty-five years, the most common pattern has been a rather dramatic collapse of authoritarian rule and at least some short-term political dislocation while a new pluralistic system is constructed. Incremental, top-down processes of democratization have been rare. This does not mean that democratization in the Middle East would necessarily have to entail political chaos or violent instability, but any assumption that one modest, incremental top-down reform after another will somehow result in deep-reaching political transformation is rooted more in hope than actual experience.

Dilemmas and Choices

The chapters in this book seek to provide insights into the core questions about the challenges of promoting democracy in the Middle East, with the intention of helping advance the ongoing discussion and debates on the subject past some of the deficits outlined above. The chapters are diverse and do not reflect any one view of how Western policy makers and aid providers should proceed. However, they share a general sympathy for the idea that U.S. and European policy should take very seriously the imperative of attempting to support positive political change in the region. They also share the overarching belief that there are no magic bullets of democracy promotion and that the experience of democracy promotion in other regions makes clear a strong need for humility and patience.

The first group of chapters, by Daniel Brumberg, Graham Fuller, and Amy Hawthorne, under the heading "Regional Realities," takes the measure of the current state of Arab politics. It does not attempt a comprehensive survey but rather focuses on several key questions. First, what is the difference between liberalization and democratization, and how do Arab political reforms of the past two decades fit into these two different patterns? Second, what are Islamists' political goals and to what extent are they likely to contribute to or impede democratization? And third, how significant is the new, post–September 11 reform ferment in the Arab world? Do the new debates on reform and the reform measures taken by some Arab governments constitute a potential breakthrough for Arab democracy?

The next section, titled "No Easy Answers," with chapters by Amy Hawthorne, Marina Ottaway, and Eva Bellin, explores some of the dilemmas and difficulties that arise in different approaches to supporting reform. The first chapter in this section asks whether civil society promotion could or should serve as the main thrust of democracy-promotion efforts, as some democracy promoters believe. The second takes up an equally challenging question, that of whether promoting women's rights in the Arab world is a fruitful method for promoting Arab democracy. The third tackles the much-debated issue of the likely or ideal relationship between economic and political reform in the Arab world. And the fourth probes the troubling absence of mass-based constituencies for democratic change in the Middle East and looks for possible future sources of such constituencies.

The next section, "Policy Choices," with chapters by Marina Ottaway, Thomas Carothers, Michele Dunne, and Richard Youngs, analyzes some of the key choices that Western policy makers and aid practitioners face in attempting to institutionalize a policy of support for democracy in the Middle East. The first chapter in the section emphasizes the problem of credibility that dogs all U.S. efforts in the democracy-promotion realm. The second questions whether Western democracy promoters have really come to terms with the need to choose a strategy of democracy promotion and outlines the available options. The third makes the case for how the United States can better integrate democracy concerns into its overall policy for the region. And the fourth looks at Europe's past and present efforts to support Middle Eastern reform, focusing on the common elements of the varied European efforts, as well as their shortcomings.

The final section, "Conclusion," by Marina Ottaway and Thomas Carothers, highlights how the United States and other countries interested in supporting positive political change in the Middle East can start dealing with the problem of credibility and with the complexities of Arab politics that make democracy promotion especially challenging. It emphasizes the need to get to the core issues at stake, above all building constituencies for democratic change and broadening political contestation. The section also stresses the need to calibrate expectations about the pace of political change and the impact of external actors in the Middle East to a level corresponding to the experience of other regions where similar democracy promotion efforts have been made.

Part One

Regional Realities

2

Liberalization versus Democracy

Daniel Brumberg

NO U.S. PRESIDENT has talked more about democracy in the Middle East than George W. Bush in the years 2002–2004. The president and his advisers spoke optimistically, at least for a time, about a post-Saddam democracy in Iraq—one that might eventually become a veritable light to other Arab nations. Their grand vision assumes that sooner or later, advocates of democracy throughout the Middle East will demand the same freedoms and rights that Iraqis are now claiming. Yet, however inspiring this vision appears, the actual reform plan that the administration put into place in 2003-2004 is unlikely to produce radical changes in the Arab world. The Middle East Partnership Initiative and the Broader Middle East and North Africa Initiative indicate that the United States will work with Arab leaders to carefully and slowly reform their autocracies. Regardless how dramatic the decisive approach to change in Baghdad, when it comes to our friends in Egypt, Jordan, Kuwait, Morocco, and Yemen, Washington's plan points to evolution rather than revolution.

Is this gradualist approach the right remedy? And, if not, should the United States press for the grander vision of radical change that some in the administration advocate? Before we can even begin to answer these questions, before we write out the prescription, we must carefully examine the patient. We need to understand how Arab autocracies actually work, and, in particular, how the "liberalized autocracies" of the region endure despite frequent prediction of their imminent death. Such regimes do not conform to the American media's portrayal of Arab politics. When we think of the region, we usually envision dictatorships or, as I prefer to call them, "full autocracies." Such regimes have zero tolerance for free debate or competitive politics. Indeed, in full autocracies, dissent warrants jail, or worse, execution. By contrast, the liberal autocracies of the Arab world temper authoritarianism with pluralism. They are liberal in the sense that their leaders not only tolerate but promote a measure of political openness in civil society, in the press, and even in the electoral system of their country. Elections give opposition leaders a chance to compete, to enter parliaments, and, what is more, occasionally to serve as ministers. But they are autocratic in that their rulers always retain the upper hand. They control the security establishment, dominate the media, and dole out economic rewards to their favorite clients. With their ultimate reliance on the supreme authority of the monarch or president, liberalized autocracies provide a kind of virtual democracy.

It is far from clear how to reform liberalized autocracies, given their multifaceted and ambiguous nature, and given how deeply entrenched they are. Encouraging rapid change, such as completely free elections, might invite radical forces and even a retreat to full autocracy. Arab leaders—many of whom will remain our allies for the foreseeable future—are not about to commit political suicide. But a go-slow approach also has drawbacks. Among these, the most corrosive is the tendency of liberalized autocracies to hang onto power without developing representative institutions that have wide popular support or legitimacy. After all, their very survival hinges on not allowing for the emergence of effective party systems or truly representative parliaments. For this reason, little might be gained by an incrementalist strategy that offers few incentives for Arab leaders to move beyond the politics of day-to-day survival. As the United States moves ahead with efforts to promote democracy in the region, it will quickly discover that promoting reforms in the liberalized autocracies of the Arab world poses dilemmas for which there are no easy answers.

Full versus Liberalized Autocracy

At the end of the day, all autocrats want to survive. But how they survive makes a difference. The full autocracies of the Arab world—which include Iraq, Libya, Saudi Arabia, Syria, and Tunisia—survive by relying on two mechanisms: the provision of jobs and economic benefits in return for political support, and the use of sheer force and intimidation. Regimes use these instruments to isolate, silence, or repress almost all contending forces outside the ruling circle. Liberalized autocracies also use money and intimidation to both co-opt and repress potential opponents, but, unlike full autocracies, they have a fairly high threshold of tolerance for political openness. For full autocracies, any political change is a slippery slope into self-destruction, whereas for liberalized autocracies, state-controlled political change is necessary for survival. Why does the first fear reform while the second tolerates and even invites it?

At least three factors explain why leaders of full autocracies dread reform. First, Iraq, Libya, Syria, and to a lesser extent Saudi Arabia boast an extensive security apparatus whose very existence depends on the regime's direct or indirect control over the economy. Because the slightest opening might deprive the most powerful members of the ruling establishment of their hard-earned booty, there are few (if any) leaders in full autocracies willing to risk political reform. Second, having failed to create truly representative institutions, the leaders of full autocracies are not well placed to create effective alternatives to sheer repression. For them, democracy is a black hole that promises only chaos and violence. Third, although total autocracies claim the undying loyalty of "the people," they are often controlled by tribal or clan bosses who hail from ethno-religious minorities, such as Alawites in Syria or Sunni Muslims in Saddam Hussein's Iraq. By repressing the majority—such as Syria's Sunni Muslims or Iraq's Shiites—they leave a trail of bitter foes whose supreme goal is revenge. Thus Syria's new leader, Bashar Al Assad, first promised democracy but then quickly retreated. A regime that massacred tens of thousands of Sunni Muslims in 1982 could hardly take the political risk typical of their liberalizing cousins in Egypt, Morocco, or Jordan. Full autocracies are trapped by an either-me-or-you logic that makes reform seem like suicide.

To be sure, liberalized autocracies also have extensive security establishments whose survival depends in part on the regime's control of economic resources. But in contrast to full autocracies, which were built on an edifice of total or near total control and exclusion, liberalized autocracies were constructed on a foundation of partial inclusion. Early in their history, their leaders had the good sense to partly dispense power to a wider universe of groups and institutions. As a result, they could afford to share power without risking a potentially suicidal win-lose confrontation with the opposition. In fact, the leaders of Algeria, Egypt, Jordan, Kuwait, Morocco, and Yemen have built alliances with forces that are officially part of the "opposition." This is simply unheard of in Iraq, Libya, Syria, or Tunisia.

Consider two arenas in which a measure of pluralism has made it easier for liberalized autocracies to initiate partial reforms without losing power. In economics, liberalized autocracies traditionally have pursued development strategies that necessitate the inclusion of competing economic forces. By reaching out to private businessmen, white-collar bureaucrats, blue-collar state workers, and professionals, they avoid becoming beholden to any one group. This usefully permits rulers to create different alliances and, on that basis, experiment with a variety of economic approaches. Because economic power is not totally fused with the political power, the ruling elite can loosen its grip without losing all the economic benefits that accrued from autocracy. (This is true even in oil-dependent states, such as Kuwait, which, despite the prominence of oil in their economies, boast different classes of merchants, professionals, and others.) Such advantages are unavailable to the leaders of full autocracies, such as Syria, who have hitched their political future to only a few key economic groups. This is why there has been nearly zero market reform in Syria, whereas in Morocco, Egypt, and Jordan, leaders could afford to partly let go of the state's control over the economy.

A more pluralistic political arena also makes it easier for autocrats to open up without fearing loss of ultimate power. Having given labor unions, professional syndicates, businessmen's associations, and civic organizations a measure of freedom from state interference, the leaders of liberalized autocracies are well placed to pursue a divide-and-rule strategy by which they play one group off against another. This game blurs the line between friend and foe, thus making it possible for rulers to constantly build different alliances with leaders inside and outside the regime. The leaders of Egypt, Jordan, Morocco, Yemen, and to some extent Algeria are expert at this kind of juggling. But in Iraq, Libya, Syria, and Tunisia, there are fewer balls to juggle and thus little incentive to liberalize.

One factor that makes it easier or harder to sustain the juggling act so crucial to liberalized autocracies is regime type. To some extent, it makes a difference whether a state is ruled by a monarch or a president. By and large, kings have an advantage. Because they act as referees of the political field, rather than captains of any one team, they have more freedom of maneuver to divide, manipulate, and thus control society's competing groups. This strategy works especially well when a monarch can add a dash of Islamic legitimacy to the recipe. Thus, in Morocco and Jordan, respectively, the authority of King Muhammad VI and King Abdullah II as ultimate arbiters has been enhanced by their purported lineage from the Prophet Muhammad, the founder of Islam. Presidents, by contrast, are tied to ruling parties, many of which oppose reform. As a result, they often have less room to maneuver or innovate. Paradoxically, "traditional" monarchies are sometimes better modernizers than "modern" presidents.

A quick comparison of Morocco and Algeria illustrates this paradox. In the early 1990s, Morocco's King Hassan II was pressed to revise the Family Code. As *Amir il Mu'minim* (Commander of the Faithful), he welcomed this chance to promote reforms in ways that reinforced his own authority. He did this by skillfully playing off the various women's and religious associations that constitute Morocco's civil society. Although the revised law pleased no one, passage of the new Family Code reminded Moroccans that in the final analysis the king decides the limits of reform. By contrast, Algeria's presidents have been wedded to a presidential system and ruling party that long ago tried to placate Islamic sentiments by upholding a traditional Family Code. As a result, not a single president has dared toy with the Family Code since Algeria tried in 1997 to reinvigorate its battered political system. This is not a matter of the personal character of any particular president. Rather, it a consequence of the very nature of the political system. In Algeria, the president lacks the legitimacy, stature, and relatively pluralistic playing field that makes divide-and-rule an easier and more successful strategy in Morocco's relatively pluralistic monarchy.

Nevertheless, it is misleading to focus too intensely on the issue of regime type, since kings and presidents rule both full and liberalized autocracies. The most critical factor in gauging the future of autocracy in the Arab world is the degree of pluralism kings or presidents tolerate. Keeping this point in mind, we can draw a simple but useful continuum running from less to more pluralism, or from full autocracy to liberalized autocracy (see Figure 1, next page). The more pluralism, the easier it is to sustain liberalization strategies and the divide-and-rule juggling acts so central to them.

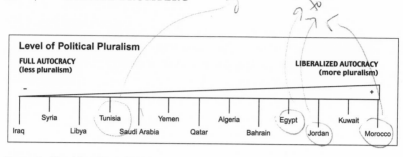

Figure 1: The Pluralism Continuum

Characteristics of Liberalized Autocracy

Partial Legitimacy and National Reconciliation

The goal of state-managed liberalization is to give opposition groups a way to blow off steam. The steam valve must meet opponents' minimal expectations for political openness and participation but prevent them from undermining the regime's ultimate control. In an ideal sense, it might be said that such limitations on political action undercut the legitimacy of liberalized autocracy. But for countries trying to exit a period of conflict, even an experiment in state-controlled opening can create space for political dialogues and accommodation in ways that give liberalized autocracies a measure of legitimacy—at least at the outset. For example, after Anwar Sadat's assassination in 1981, Egypt's new president, Hosni Mubarak, embarked on a political opening that brought many of Sadat's critics into the political arena. The leaders of Jordan, Kuwait, and Algeria have completed this model. In the wake of Jordan's 1989 bread riots, the late King Hussein oversaw the creation of a national charter to define the new parameters of a more open political system. He then held the first competitive national elections in the modern history of the country. Similarly after the liberation of Kuwait from Iraqi occupation in 1991, and in an effort to overcome the deep chasm that had long marred regime-opposition relations, the Sabah family held discussions with a diverse range of opposition leaders. The 1992 elections were meant to signal a return to parliamentary life and thus a new era of cooperation in Kuwait politics. In Algeria, then-President Amin Zeroual initiated a national reconciliation program that sought to end a bloody civil war that had claimed some 100,000 lives. The 1997 parliamentary elections were followed by a new amnesty law that brought into the parliament some former members of the Islamic Salvation Front (FIS) and other Islamists. Similarly, Yemen's 1993 parliamentary elections capped a two-year effort to create one unified state, after years of conflict between North and South Yemen.

These initiatives not only helped secure a measure of social and political peace at home, they also made it easier for regimes to gain U.S. economic and military support. From Washington's perspective, such political openings represent a major step forward. Thus, for both Arab and U.S. leaders, liberalization minus substantive democracy came to be viewed as a winning formula.

Still, it would be inaccurate to see this formula as merely a "Potemkin democracy" whose facade will collapse with the slightest push. State-managed political liberalization works because it entails real, if partial and limited, reforms in civil society, the economy, the electoral system, and the parliament. These reforms bring additional benefits to the regimes in question, and to some extent, to their opposition as well. Indeed, it is precisely the fact that both sides get something out of the bargain that partly explains the endurance of liberalized autocracy.

Partial Reform of Civil Society Laws and Organizations

Liberalized autocracies not only permit but also promote the growth of nongovernmental or quasigovernmental organizations. Where centralized states can no longer provide adequate schooling or social and health services, regimes will encourage civic organizations to assume some of these tasks. (Of course, the state retains ultimate control of the purse strings.) Striking just the right balance requires "reforming" those laws that define how civic, professional, and labor associations govern and finance their activities. Yet as Egypt's infamous Laws of Association remind us, such reforms often place civil society organizations in a strange limbo, partly autonomous, partly captured. Still, for many social activists in the Arab world, this is not a bad trade-off. Because they often lack independent sources of finance or get in trouble when they acquire foreign funds (as did Egypt's Saad Eddin Ibrahim, a sociology professor and civic activist who was recently acquitted of charges that his nongovernmental organization [NGO] unlawfully used foreign funds), they sometimes learn to tolerate such ambiguous laws. Regimes, in turn, not only retain final control; they further divide the opposition. For wily "reformists" such as Egypt's Mubarak, it is better to have 5,000 small civil society organizations than five big ones, because many competing NGOs impede social activists' cooperation. This is one reason why in the 1990s the rulers of Morocco and Egypt fostered the growth of thousands of semi-independent organizations. American democracy promoters encouraged this trend because they mistakenly assumed that civil society organizations had the capacity to push for democratic changes. What these democracy promoters failed to recognize is that such organizations could not compensate for the absence of well-organized political parties or truly representative parliaments.

Partial Reform of Economies

By bringing a variety of social and professional groups into the political arena, liberal autocracies also create space for partial economic reforms. During the 1980s and 1990s, decreasing oil revenues, rising foreign debts, and the paralysis of state-run industries all created a strong impetus to reinvigorate the private sector. Liberalized autocracies from Rabat to Amman looked to the business community to encourage foreign investment in ailing economies. This strategy often left many public sector industries intact because Arab leaders did not want to provoke an outcry from the many groups who would have paid a price for structural reforms, such as labor, state bureaucrats, and public sector managers. Yet, if partial reforms have not removed the actual causes of economic crises, they have slowly expanded the private sectors in Morocco, Egypt, and Jordan by attracting some foreign and domestic investment.

Partial Reform of Parliaments and Electoral Systems

To attract a modicum of legitimacy and popular support, liberalized autocracies almost always allow elections and the creation of parliaments. More or less regular national elections have been held in Morocco since the 1960s, Egypt since 1976, Jordan since 1989, Kuwait since 1991, and Yemen since 1993. But elections and parliaments do not a democracy make. The essential elements for democracy are political parties that speak for organized constituencies, parliaments that have the constitutional authority to speak on behalf of the electorate, and constitutions that impose limits on executive authority. Because all three of these fundamental requirements are missing in the liberalized autocracies of the Arab world, no government in the region can credibly claim a democratic mandate.

The absence of strong political parties makes it difficult to build on the enthusiasm and hopes that a first round of competitive elections invariably generates. With the possible exception of some Islamist parties, the Arab world lacks strong political parties that can mobilize and—most important—sustain a mass following. Parties may exist in name, but in practice their leaders are usually drawn from the elite who have close family, personal, or economic ties to the rulers but little support in society itself. Such state-focused ties are buttressed by payoffs, favors, and bribes to ensure that most "opposition" politicians will only rarely defy the ruling authority. Moreover, when opposition groups do begin exhibiting excessive independence—as in Jordan and Kuwait during the early and mid-1990s—liberal autocracies have all kinds of mechanisms on hand to deal with such upstarts.

The most important of these mechanisms are constitutions and the autocratic laws they sanction. To the American reader, this sounds strange. We think of a constitution as the first guarantor of freedom and civil rights. But in the Arab world, constitutions are written to ensure that the president or king has ultimate power. Cabinets are formed and prime ministers chosen by an unelected executive. With the possible, and partial, exceptions of Morocco and Kuwait, these cabinets are not responsible before an elected majority in parliament. As a result, parliaments are more like debating societies than law-making institutions. Although they sometimes assail this or that technical measure coming from the executive (as has occasionally been the case in Kuwait, for example), parliaments lack the constitutional authority to actually represent the will of the elected.

The laws passed by parliaments in liberalized autocracies almost always reflect the wishes of presidents and their allies, or kings and their princes; therefore, many of these laws are explicitly designed to enhance state power and punish dissent. This is what legal experts mean when they observe that in the Arab world, there is rule by law rather than rule *of* law. In liberalized autocracies, unelected leaders are not so much above the law as they are its creator and ultimate dispenser. It is the job of parliaments to rubber-stamp these laws, and it is the mission of state-controlled judiciaries to enforce them. Even if appellate courts occasionally defy the will of the executive (as has happened in Egypt), at the end of the day they know their place. What is more, this entire legal machinery is sanctioned by constitutions replete with loopholes that provide for "complete freedom of speech and assembly"—so long as those freedoms do not harm "national" or "Islamic" values. Such conditioned liberties guarantee freedom of speech but not freedom after speech.

Rule by law not only creates weak parliaments and illiberal laws, but also gives executives the legal means to clamp down on parliaments that get too critical of government policies. One such tool is the manipulation of electoral laws. For example, before national elections in 1998, Jordan's electoral law was revised in ways that dramatically reduced Islamist representation in the new parliament. Elsewhere, as in Egypt, the electoral laws make it hard for Islamists to run in political parties. Finally, as we have seen most recently in Jordan, when such tools become unreliable, leaders can invoke their constitutional authority to suspend parliament. In the Gulf, such suspensions have been a regular part of parliamentary life for decades, a point that no politician in the ruling establishment or opposition forgets.

Partial Inclusion (and Containment) of Islamists and Secularists

One of the main obstacles to democracy in the Arab world is the absence of consensus regarding national identity, particularly as it relates to the controversial question of Islam's place in public life. Many Islamists, including mainstream activists in parliaments and civil society, believe the state should enforce or even impose Islamic laws, whereas nominal or secular Muslims and non-Muslims want the state to protect their right to practice—or not practice—their religion. Ethnic groups (such as Sunni Muslim Kurds in Iraq and Syria, the Berbers in Morocco and Algeria, Christian minorities such as Egypt's Copts) and myriad civil society groups (such as women's rights organizations, labor unions, and professional syndicates) often fear Islamist domination. Lacking the capacity for mobilization that Islamists command via the mosque, such non-Islamist groups have sometimes tacitly backed autocracies rather than press for open elections. After all, many of these would-be democrats are not ready to give Islamists a "democratic mandate" to limit or even obliterate their civil and human rights. This happened in Algeria in 1992, when secularists in the labor unions and professional associations backed the coup that prevented the FIS from winning a majority of seats in the country's parliament. From the perspective of these secularists, full autocracy was preferable to the risks of a truly competitive political game.

Yet, if conflicts over national identity hinder democratization, they do not necessarily lead to total autocracy. Liberalizing autocracies can sometimes reduce or contain conflict between Islamists and non-Islamists through a process of partial and controlled inclusion that allows mainstream Islamists, Arab nationalists, and liberals to enter parliament as independents or as a formal political party. Islamists invariably make major gains when regimes allow them to compete in such semicompetitive elections. This occurred in Jordan in 1989, Yemen in 1993, Algeria in 1997, and Bahrain and Morocco in 2002. But these victories have their limits. By funneling patronage to ruling parties and bureaucracies, to state-controlled organizations such as labor unions and professional associations, or to traditional tribes or ethnic groups such as Kurds or Berbers, liberal autocracies mobilize their own allies and thus make it hard for Islamists to attain electoral majorities. From the vantage point of regimes, state-controlled power sharing can make sense.

But why, one might ask, should Islamists accept such an arrangement? They do so because the alternatives—a rush into full democracy or a return to full autocracy—can be much worse for both the regime and its opposition. Algeria's sad experience illustrates this lesson. The 1992 coup that prevented the Islamists from winning a majority in the parliament hardly provided an enduring solution to Algeria's profound political and ideological conflict. On the contrary, as the subsequent seven-year civil war clearly shows, when the military tries to re-impose a full autocracy that completely shuts Islamists out of the political system, new horrors can emerge that eventually engulf the entire society. Given the drawbacks of both full democracy and full autocracy, the remaining solution is a state-enforced power-sharing formula that favors regimes but does not exclude any group that accepts the ultimate authority of the regime itself. So long as both sides play by these quasi-autocratic rules of the game, some measure of coexistence between Islamists and non-Islamists seems possible.

Some of Algeria's neighbors apparently have learned this lesson. For example, Morocco's Islamist Party of Justice and Development won some

12 percent of seats in the Lower House during the September 2002 parliamentary elections. Although it probably could have taken at least 50 percent, its leaders chose not to run a full slate of candidates and thus avoided a head-on collision with the ruling establishment. As a result, the country's liberalized autocracy has weathered the storm that might have emerged from a fully democratic election.

Still, the logic of state-enforced power sharing does not always prevail. Indeed, it can prove elusive when especially sharp ideological or sectarian divisions pit a ruler against the opposition. In Egypt, for example, the regime has barred members of the Muslim Brotherhood from creating a political party and has obstructed their efforts to run as independents. The Brotherhood's quest for an Islamic state is viewed simply as too threatening to be accommodated by any power-sharing formula. In Bahrain, meanwhile, the split between the minority Sunnis and the majority Shiites has hindered recent attempts to promote power sharing. In October 2002, the royal family (who are Sunni) held elections under rules designed to benefit Sunni candidates. Many Shiites boycotted the polls, thus setting the stage for a new parliament whose legitimacy is called into question by a significant part of the population. Finally, in Lebanon, a formal power-sharing arrangement has survived only because Syrian troops protect it. Power sharing is hard to sustain absent a strong state or an outside power to enforce it.[1]

Yet if its record is mixed, state-managed partial inclusion has fared pretty well in Jordan, Kuwait, and to a lesser extent in Algeria. It has done so because it offers both Islamists and secularists some advantages. The crucial benefit, especially for Islamists, is the chance to sink roots in society. Even if parliaments have no real power, Islamists can use the cover gained from participating in them to spread the "good word." This has been the case in Jordan, Kuwait, Yemen, and more recently Morocco. Parliaments can also offer secularists and Islamists their first chance to pursue dialogue after years of conflict. For example, although radical Islamists continue to use violence in Algeria, a measure of peaceful coexistence prevailed among mainstream Islamist, secular, and Berber parties during the first three years of Algeria's 1997 parliament. In Kuwait and Jordan, Islamists have joined forces with Arab nationalists and leftists to challenge privatization laws. In Jordan all three groups have assailed the country's peace treaty with Israel. Moreover, in all three countries, Islamists and secularists have on occasion served in the same government. Still, whether such limited power sharing promotes endur-ing ideological moderation and national reconciliation is another ques-tion. Instead, it might merely provide a convenient way for Islamists and secularists to avoid further conflict, a kind of ideological cease-fire that does little to enhance the legitimacy of parliament or national rec-onciliation. Partial inclusion has long-term political costs, as does the very institution of liberalized autocracy in the Arab world.

Costs of Liberalized Autocracy

Regimes that embark on partial societal, economic, or political reforms know that the short-term gains that come with liberalizing the political and social system often exact a long-term price. But since most Arab leaders, as do most politicians, deal with short time horizons, they are less concerned about the cumulative consequences of day-to-day politi-cal survival. We can briefly assess the costs that accrue from the partial reform of civil society, the economy, the electoral field, and regime-controlled power sharing.

Ideologically Fragmented Civil Society and Weak Political Society

One of the most significant costs of partial civil society reform is the aggravation of ideological conflicts. In the Arab world, many human rights organizations, women's associations, and even "nonpolitical" en-vironmental groups are torn by disputes pitting Marxists, liberal secu-larists, Arab nationalists, Islamists, tribes, or ethnic groups against one another. Anyone who has tried to get NGOs to cooperate in Egypt or Morocco has seen how ethno-religious or ideological conflicts play into the hands of rulers.

However, elite manipulation is not the sole source of such divisive-ness. Rather, ideological conflict is a by-product of a system that inhibits the growth of political society (that is, an independent realm of political parties that can mobilize constituencies that have a stake in what their leaders say and do). This is a second cost of liberalized autocracies. Be-cause they lack effective parties, they create an incentive for civil society organizations to take up political roles for which they are badly suited.

In Egypt, Jordan, and Morocco, professional syndicates often spend more time championing rival ideologies than using their expertise to solve concrete problems. The polemical nature of the Arab press can also be partly attributed to the role that opposition newspapers play as surrogate political parties. Rather than focus on reporting or analysis, they use rumor, innuendo, and pandering to the "man on the street" to get the regime's attention. Since September 11, 2001, the American press has featured stories about how such yellow journalism includes doses of anti-Americanism and even anti-Semitism. But the American press has failed to emphasize the costs of such polemics for Arabs. In its wake, civil society fails to sprout its own wings, and political society remains stunted and ineffective.

Partial Economic Reforms: Giving Capitalism a Bad Name

Partial economic reforms exact long-term costs. Because they often open the economy to private sector investment while leaving public sector industries largely intact, they create a dualistic economy whose inefficient public sector industries and bureaucracies continue to cost governments millions of dollars. Moreover, because partial economic reforms leave bureaucrats in charge, the resulting red tape and corruption discourage more productive forms of private investment and trade. Anyone who has walked the streets of Cairo, Rabat, or Amman knows that many of the real moneymakers are the new businessmen who rake in quick profits from real estate, the import (or smuggling) of luxury and consumer goods, and currency speculation. Finally, partial economic reforms, absent democratization, do not ensure transparency. In Algeria, Egypt, Morocco, and to a lesser extent Jordan, the cronies of the ruling establishment have not just given capitalism a bad name: Their visible profit making also feeds anti-Western resentment and thus stokes the flames of Islamic fundamentalism against "Western-style democracy."

Partial Political Reform: A Big Trap?

The biggest price of liberalized autocracy is political. The longer liberalized autocracies depend on weak political parties and impotent legislatures, the more difficult it becomes to move from state-managed liberalization to genuine democratization. Because where you can go depends on where you have been, the very success of liberalized autocracy can become a trap for even the most well-intentioned leader. Thus, while the new and decidedly Westernized kings of Morocco and Jordan came to the throne promising all kinds of democratic initiatives, they both eventually fell back on the instruments of liberalized autocracy. Having done so, they must now learn to live with the negative consequences of partial political reform, among which are reinforcing Islamist power, increased ideological confusion and weak legitimacy, growing civil conflict, and what I call transitions to nowhere.

REINFORCING ISLAMIST POWER. Through their mosques, charitable institutions, and health clinics, Islamists advance their cause, to the detriment of their secular and ethnic competitors. This is inevitable, since Islamists, unlike their non-Islamist rivals, benefit from weakly institutionalized party systems. When such unequal competition produces Islamist successes at the polls, governments react by changing the electoral rules of the game, as they have in Egypt and Jordan, or by embarking on a strategy of deliberalization. This can take the form of more repression of opposition newspapers, civil society activists, or politicians. Or it can be achieved by narrowing the scope of parliamentary life, a trend that became visible in Egypt and Jordan during the 1990s.

INCREASED IDEOLOGICAL CONFUSION AND WEAK LEGITIMACY. Because liberalizing autocrats sustain their rule by manipulating different groups and the competing notions of authority they espouse, even the most well meaning of reformists may not be well placed to advance a democratic vision of rule. When Jordan's new king, Abdullah II, appears as a Westernized businessman on Monday, a liberal thinker on Wednesday, an army officer on Thursday, and a pious sheikh on Friday, the resulting ideological mishmash points in no single direction. Such confusion obscures the fact that at the end of the day, all liberalizing autocrats fall back on the state's dissemination of a patrimonial vision of politics. This vision demands that all groups—secular, liberal, Islamist, leftist, or ethnic—accept the king or the president's ultimate authority. Wedded to this ideological default mechanism, the rulers of liberalized autocracies have not, at least until recently, challenged their public education systems to promote democratic ideals. Indeed, the leaders of Egypt, Kuwait, and Yemen have occasionally sought to appease, co-opt, echo, or more rarely align themselves with illiberal Islamic groups. Such Islamicizing tactics can sometimes strengthen Islamists, thus hastening the day when the regime must narrow the political field and thus deliberalize.

NURTURING CIVIL CONFLICT. State-enforced power sharing and partial inclusion can give elected officials an opportunity for dialogue. But because parliaments rarely represent the electorate and therefore do not wield real power, parliamentarians often find plenty of incentives to indulge in ideological one-upmanship rather than pursue concrete programs that might help bridge the divide between secularists and Islamists. This has been Kuwait's unfortunate experience. Despite occasional cooperation between mainstream Islamists and secularists, the gulf between them has only grown. There, as elsewhere in the Arab world, partial inclusion acts more like an extended cease-fire than a path toward reconciliation and political maturity. Some might argue that the only way to resolve this dilemma is to have a real democracy—one that would force the population to choose between competing identities, or compel rival leaders to offer a new vision of national unity. But since such a bold move would probably magnify rather than diminish religious or ethnic conflict (at least initially), liberalizing autocrats prefer holding onto the life raft of state-managed partial inclusion rather than abandoning it for the stormy waters of full democratization. Moreover, if power sharing fails to bring a measure of stability, rulers can deliberalize by using the many tools of repression at their disposal. This choice, of course, only widens the gap between regime and opposition, thus further weakening the legitimacy of liberalized autocracy.

TRANSITIONS TO NOWHERE. Because most autocrats (and even some opposition groups) are loath to give up the benefits of partial reform, they have sometimes flirted with, but thus far never crossed, the line into full autocracy. Instead, they go through unstable cycles of opening and closing, liberalization and deliberalization. The bumpy duration of these cycles depends in part on how much threat their leaders perceive. But what does not happen is a decisive move forward that would allow regimes and oppositions to define a new political system based on a common set of values and aspirations. This is the biggest problem liberalized autocracy creates: It snares regimes in a *marhalla intiqaliyya mustamirra* (endless transition) that eventually robs each new generation of what little hope it had when a new king or president invariably inaugurated a "new" era of reconciliation, openness, and reform.

Which Arab States Can (or Should) Exit the Trap of Liberalized Autocracy?

Even though liberalized autocracy can be a trap, the severity of this trap varies from country to country. And, since some Arab states are more trapped than others, the cost they pay for trying to get un-trapped also varies. This is an important point for democracy promoters. Those in the U.S. government who favor a go-slow approach fear that any attempt to quickly remove the snare of liberalized autocracy will breed instability. Others apparently believe that in the wake of a regime change in Iraq and the creation of a reasonably pluralistic government in Baghdad, a go-fast approach will be possible. In point of fact, a one-size-fits-all strategy, be it incrementalist or rapid, will never be appropriate for all liberalized autocracies. Because they are not all equally ensnared, the challenge is to devise a rough guide that will help distinguish where and when a go-slow approach is preferable, and where and when more radical surgery may be in order. Among the factors such a guide should include are: the longevity of liberalized autocracies; the size of the population and the level of economic crisis; the level of political and institutional pluralism in civil society and party system; and the type of regime.

- *Factor 1: Longevity.* The longer Arab states bear the cost of liberalized autocracy, the harder it becomes to create functioning civil and political societies that encourage rival forces to find democratic ways to resolve their conflicts. Paradoxically, because success makes a move from liberalization to democracy risky, some of the most experienced liberalizers are likely to devise new kinds of "reform" to skirt democracy. Thus, for example, the goal of the current effort to reform Egypt's National Democratic Party (NDP) is not to democratize; rather, the goal of this reform is to infuse new blood into a ruling party whose political body has ossified. By contrast, regimes that have just embarked on political liberalization, such as in Bahrain and Qatar, have a window of opportunity to plant the institutional and constitutional seeds of political society and genuine parliamentary representation. In short, regimes that are less practiced in the art of survival are better placed than those with ample experience to devise a political liberalization strategy whose purpose is to open the door to democracy rather than close it.

- *Factor 2: Size of Population and Level of Economic Crisis.* Countries such as Egypt, Morocco, and Algeria—which boast huge populations and economies hamstrung by extensive public sector industries, corruption, and external debts—are not good candidates for a quick move from liberalized autocracy to competitive democracy. Having pursued a dualistic development strategy that has sown ever greater levels of social discontent, the leaders of big countries assume that any effort to deepen democracy by holding free elections will only create big problems by mobilizing the opponents of market reform. By contrast, smaller and richer countries are better placed to advance both market and political reforms. Of course, the source of wealth is also important. The oil-based economies of the Gulf states link economic and political power in ways that inhibit political reform. Still, because countries such as Bahrain, Kuwait, and Qatar have great wealth and a small native population, their leaders have far more room to advance political reforms than their counterparts in states such as Egypt or Morocco.
- *Factor 3: Level of Organized Pluralism.* By pluralism, I am not referring to the often vaunted role of civil society organizations or NGOs. Although they frequently foster liberalization, civil society organizations cannot substitute for the vital role that political parties must play in promoting democratization. Although all liberalized autocracies have weak party systems, those that have promoted a more competitive electoral arena are better off than those that have limited competition. This point is especially important given the challenge posed by mainstream Islamist parties. As Morocco illustrates, where Islamist parties must compete with secular parties that command some mea-

sure of support, they pose less of a threat to the regime. Less threat makes more reform possible. By contrast, where they have been excluded from politics (as in Egypt), or where Islamists do not face significant competition from other secular, ethnic, or even Islamic opposition parties, the sudden entrance of Islamists into an open political arena will threaten the regime. Increased threat hinders a move from liberalized autocracy to real democratization.

- *Factor 4: Regime Type.* As noted, most monarchs are better positioned than most presidents to promote the kinds of regime opposition understandings that will facilitate reforms. Presidents are usually wedded to ruling parties or ruling establishments that are loath to let go of "their" presidents and the authority they provide. By contrast (and with the exception of the monarchy in Saudi Arabia, which is closely tied to and thus constrained by the Wahhabi clerical establishment), most Arab kings are well placed to stand above the fray and encourage accommodation of opposition to the regime. Thus, the presidents of Egypt and Algeria are less likely to promote a move forward from liberalization to democracy, whereas the kings of Bahrain, Jordan, Kuwait, and Morocco have relatively more freedom to do so.

These four criteria suggest that recent liberalizers, such as Bahrain and Qatar, as well as more well-entrenched liberalized autocracies that benefit from the arbitrating role of monarchs, such as Kuwait and Morocco, are potential candidates for moving beyond liberalization toward democracy. Morocco's legacy of party competition, however imperfect, should also help lower the costs entailed in genuine democratization. Still, forward movement does not require a sudden leap into the unknown. Rather, it requires carefully targeted constitutional and legal reforms that give parliament and political parties real authority to represent their constituency. Broader educational reforms that promote democratic and pluralistic values are also necessary. These reforms would give electoral systems and the parliament they create the kind of legitimacy they sorely need.

Such bold changes will also require bold leadership from reformers who are ready to seize opportunities when they arise. Recent liberalizers, such as those in Bahrain and Qatar, have a chance to avoid ensnaring themselves in the kinds of traps that older, more experienced liberalizers have fostered. But beware! In the Middle East, windows of opportunity tend to close quickly. Unfortunately, the signals from both countries (such as the banning of political parties) suggest that their leaders have chosen the liberalized autocracy path. Once they go down it, even the most visionary reformer will have difficulty switching to competitive democracy.

By contrast, the leaders of Algeria, Egypt, and to some extent Jordan are candidates for a more incrementalist approach. As they face daunting economic challenges, as their Islamists would make gains in open elections without facing significant competition from non-Islamist parties, and as their leaders face growing discontent over regional conflicts in Israel–Palestine and Iraq, any effort to push for rapid political change would only set the stage for regime opposition conflicts and thus more deliberalization. That said, a go-slow approach should not be limited to the same-old reforms the United States has promoted before, such as building civil society, promoting women's political participation, and accelerating economic development. These are all good things. But even a go-slow approach must tackle more fundamental political challenges, such as strengthening political parties, reforming education, promoting the rule of law, and pressing for constitutionally mandated organizations to protect human rights.

Conclusion

Whatever the approach, Washington will not be able to simply impose its preferences on the region. For the foreseeable future, the United States will have to work with Arab leaders whose principal concern will be to shore up their legitimacy in the wake of a highly unpopular war. Indeed, because the war in Iraq has reinforced the influence of radical Arab nationalists and Islamists, Arab leaders will resist Washington's calls for political reform. In the short run, even a go-slow approach may encounter resistance. That said, in the medium and the longer term, the public outcry in the Arab world against the Iraq war will probably wane, and with that, the question of domestic political reform will emerge as a central issue throughout the Arab world. The creation of a reasonably stable, open, and most of all popular government in Baghdad—if we are lucky and skillful enough to help Iraqis achieve it—may in turn reinforce the pressures for change in liberalized autocracies, and even in some full autocracies, such as Tunisia or Saudi Arabia. When this moment comes, Washington will have to face some difficult decisions about how to encourage both regimes and oppositions to think beyond the day-to-day politics of political survival. This will require paying close attention to the costs and benefits of liberalized autocracy.

Notes

An earlier version of this chapter was originally published as Carnegie Working Paper 37 (May 2003).

1. I have not included Lebanon among my cases of liberalized autocracy because the country's political system is not a liberalized autocracy. Lebanon is a "consociational democracy" whose parliamentary system is designed to provide all groups—Christian, Shiite, Sunni, and Druze—some representation in an elected government. Syria's military and political presence in Lebanon helps to sustain this formal power-sharing system while imposing limits on it. It is impossible to gauge Lebanon's potential for democracy so long as Damascus maintains the ultimate say over the country's political system.

3

Islamists and Democracy

Graham Fuller

ARE ISLAM AND DEMOCRACY COMPATIBLE? And are Islamists willing to accept a democratic order and work within it? Debate has swirled around these two grand questions for decades and has produced a broad variety of responses, often quite polarized. Whatever we may think about Islamists, the topic matters vitally because in the Middle East today they have few serious ideological rivals in leading opposition movements against a failing status quo. These Islamist movements are characterized by rapid growth, evolution, change, and diversification. In the Arab world the only ideological competition comes from Arab nationalism, the left, and liberal democracy, in diminishing order of size and importance. More significantly, since the Al Qaeda attacks of September 11, 2001, and the declaration of the George W. Bush administration's war on terrorism, Arab nationalists and the left increasingly share a common cause with the Islamists in the face of growing political confrontation with the United States. This rising hostility shows no abatement as yet and permits political Islam (Islamism) to gain ever greater ground.

This chapter will argue that democracy and political Islam are potentially quite compatible in principle, and the record indicates as much. I am optimistic about the long-term strength of this trend. Yet real world events damage the practice of such compatibility; the present anger and increasing radicalization of a Muslim world that feels itself under siege is creating a highly negative environment that is not conducive to the emergence of Islamist moderates—indeed for moderates of any stripe. Ultimately, this relationship between democracy and political Islam will not work itself out in the abstract but in the real world. Its actual character on the ground will depend on some concrete variables: country, time, given personalities, local political cultures, and ambient regional and global politics.

First we need to define terms. What is an Islamist? Defined broadly, in keeping with the reality of the phenomenon, an Islamist is anyone who believes that the Koran and the Hadith (traditions of the Prophet's life, actions, and word) contain important principles about Muslim governance and society, and who tries to implement these principles in some way. This definition embraces a broad spectrum that includes both radical and moderate, violent and peaceful, traditional and modern, democratic and antidemocratic. At one extreme it includes Osama bin Laden and Al Qaeda; on the other, the ruling moderate Justice and Development Party (AKP) in Turkey, which seeks membership in the European Union and cooperates with Washington on key aspects of regional politics. The moderate side of the spectrum vastly outweighs the more dangerous, violent, and radical segment, yet it is these latter radical forces that constitute the focus of most governments and the media. Islamism also includes *fundamentalist* views (literalist, narrow, intolerant) but does not equate with it. If we are to understand the long-term issues of Islamism and democracy, we need to look at both "good" Islamists (from the viewpoint of Western policy makers) as well as the "bad." There is an ongoing struggle among them.

Islam versus Democracy: The Theoretical Argument

The debate about the compatibility between Islam and democracy is perhaps the most passionate at the theoretical level—and probably the least important. Some Western scholars examine the Koran and Islamic law and tradition to textually "demonstrate" that Islam is not compatible with democracy. Ironically, their views are bolstered by *radical Islamists* in the Muslim world who similarly argue the incompatibility of these two concepts. The essence of the radical argument rests on the divine source of Islamic law: If God has revealed clear principles of what is to be encouraged and what is to be proscribed, then human desire and man-made law have no place in tampering with these prescriptions and prohibitions. (In a simple example, if Islam has clearly banned the consumption of alcohol, then in an Islamic state no democratic leader or elected parliament has the right to decide that drinking beer is permissible.) Many fundamentalists argue further that "all of life" is about religion, thus making it theoretically impossible to delink Islam from any aspect of society, life, or even governance. Because the state has the primary role in shaping human society, the argument goes, it is imperative that the state be based strictly on Islamic principles to mold an Islamic society, informed first and foremost by religion. In this more radical vision, religion and state are inextricably linked; the sole proper form of government is only rule by just and wise Islamic scholars and not by the uninformed masses. Most Muslims, however, do not agree with this theoretical incompatibility.

But the question, then, is really not only about Islam but about whether *any* revealed religion is compatible with democracy: All major religions have authoritarian bases, are patriarchal, have no democratic foundation, are dogmatic about what constitutes the truth, and do not emphasize reason as a path to God. But the *theory* of incompatibility is belied by reality. Both Protestant and Catholic states in the West, by different paths, have evolved forms of democratic practice that defy any theoretical considerations. In most cases this compromise between ideology and practice has been facilitated by social contract over the extent of public religious authority exercised within a society.

The same process applies to Islam. We are talking here not about what Islam *is*, but about what Muslims *want*. If the course of Muslim political evolution inspires Muslims today to live under democracy—to be able to get rid of bad rulers and have a voice in their own governance—then they will call for democracy, as most in fact do. This reality will define the relationship between Islam and democracy.

Even on a theoretical basis, few Muslims see a contradiction between the two values. Some fundamentalists will argue simplistically that in Islam sovereignty comes from God, whereas in democracy it comes from human beings. (U.S. Supreme Court Justice Antonin Scalia, too, has commented that ultimate sovereignty comes from God.) On this basis, many fundamentalists will argue that human beings cannot pass legislation that infringes on the moral principles of Islam and its traditions: In short, human beings cannot "make law." But even here, modernist Muslims can comfortably agree that all sovereignty derives from God but still point out that Islam does not specify in any way what form the state should take. God furthermore gave humanity the power of reason with which to formulate public policy. The state, even the Islamic state, must still be constructed in conformity with human understanding of how Islam translates into practice and institutions—a process always open to debate and new interpretation over time. In the end then, dicta about what is or is not permissible within Islamist thinking are strictly theoretical; supposed contradictions are belied by the facts on the ground and the actual *experience* of Muslims with democracy.

The Arab Experience with Democracy

To date no Arab state, with the possible exception of Lebanon, qualifies as "democratic"—defined by the ability to change the ruling authority through elections. Advances in democracy in the broader Muslim world have occurred primarily in the non-Arab states of Indonesia, Malaysia, and Turkey, and to a lesser extent in Pakistan, Bangladesh, and even Iran. Nonetheless, some Arab states are moving in encouraging directions, including Jordan, Kuwait, Morocco, and Yemen. But in no Arab country except Lebanon are heads of state and government (presidents, prime ministers) chosen by honest popular elections. Nearly all Arab states now possess pro forma parliaments, but few of them wield any significant power or are able to overturn decisions by an unelected executive. Saudi Arabia actually challenges outright the appropriateness of democracy for Muslims, dismisses democracy as non-Islamic, and claims that its own system is based on the Koran. Yet even the Kingdom has been obliged to inch toward broadening the representative nature of its Consultative Assembly, still largely appointed.

Genuine political parties in the Arab world are generally either absent from the political scene or else severely constrained by the state. In nearly all Arab countries, "ruling parties" dominate the scene and only permit token representation of selected other parties as long as they do not seriously challenge the existing order. The role of any "opposition" is invariably a negotiated process between the ruler and the given party as to how much power and latitude it will be given at any one time.

Why in fact is democracy so weak in the Arab world? The development of democracy there compares unfavorably to all other regions of the world except Africa. This reality prompts some observers to provide a simplistic religious explanation for the phenomenon: Islam is "authoritarian" in character and thus hostile to the emergence of democratic societies. Such a sweeping generalization is belied by the past authoritarian nature of nearly all religions and requires far more detailed and concrete arguments about the nature of political culture in the Arab world. But to what then do we attribute this weak democratic development in Arab states, if not to Islam? Failure to diagnose the problem accurately means near certain failure in finding the correct prescription for a remedy. Some of the following factors rank high in diagnosing problems of the Arab world in developing more democratic orders.

- *Oil.* Oil-producing states in the developing world share particularly poor records in developing democracy, for quite concrete reasons. Large oil revenues inhibit the development of democracy because the state "graciously and generously" distributes oil largesse to a "grateful" public that can make only limited demands on the paternalistic state in return. Conversely, when public taxation provides the fiscal basis for the maintenance of government, people traditionally quickly demand a voice: "No taxation without representation" and hence, "there can be no representation without taxation."
- *Income Levels.* Non-oil Arab states have low per capita income levels, a fact that is typically uncongenial to democracy everywhere.
- *Nature of the Arab State.* The largely arbitrary and "artificial" nature of the modern Arab state and its borders, drawn by colonial powers, has tended to diminish the legitimacy and sovereignty of the individual Arab state. Furthermore, the nearly unique existence of an "Arab world"—where else does such a "world" exist?—weakens the identity of individual Arab states. With a broadly shared culture and language, Arabs tend to feel that developments within other Arab states directly affect their own local interests, giving them a right to a voice, or even interference, in affairs across borders of the greater "Arab nation." Popular identification with the local state has been arguably weaker than in many other parts of the world—sub-Saharan Africa excepted—thus weakening the legitimacy of state structures and the evolution of the democratic process. The ideal of pan-Arabism weakens commitment to local autonomy.

- *Arab–Israeli Tensions.* The creation of the state of Israel on Palestinian soil came at a time when most Arab states themselves were just gaining their own independence. The quick Arab rejection of the new Israeli state and subsequent wars and Arab defeats have encouraged the development of military regimes and security-focused states that are readily exploited by dictators.
- *Geography.* The location of the Arab world on a central East–West axis and the geopolitical reality of over half of the world's oil reserves have made the Middle East a key focus of European colonialism in the nineteenth and twentieth centuries. Struggles between Arab states and colonial powers for control over oil and its pricing have led to frequent Western military intervention that is still ongoing. These conditions and continuing regional tensions have not been conducive to democratic development.
- *Longtime Western Support for "Friendly Tyrants" in the Middle East.* This phenomenon began with the Cold War and systematically weakened democratic forces within the region and elsewhere in the Third World. After the end of the Cold War, the emergence of international terrorism and the Bush administration's war on terrorism have continued to favor the maintenance of "friendly" authoritarian regimes. The Bush administration's call for democratization invariably takes a back seat to security considerations, perpetuating tolerance for cooperative dictators who are supportive of the war on terrorism.
- *Islamism.* The increasing emergence of Islamist movements over the past few decades as the primary opposition to Middle East autocracy has further discouraged the West from pressing the democratic agenda there. Arab dictators facing rising opposition from their own peoples regularly peddle fear of Islamist victories at the polls to discourage support for democracy among Western powers.

The factors cited above offer significant alternative explanations for the present weakness of democracy in the Arab world. But they still amount to a broader argument that specific cultural and historical reasons in the Arab world—both internally and externally generated—have created a contemporary Arab political culture that complicates democratization at this stage of development.

The Evolution of Islamist Thought

Despite the historical obstacles to quick evolution of democracy in the Arab world, the region has seen considerable political evolution over the past few decades, most notably in the development of political Islam. Islamists have particularly shifted in their view of democracy over the past half century. For a long time, democracy was discredited on several grounds. First, it was perceived as a Western, indeed colonial, importation that had no roots in the Arab world. It was propounded mainly by a small group of Westernizers, a tiny elite who lacked broad acceptability in society and were seen to be linked to colonial and Western values in ways that threatened Muslim culture. It was an "alien" importation suspected of furthering the designs of imperial powers.

But political thought in Islam has long been aware of the requirement for good governance, particularly defined over the centuries as the need for *just* governance. Until recent centuries, few rulers anywhere in the world derived their legitimacy from an electoral process; in Islam, rulers derived legitimacy, at least in the eyes of the *'ulama* (clerics), primarily through the rulers' attentiveness to application of Islamic law and implementation of justice on the social level. But if rulers turned out not to be just or Islamically legitimate, there were no legal mechanisms for getting rid of them.

The problem was compounded when jurisprudential authority during the chaos and destruction of the Mongol invasions propounded the concept that even unjust rule was preferable to chaos and anarchy. This legal opinion has comfortably served autocrats well ever since, because it provides virtual de facto sanction for tyranny. These theories have not prevented Muslims, just like people in other parts of the world, from engaging in periodic revolts against oppressive rulers. Interestingly, mainstream Islamists in the twentieth century were the first to widely break with the clerical concept that "oppression is preferable to anarchy" and to demand that rulers must indeed be just and good Muslims, free of corruption or misrule. In this new view, if rulers failed to deliver justice, they could and should be legitimately overthrown—a near

Jeffersonian vision that the tyrannical state should be resisted, even by force. As a result, Islamists have developed new regard for some aspects of Western democratic practice that include checks and balances and instrumentalities for getting rid of unwanted and illegitimate rulers.

How far does the Islamists' embrace of democratic principles go? For several decades Islamists across the Muslim world have been steadily moving toward acceptance of the concept of democracy, at least in principle. The rationale has little to do with convoluted arguments about the source of sovereignty, or whether democracy is an alien Western institution. Islamist appreciation for the values of a democratic order has been most strengthened by the very reality that they themselves would be among the primary beneficiaries of it. The same goes for their growing support for concepts of human rights: Even nonviolent Islamists are now victims of arbitrary authoritarian rule and extralegal punishment by the state (arrests, persecution, and execution). And as Islamists have assumed the role of the major opposition movement in most Arab states, the greater becomes the attraction of democracy that would likely grant them a dominant voice in initial elections.

Would Islamists still embrace democratization and human rights if they did not see themselves as the primary beneficiaries? This is a valid question, since much of this more recent Islamist appreciation for democracy is based on pragmatic reasons. But is there any reason why pragmatic thinking is not desirable? Pragmatism, for example, has led to clear long-term political change in the thinking of the Muslim Brotherhood across most of the Arab world. (Yet even here the conversion is not complete: There is the disturbing case of Sudan, where in 1989 the Brotherhood participated in a military coup against a semidemocratic regime because it believed it could not win power by democratic means. The Brotherhood is still the key element of an authoritarian order in Sudan today.)

Caution is thus needed in evaluating the newfound Islamist enthusiasm for democracy. First, Islamists *in power* in the Muslim world—in Sudan, Iran, and the Taliban's Afghanistan—so far have not shown a serious commitment to democracy, although Iran has shown encouraging progress in holding honest elections, even while circumscribing the kinds of candidates permitted to run. Even Sudan is groping its way toward greater opening with some of the former opposition parties, although the terrible human rights abuses endemic there for decades continue in parts of the country. In these cases, Islamists behave in patterns typical of most regimes across the Muslim world: They are reluctant to give up power once they have attained it.

A more important reality, however, is that in all three of these cases, Islamists came to power through nondemocratic processes—revolution, military coup, and civil war, respectively. *Any* party that gains power by these means is unlikely to open up the system to greater democracy. The real test of Islamist commitment to democracy comes when they win power through democratic elections and then face the prospect of loss in future elections. In the Arab world there is no democratic precedent as yet—the old fear about Islamists supporting only "one man, one vote, one time" style elections has never actually happened in the Islamist experience because Islamists have not been permitted to participate fully or win in open elections. The real question about whether Islamists are ready to win—and lose—elections has less to do with Islam and more to do with the political culture of the given country in question. Where democratic concepts and practice have some historical roots or track record, the chances are good that Islamists—indeed any political party— will honor constitutional precepts and accept defeat as well as victory. I have great confidence, for example, that the present ruling Islamists in Turkey will relinquish power constitutionally when at some point they lose an election, because Turkish democratic culture by now has taken root and is quite advanced. However, in states such as Algeria that have no tradition of democratic practice, there is no guarantee that if Islamists—or any other political party—win a legitimate electoral victory that they would hold subsequent elections or agree to leave power upon losing such an election.

Confronting Strategic Dilemmas

As Islamists gain opportunities to move into the political arena with greater freedom, they face key strategic choices involving dilemmas of choosing between principles and the use of power.

Play the Political Game, or Resort to Violence?

Islamists first need to decide whether they want to enter the political process at all. Many Western political commentators emphasize that if allowed to enter the system, Islamists (or any other opposition) must play by the "rules of the game." But the rules of the game in Arab countries are generally designed by authoritarian regimes to weaken and marginalize all opposition. Such methods include holding presidential referendums in place of elections, dishonest elections, arbitrary barring of religiously based parties when they constitute the primary opposition, arrest of leading Islamist figures on the eve of elections, other forms of individual electoral disbarment, gerrymandering of electoral districts, state control of media, and government denial of airtime to opposition elements on government-controlled radio and television to promote platforms. These processes are widespread in Algeria, Bahrain, Egypt, Jordan, Kuwait, and other states that make some claim to adoption of democratic processes. Under such conditions, the rules of the game are themselves the problem and are not seen as acceptable by the marginalized opposition.

As a result, some radical movements have rejected the state outright and adopted violence or armed struggle against it, particularly in Algeria, Egypt, Libya, Saudi Arabia, and Yemen.

In Egypt, two dangerous Islamist terrorist organizations emerged in the 1980s: Islamic Societies (*al-Jama'at al-Islamiyya*) and Islamic Jihad (*al-Jihad al-Islami*). These movements have by now been almost completely eliminated by state security organizations, at least for the interim, and their leadership has subsequently renounced violence as a political tool inappropriate to Islam. Some of these conversions to "true, nonviolent" Islam may be viewed with some skepticism because they took place within prison walls where the logic of the state's theological arguments no doubt carries greater weight. But such movements may also have recognized that they cannot defeat the state at this juncture and that renunciation of violence is the wiser path. For some radical Islamists, then, the change of heart may be quite sincere as they gain experience and confront reality. But given the huge political tensions within a state such as Egypt, the reasonable likelihood of political explosion, the rising regional polarization, and the ongoing discrediting of all authoritarian leadership, we cannot rule out the possibility that remnants of these earlier movements may once again adopt violence as a way to combat the state, especially should it show signs of tottering. In Libya and Saudi Arabia, it is even more likely that Islamists will turn to violence, because they do not have a democratic option in the first place.

Reopening of Armed Violence

If the repressive powers of the authoritarian state had generally prevailed in the struggle against most violent Islamists before September 11, the events of September 11 may have regrettably reopened the path to violence. The Bush administration's war on terrorism and the prolonged violence of the U.S. war in Iraq have revivified movements of violence in an expanded armed struggle against the American presence in the Middle East. Arab regimes that support the U.S. presence have likewise become new targets. This reemergence of regional violence undoubtedly stems in the first instance from the activities of Al Qaeda and the U.S. military response to it. The spread of regional violence unfortunately has greatly strengthened the voice of the radicals against the moderates, especially when the moderates seemingly cannot demonstrate that their peaceful path has borne fruit and when the Arab homeland seems to be under a state of siege, radicalizing the general population against both the United States and compliant Arab regimes.

Violence of course need not be the only path to rejection of the existing political order. Several movements have adopted (generally) nonviolent and nonpolitical means. Typical of this phenomenon is *al-Takfir wa'l Hijra*, literally the denunciation of the existing political society as non-Islamic (*kafir*) and the search for refuge from it, in the form of underground organization. Similarly, the Liberation Party (*Hizb al-Tahrir*), a radical movement, has spread outside its original base in Palestine to become a major nonviolent underground force in Central Asia and other Muslim locales. Many Wahhabi (*Tawhidi*) organizations likewise propagate a radical analysis of the ills of the Arab and Muslim world and call for a change in the political order, even when not engaging in violence. All these groups denounce existing political orders as Islamically illegitimate and call for adoption of strict Islamic (*Sharia*) law and noncooperation with the West as the only way to revitalize the moral underpinnings of the Arab world and set it on a path of renewed legitimacy and power. These groups see a change in public attitudes and values as a necessary prelude to any political change.

Before September 11 most Islamist organizations in the Arab world had seemingly accepted the futility and even error of engaging in armed struggle, but the radicalizing tensions of the post–September 11 Middle East have rekindled this debate, at least in the short to medium term, with unpredictable impact on the longer range evolution of many Islamist movements.

Movements versus Parties

Political participation by definition requires compromise. If a movement possesses clearly established political and religious values, is it appropriate to compromise those values by cooperation with other political movements whose values might be quite alien? And if the rules of the game, as noted above, are skewed or unfair, is there any value in cooperating with an unjust political order for marginal gain? The virtue of a *movement*, as opposed to a party, is that it can espouse its moral and political values without working with the regime, without compromising its own principles. Many Islamists have argued further that it is nearly impossible to change the political order without first changing the ideas, values, and attitudes of society itself. If a transition in public values and understanding has not taken place, then even a popular Islamist party faces the issue of whether to try to *impose* its views on the public—at some risk if the public is not ready. Indeed, one major Islamist thinker, Rashid Al Ghannushi of Tunisia, living in exile in London, has famously commented that "the most dangerous thing is for the Islamists to be loved by the people before they get to power and then hated afterwards."[1] Such is precisely the case in Iran today, for example, where political Islam has become synonymous with a repressive state order, leading the people to "hate" Islam when it becomes the justification for regime oppression.

Yet in the end, the temptations of competing in the political order as a political party have proven irresistible for most Islamists, even when the rules of the game are perceived as unfair. Power is perceived as the ultimate instrument of change. The state itself is the prize, however used to fulfill political goals.

As a result, most Islamist movements in the Arab world have opted to move in the direction of establishing political parties where permitted. The most important example is the Muslim Brotherhood, the oldest, most important, and most influential of all Islamist movements. The Brotherhood led the way with the establishment of political parties in most Arab countries, under a variety of different names. The Brotherhood in Jordan, for example, has cooperated for decades with the throne, at one point providing a valuable counterweight to the power of radical Arab nationalist parties in the 1960s. The Brotherhood is active in Egypt as well (the seat of the original movement and still its unofficial head-quarters). It has contested elections regularly in Algeria since the Algerian political order was partially opened in 1991 and where it was viewed by the regime as a moderate force compared with the largest and slightly more radical umbrella organization, the Islamic Salvation Front. Parties linked with the Brotherhood are also legally active in politics in Kuwait, Lebanon, Morocco, Palestine, and Yemen. It remains a movement in other Arab states where political parties are banned. It is permitted to exist as a movement in Egypt but is not allowed to form an official party—although Brotherhood members are sometimes permitted to run on the slate of other parties and win seats in the very tame and controlled parliament. The Brotherhood is banned outright in Syria and Tunisia, but it is allowed to function as a movement under very close supervision in Saudi Arabia. It has reemerged strongly in Iraq after the fall of Saddam Hussein.

In all of these states, the Muslim Brotherhood has demonstrated a willingness to work with other parties toward common goals, even with communist parties whose ideology is anathema to its values. The Brotherhood works increasingly more closely with Arab nationalists and liberals on two key shared goals: liberalization of regimes in all Arab countries (which would strengthen the Brotherhood at the polls), and an "anti-imperialist" agenda of opposing U.S. interventionist policies in the Muslim world. Ironically, the heightened anti-Americanism across a wide spectrum of the Arab world is likely to help integrate the Islamists into the mainstream of Arab politics and to diminish their differences with other major ideological trends. Although this is not good news for current U.S. policy in the region, it suggests that all but the most radical and violent Islamists will gain the practical experience of compromise on national goals. This experience is serving to move Islamists away from doctrinaire or pseudotheological approaches to political problems. In short, even though the whole Arab world is moving toward greater radicalism and anti-Americanism, Islamist parties are entering the system more vigorously in nearly every country and becoming part of that new mainstream. Anti-Americanism facilitates the integration of Islamism everywhere.

Diversification of Islamist Parties

State repression of Islamist movements and parties over past decades pushed them toward a certain sense of solidarity with one another and avoidance of mutual public criticism. But that reality is changing as movements expand and diversify, producing a far healthier phenomenon of more open debate and rivalry among them. Some Islamist parties have tried to put themselves beyond criticism by assuming conspicuously religious names linked to God or the Prophet, a practice denounced by secularists as arrogant and dangerous: How could a party with the name of Party of God (*Hizballah*) be beyond political criticism or attack? How can a specific political party speak in the name of God? Today, there are not only several Parties of God, but several Islamic Jihads, an Army of Muhammad (*Jaysh Muhammad*), Troops of God (*Jund Allah*), Partisans of Islam (*Ansar al-Islam*), and others of similar ilk. By becoming commonplace, religiously freighted names such as these are actually frittering away their religious impact. And with the multiplication of Islamist parties, debate and rivalry among them has opened up, an extremely important and healthy phenomenon. No Islamist party can now claim any serious *religious* authority, even if it wields political, financial, or guerrilla power. Radical and intolerant movements cannot claim monopoly on religious truth, and the public has opportunity to hear debate over religion as it affects politics. Already there has been a very significant public break between the major forces of Wahhabism (*Tawhidis* or *Salafis*) in Saudi Arabia and the Muslim Brotherhood over the narrowness and intolerance of the Wahhabis, from whose ranks Al Qaeda emerged.

Divisions, debate, and rivalry among Islamist parties now occurs not only between countries, but within a single country as in Algeria, Egypt, Jordan, Kuwait, Lebanon, Morocco, Sudan, and Yemen. Interestingly, in Egypt a more modernist offshoot of the Muslim Brotherhood has emerged in the form of the Center Party (*Hizb al-Wasat*), which calls for far greater women's representation within the party and for the extension of membership to the Coptic Christian minority—using the values, not the theology, of Islam as a common denominator. The old-line Brotherhood has opportunistically cooperated with the regime in preventing the Center Party from gaining legal status within the country. Nonetheless, further debate among all these parties is welcome and important. Islamist ideology must be exposed to full public debate if it is to evolve, mature, and deal with the real world responsibly, constructively, and pragmatically.

Playing Politics

Another development that augurs well for the future is that as Islamist parties legally enter the political order, they start playing politics. They have proven adept at forming coalitions with other parties, regardless of ideology, to achieve common short-term goals, usually conservative ones. In Kuwait, the Muslim Brotherhood and the fundamentalists (*Salafis*) are rivals, but they often agree on conservative approaches to social issues such as separate male-female education and issues of public morality. In Jordan, because of the preponderance of Palestinians in the country, the Brotherhood has played heavily to the agenda of struggle for Palestinian rights in Israel. Although the Brotherhood as an organization does not engage in political violence, it draws a clear distinction, as does most of the Arab world, between the apocalyptic terrorism of the Al Qaeda type, which it condemns, and the armed struggle for Palestinian national liberation, which it condones. The Brotherhood in Jordan seeks to push the regime into greater confrontation with Israel, partly as a tactic to embarrass the regime. Within Palestine itself, the Brotherhood has sponsored the guerrilla-terrorist movement Hamas to engage in the armed struggle along with secular Palestinian guerrilla organizations.

Islamists also play politics through exploiting Islam in the debate of religious issues that do not lead in the direction of liberalization at all. In Egypt and Kuwait, for example, Islamists have often demanded the government ban specific books or arrest certain leading liberal thinkers for blasphemy. This role is hardly constructive and indeed has the undesirable effect of inhibiting the very debate that would lead to greater evolution and interpretation of Islam in a modern context. In most cases, the Islamists, like other politicians, are strictly playing politics—seeking to embarrass and weaken the state by charging it with insufficient zeal in protecting Islam. Sometimes Islamists will call for the state to adopt far more conservative positions in conformity with ostensible "Islamic law" as a way of pressuring the state. These tactics are familiar in all democracies as some political leaders adopt extreme agendas designed to tactically embarrass the incumbent government and appease key segments of the public even when such agendas are unrealistic.

At the same time, however, politics also forced some degree of liberalization on Islamists. Women's roles within Islamist parties have grown in all Muslim countries as soon as elections are held because female votes are as valuable as male votes in winning elections. Women's wings of Islamist parties, and even women on the central committees of these parties, are now commonplace.

In my view, therefore, we can see within Islamist politics some key developments that evoke cautious optimism about its future evolution in the Arab world:

- Broad understanding of the importance of democratization and the benefits that accrue for Islamist parties themselves in calling for more participatory government.
- Willingness of many parties to work pragmatically with other parties with differing ideologies toward common goals without becoming rigidly committed to a narrow vision.
- Exposure of Islamist parties to the political and social realities of the contemporary Arab world in which mere slogans about "Islam is the answer" simply will not suffice; their growing awareness that they need to find concrete answers to concrete problems if they are to succeed in the political arena.
- Broadening of the ideological debate among Islamists themselves, thus opening space for greater intellectual and theoretical development and evolution.
- Signs of growing pragmatism and realism based on experience.
- The nonviolent nature of the vast majority of such parties.
- The likelihood that most of the grand debates of Arab politics in the next decade will be *within* the framework of Islamist politics more broadly. In other words, Islamist debate is just beginning. Political debate must encompass Islam if the debate is to be meaningful. Excluding the Islamic factor in Arab politics will simply be one-sided and unrealistic given the critical importance of Islamists in many Arab societies.

The International Factor in Islamist Politics

If the Arab world were operating in isolation, the factors discussed above might be the dominant ones in forging the politics of a new

Middle East. A review of these trends would provide ample grounds for optimism about the successful integration of a great segment of the powerful forces of Islamist politics into a democratization process across the Arab world. But the Arab world is not operating in isolation. Indeed, it is now operating within an intensely negative international environment with tensions perhaps unprecedented in the modern history of the Middle East.

The Al Qaeda attacks of September 11 transformed U.S. policy under the Bush administration, placing the war on terrorism at the center of U.S. foreign policy. This goal of eliminating terrorism worldwide has focused almost exclusively on the Muslim world where the majority of radical terrorist movements now exist. The war against the Taliban, the invasion of Iraq, the overthrow of Saddam Hussein, the U.S. occupation of Iraq, the spread of U.S. military presence across the Muslim world, the new embrace of authoritarian Muslim regimes as allies in the war on terrorism, the ongoing deterioration of the situation in Palestine, and America's close identification with the Likud Party's hard-line policy toward the occupied territories—all have led to a massive growth of anti-American feeling in the Arab world at nearly all levels of society. This sentiment is reflected and deepened by independent satellite television channels and is now beginning to affect the views of an entire generation of young Arabs.

At the same time, Arab regimes are under greater pressure—from the United States on the one hand and their own people on the other—more than ever before, at a time when the gap between the rulers and ruled has never been so wide. Nearly all regimes are viewed with contempt by publics that see them as led by supine dictators, who depend on harsh security services to stay in power, who are powerless to change realities in the Arab world, who cling to tight relations with Washington at any cost to preserve their power and thus are even more subservient to U.S. interests than more democratic allies of the United States such as Turkey or Europe. There is almost no regime in the region whose fall would not elicit widespread public enthusiasm—with possible exceptions in the United Arab Emirates, Qatar, and maybe Morocco. This places Islamists at the forefront of the opposition and in command of much popular support. The public may also show some cynicism on occasion about the opportunism of Islamists as well, but Islamists are the current masters of anti-imperial and anti-regime rhetoric.

Muslims, furthermore, feel uniquely under siege from the West—read the United States—at this stage in their history and react strictly defensively. They are in a hunker-down mode, feeling their culture and religion under attack and under legal discrimination even in the West. Any culture feeling itself under siege turns to basics. As a result, Muslims are embracing Islamic practice more deeply, an essential element of their identity. When their religion is vilified or portrayed in the West as part of the problem, Muslims not surprisingly react by intensifying their identification with Islam as a source of strength, solace, and solidarity. Islamic emotions are stronger than ever. Those Arabs who identify with other ideological trends—Arab nationalism, or the smaller leftist/socialist/Marxist elite, or the smaller yet liberal Westernizing elite—all find it difficult to avoid being drawn into a broader wave of Islamist–nationalist rhetoric and action dedicated to repelling the foreign invader, militarily, politically, and culturally. The line between nationalism and the Islamic identity is now nearly obliterated: Even *non*-Muslim Arabs generally identify with the broader Islamist–nationalist trend.

Prognosis

In the face of these immense international pressures and "civilizational" confrontations, conditions for continuing a moderate evolution of Islamist movements are at their worst. Anti-imperial and anti-regime instincts now motivate the public at large and generate more radicalized attitudes. A process of polarization is under way in which anti-Western and anti-American violence is now perceived, if not as acceptable, at least as "understandable" in defense of the Islamic homeland and its culture. Radicalism on both the secular and religious levels is merging. Regrettably, it is unrealistic to think that at this juncture in Arab history we will find greater tolerance and openness toward the West or greater interest in Western political institutions or moderation. In the struggle against local regimes, radical ideologies are likely to shout down more moderate and liberal interpretations of Islam and Islamic politics in particular.

The prognosis for political Islam under these conditions—indeed for almost any form of moderate politics—is not good. Moderate voices, Islamist or non-Islamist, dare not speak up in the mood of rising radicalism. Indeed, we might speculate that at least two things must occur before we can hope to see any longer term trend of moderation within Arab Islamist politics. Only after existing regimes fall, or throw open the political process, will there be a chance for genuinely open and democratic orders to emerge. But this in itself is not enough, because the mood of the new more populist regimes will initially be anti-American. The external sources of radicalization must also be curtailed. This means an end to the radical right-wing policies of the Likud in Israel and a just settlement of the Palestinian problem, a departure of U.S. troops from the region, and an end to the more intimidating and broad-brush anti-Muslim discrimination that has unfortunately come to mark the new global alert against Muslim terrorism.

Until this happens, the region will remain radicalized and without political outlet, except through Islamist parties and movements. Anti-American and anti-regime terrorism, if not condoned, will be viewed with immense ambiguity or even indulged by publics at large. These conditions are the worst possible for the moderate evolution of the Arab world. But all is not lost. If the conditions that are generating such radicalism today can be addressed or ameliorated, then the longer term future of the Arab world is likely to be quite different. Islamist parties will simply become a part of a broader political spectrum and less a source of anxiety to all—as has happened in Turkey. Unfortunately, getting there is not likely to be quick or easy.

Note

This chapter was originally published as Carnegie Paper 49 (August 2004).

1. Rashid Al Ghannushi, "Islamist Movements: Self-Criticism and Reconsideration," *Palestine Times*, no. 94 (April 1999).

4

The New Reform Ferment

Amy Hawthorne

IN THE THREE YEARS SINCE the terrorist attacks of September 11, 2001, the question of Arab reform not only has become closely linked in the minds of Western policy makers to the fight against Al Qaeda, but also a dominant theme of discussion in the region itself. Arab satellite television stations broadcast talk shows featuring vigorous discussions about the persistence of authoritarian rule in Arab countries and the incompetence of incumbent regimes. The opinion pages of Arab newspapers are replete with articles championing democratic reform as the only way to strengthen the region against Western control, or, conversely, to connect it with globalization and "modernity." Civil society groups, political parties, and even business organizations are promulgating reform manifestos with increasing regularity. Political reform is also the focus of heated debates in unexpected circles such as the Egyptian Muslim Brotherhood and the Saudi royal family. All Arab governments have acknowledged the need for reform in principle (some have even talked of democracy), and many have announced their own reform initiatives.

The nascent reform trend has inspired optimistic predictions that the region is finally responding to the global trend toward democracy. Egyptian sociologist Saad Eddin Ibrahim, one of the Arab world's best-known democracy activists, argues that the prospects for liberal democracy in the region have never been so bright.[1] Influential American journalist Fareed Zakaria concluded after a visit to the region that "everywhere in the Arab world, people are talking about reform . . . the wind is behind those who advocate free-market, modern, Western-style reforms."[2] And in 2003 and 2004, President George W. Bush spoke of Arab democratization as a certainty. As he declared in a June 2004 speech, "voices in that region are increasingly demanding reform and democratic change . . . now freedom is stirring in the Middle East and no one should bet against it."[3]

Such enthusiasm about the inevitability of democratic change in the Middle East is premature. So far, talk about reform exceeds actual reform implemented, and the reforms that Arab governments have actually carried out in the past three years are quite modest and do not affect their fundamentally authoritarian character. Furthermore, there is no popular movement for democratic change in the Arab world, only a growing willingness among some members of the elite to question existing systems and deliberate future options.

Nonetheless, an important debate about political change is clearly under way. The point at which discourse penetrates the surface of politics and reshapes norms and values on a broad scale is difficult to predict, and the context for reform varies considerably from country to country. But the ferment is real and should not be dismissed as inconsequential.[4]

The Long Road

Some Western commentators have portrayed the Arab world as a politically stagnant region that suddenly has awakened to the idea of change in the aftermath of the September 11 attacks. Such a depiction is quite misleading. With the exception, until recently, of the Gulf countries, Arab states have been buffeted by strong currents of political change throughout the twentieth century. The first half of the century was a period of considerable instability. In the space of a few decades, the Ottoman Empire collapsed and Britain and France successfully asserted control over much of the region, though some states gained or retained nominal independence. The new imperial arrangements were often sharply contested, however, and the European imperial presence began to decline after the Second World War. Nationalism, often with a liberal, secular ethos, was the dominant factor in Arab politics during this period. By mid-century, particularly after the 1952 Free Officers' coup and the rise of Gamal Abdel Nasser in Egypt, liberalism receded and ideologies of Arab socialism and pan-Arabism took hold, inspiring efforts to reshape political systems into one-party states with centrally controlled economies. By the 1980s and 1990s, as regimes faced the twin challenges of economic contraction and Islamist opposition movements, a mild liberalizing trend reemerged. Seeking to shore up their legitimacy, many rulers experimented with heavily manipulated multiparty elections and lifted some controls on political activity. Civic organizations dedicated to democracy and human rights, along with pan-Arab satellite television stations and other forms of new, more open media, came into being across the region during these years.

Political reform—at least demands for it by domestic critics of Arab regimes and pledges of it by rulers in times of crisis—has been a recurring motif in modern Arab politics. For example, since the early twentieth century, Islamic fundamentalists have urged reform according to "authentic" Islamic principles—to fight what they see as the deterioration of Arab society resulting from Western influences. In Egypt, after calls for reform from judges and intellectuals following the Arab defeat in the 1967 war with Israel, President Nasser tried to regain his credibility by announcing limited political reforms. Demands for governance changes and anticorruption measures have convulsed the Palestinian national movement at critical junctures in the conflict with Israel. And in the 1980s and 1990s, as mentioned above, many Arab rulers adopted the rhetoric and sometimes the trappings of democracy to bolster their credentials in the face of mounting socioeconomic problems.

Calls for reform have surged and receded, however, without altering the core of authoritarian rule. Governments often have used promises of reform as a smokescreen for inaction. By 2001, the Arab world remained the least free and democratic region of the world, according to the annual surveys of the watchdog group Freedom House and the evaluations of most other analysts.[5] Liberalization programs stalled or were reversed in most countries as Arab regimes manipulated openings and closings to maintain their grip on power. To be sure, throughout the 1990s voices across the region, mainly liberal intellectuals and civil society activists, called for democracy. But they usually spoke in cautious, vague terms to avoid overstepping the narrow bounds of tolerated public discourse. They were only marginal voices in a political milieu in which pan-Arab causes such as Palestine dominated the regional agenda and any suggestion that reform should be the Arabs' priority was widely viewed as tantamount to a betrayal of such causes.

The reform ferment of the post–September 11 period represents an evolution of this earlier liberalizing trend, rather than a wholly new stage in Arab politics. Three characteristics mark the present reform environment. First, political reform has become a topic of regional concern. Advocates of democracy from most Arab countries are speaking out in the pan-Arab media and at regional conferences. Almost every Arab government has committed itself rhetorically to the concept of reform, and the issue has forced itself onto the agenda of Arab League summits and other such conclaves for the first time. This geographic broadening has had a magnifying effect on calls for reform in individual countries as Arab governments compete with one another to show a reformist face to the world, and civic activists feel solidarity with their counterparts across the region. Second, the boundaries of discourse have expanded. Liberal democrats are the most outspoken, openly raising previously taboo issues such as instituting term limits for Arab rulers and lifting emergency laws. Third, voices challenging the very need for reform are somewhat fainter. Although the Palestinian and Iraqi causes remain staples of Arab political discourse, the current debate revolves more around what reforms are needed and the role of outsiders, particularly the United States, in supporting change, than around whether change is necessary at all.

External Pressures

A combination of factors has stimulated the current reform ferment, including developments in the Arab world itself and the unprecedented international pressure for change spurred by the events of September 11. Although the internal factors carry the most weight, it is worth considering the external pressures first, because they are in a sense the most visible and novel.

Within days of the September 11 attacks, the previously obscure topic of the Arab world's "democracy deficit" suddenly became the focus of wide discussion in Western media and policy circles. A chorus of commentators, mainly in the United States, blamed the spread of terrorist groups such as Al Qaeda and the rise of politically militant Islamic fundamentalist movements on political repression and economic stagnation in Arab countries. Neoconservative analysts in particular criticized autocratic Arab governments, including close U.S. allies such as Egypt and Saudi Arabia, for spawning radical groups and stifling moderates. Likening the fight against Al Qaeda to a Manichean struggle in which the United States is the savior of Western civilization, neoconservatives appealed to the Bush administration to make the democratic transformation of the Middle East a cornerstone of the war on terrorism.

The Bush administration basically accepted this analysis of the roots of terrorism. It responded to the suddenly pervasive question "why do they hate us?" by putting the responsibility, and thus the onus of change, on Arab regimes rather than on the United States. (An alternative answer to the question, that animosity toward the United States stemmed at least in part from its policies in the Middle East, was more threatening, because it implied that the United States had contributed to the rise of terrorism and should reconsider its policies.) The idea of promoting democracy as an antidote to terrorism gained the endorsement of the realist camp in the administration and attracted bipartisan support in Congress. Democracy promotion in the Middle East thus became for the first time an important tenet of the United States' Middle East policy.

Until now at least, the main thrust of the new policy has been exhortatory rhetoric. President Bush and his top aides spoke regularly in 2003 and 2004 about the need for liberty and freedom to take hold in the Middle East, declared America's commitment to support voices of reform in the region, praised Arab leaders who have carried out reforms, and gently called on others to do so. The administration's most extensive articulation of its democracy-promotion policy came in a November 2003 speech at the National Endowment for Democracy in which President Bush announced that his administration was replacing the long-standing U.S. policy of unquestioning support for friendly authoritarian Arab regimes with a new "forward strategy of freedom" for the Middle East. The old policy, he stated, had brought stability but had failed to protect U.S. national security.

In addition, the Bush administration frequently invoked Arab reform in the context of the U.S.-led invasion and occupation of Iraq. The administration maintained that toppling Saddam Hussein and implanting a democratic government in Iraq would inspire a wave of democratic change throughout the Middle East. This assertion aimed not only to offer a rationale for the war to the American public, but also to signal to

Arab regimes that the United States is no longer wedded to upholding the region's undemocratic status quo.

Although the leading edge of the new policy is rhetoric, some diplomatic and aid initiatives have been launched. Political reform has edged its way onto the list of talking points for meetings with Arab leaders, and senior U.S. officials have made visits to the region centered on reform issues. New assistance programs include the State Department's Middle East Partnership Initiative (MEPI), launched in December 2002, and the White House's Broader Middle East and North Africa Initiative, formally unveiled at the June 2004 Group of Eight industrialized nations (G-8) summit at Sea Island, Georgia. MEPI funds political, economic, and educational reform programs in Arab countries. The Broader Middle East and North Africa Initiative is more ambitious, providing a U.S.–European framework for democracy promotion and proposing, among other initiatives, a new democracy fund and a regional forum for dialogue on reform among donors, Arab governments, and Arab civil society groups.

The U.S. government has also pursued the goal of democracy promotion through new public diplomacy programs, including radio and television stations, that deliver prodemocracy and pro-American messages to Arab audiences. Outside the administration, a growing interest in reform among members of Congress, along with the post–September 11 proliferation of American media reports, task forces, conferences, research programs, and other private initiatives on Arab democracy, represent additional forms of external pressure.

Arab governments and publics have reacted to this collective stream of unflattering attention on two levels. On one level, they have exhibited hostility and defensiveness. They have reacted with particular scorn to Washington's attempt to recast itself as a champion of democracy and as the friend of all Arab reformers. Such hostility is hardly a surprise given the unfriendliness of the environment into which the Bush administration was attempting to project its democracy message. Long-standing Arab suspicion of U.S. motives in the region was only exacerbated by the administration's unconditional support for controversial Israeli Prime Minister Ariel Sharon. On a second, deeper level, despite mistrust of the messenger, many government officials and other members of the elite have basically accepted the message that Arab countries need positive political, economic, and social change. Thus, as U.S. rhetoric on democracy became more prominent in 2003 and 2004, domestic opponents of Arab regimes coupled their criticisms of U.S. policy with calls for reform. Some Arabs who had privately supported democratic reform but had hesitated to voice their opinions publicly were also emboldened to weigh in. For their part, Arab rulers, suddenly no longer able to depend on the protection offered by U.S. silence about their poor governance and human rights records, found it difficult to reject such criticism outright as they had long done.

The U.S. occupation of Iraq added to the reform ferment, but not, as the Bush administration had predicted, by providing an inspirational democratic model. Instead, the Iraq war influenced the reform environment in other ways. Widespread anger over the war and over Arab governments' inability to prevent it exposed Arab governments to fresh charges of incompetence from their citizenry and to new expressions of discontent with the status quo. The war also enhanced many Arab governments' desire to portray themselves internationally as reformers. They sought to demonstrate that, unlike Saddam Hussein, they cared for the well-being of their citizens and thus should not be considered targets of future U.S. interventions, occupations, and social transformations launched in the name of human rights. Arab civil society groups and opposition parties also started to put forward their own reform initiatives in 2003 and 2004. They too sought to seize the reform agenda from the United States to counter neoconservative suggestions that the Middle East was a passive region subject to impending transformation by the West.

These tensions were particularly acute in Egypt, Jordan, and Saudi Arabia—close U.S. allies that had officially opposed the invasion but provided behind-the-scenes military assistance to the United States. In the months after the toppling of the Iraqi regime, Jordan moved to appease popular discontent by holding long-delayed legislative elections. The Saudi government launched a national dialogue on reform and announced its intention to hold the kingdom's first nationwide municipal elections, in which half of the members of municipal councils will be elected. In Egypt, President Hosni Mubarak pushed a package of modest political reforms through parliament, the first such reforms the government had carried out in more than a decade.

Internal Factors

External pressure alone would not have been sufficient to trigger a debate about reform in the absence of domestic factors that pushed a majority of Arab governments to accept the necessity of change and that emboldened domestic critics to speak up more openly.

From the point of view of the governments in the region, the preponderant factor that made them more amenable to the idea of reform was a combination of fear of the upsurge of terrorism and the realization that security measures, while necessary, would not be sufficient to combat radical groups. September 11 stunned not only the United States, but many Arab governments as well. Saudi Arabia was particularly shocked to discover how many of the perpetrators were Saudi citizens. Initially unwilling to believe that the information was correct, the Saudi government finally had to accept the evidence, particularly after terrorist attacks began occurring inside the Kingdom itself in 2003. Yemen had recognized the degree to which terrorists operated in the country with the attack on the *U.S.S. Cole* warship in 2000. Algeria had been battling Islamist terrorism for years. Morocco experienced a major terrorist incident in Casablanca in 2003, and Jordan foiled several plots in the past few years. Only Egypt, which had experienced its wave of terrorism earlier, appeared to have the situation under control, at least for the time being.

The reaction in all countries was to heighten security measures, which further constrained Arab citizens' already limited civil and political rights, yet also to acknowledge the need for reform and in some cases to carry out reforms. It is difficult to judge to what extent this reform impulse was based simply on a desire to project a more benign image abroad and to what extent Arab governments accepted the U.S. administration's argument that domestic repression was in itself a main cause of radicalism and terrorism. Given the limited nature of the reforms that most governments have introduced, the former appears more likely than the latter.

Some countries, furthermore, were experiencing political pressures unrelated to the threat of terrorism that forced them to face the necessity of change. Egypt was moving toward a succession crisis because of President Mubarak's advancing age and failure to appoint a vice president. Jordan, with more than half of its population of Palestinian origin, was confronted by widespread anger among its citizens because the government was maintaining its peace treaty with Israel while Palestinians in the West Bank and Gaza were under siege. Algeria was trying to reconstruct a political system that could maintain a fragile peace after a civil war between government forces and radical Islamist groups throughout the 1990s. The Gulf countries were contending with the challenge of adapting political systems originally designed to control poor, backward societies to govern increasingly educated populations seeking to join the global economy. Across the region, governments faced huge gaps between the number of entrants into the job market and the number of jobs available, education systems that failed to produce graduates suited for the needs of the global economy, and paltry foreign direct investment outside the oil and gas sectors. For all Arab governments, in other words, socioeconomic and political pressures building during the 1980s and 1990s were intensifying at the time of the September 11 attacks, making reform a necessity.

The publication in May 2002 of the United Nations Development Program's *Arab Human Development Report* enhanced the legitimacy of reform as a pressing pan-Arab issue. Highly critical of Arab regimes, the report denounced the deficits of education, good governance, freedom, and women's empowerment and described political and economic reform as essential to solving the multiple crises facing the region. The document's credibility derived from the fact that it was written by well-respected Arabs but also had the authority of the United Nations behind it. Arab governments simply could not ignore the report as they had previously managed to do with less prestigious critiques, and they set up a committee in the Arab League to study its recommendations.

Another factor that helps to explain why at least some Arab governments were more willing to talk about reform was the recent coming to power of four younger leaders: King Abdullah II in Jordan, King Hamad bin Isa Al Khalifa in Bahrain, King Muhammad VI in Morocco, and Bashar Al Assad in Syria. The three kings rose to the throne in 1999, and Bashar succeeded his father the following year. Upon assuming power, each leader tried to establish his legitimacy by enveloping himself in the rhetoric of reform. However, the expectation that the change of leadership would usher in a period of sweeping political change was quickly dashed in all four countries. A mixture of personal inclination to consolidate power and an unwillingness or inability to take on the old guard in their respective governments stymied the reform process in Syria and greatly constrained it in Jordan. A reformist trend is still alive in Bahrain and Morocco, although reforms have been modest so far. But the change of generations—along with an impending leadership change in Egypt— has helped to foster a new climate in which some domestic issues are now more open to discussion.

In addition, the declining appeal among many secular intellectuals and opposition groups of old ideologies such as pan-Arabism and Arab socialism has generated greater receptivity to the idea of liberal politics and democratic reform. Statistics that showed how the Arab world was lagging behind almost every other region of the world politically and economically were humiliating, all the more so because the evidence was irrefutable. Although most Arab intellectuals and activists remain hostile to reform proposals coming from the outside, in particular from the United States, they have become much more amenable to the idea that democracy is a legitimate aspiration of Arab societies.

A final factor has been the reformist trend within Islamist political movements such as the Muslim Brotherhood. This trend—which has been unfolding over the past decade as mainstream Islamist groups have found radicalism and violence unhelpful to their cause and have sought new strategies to compete for political power—was accelerated by the attacks of September 11. Facing increased pressure from Arab governments and anxious to distance themselves from terrorist organizations, some Islamist groups have become more open to at least debate the merits of democracy.

Reform in Theory

Although a consensus is forming within the region's political elite that political reform is necessary, there is no corresponding agreement on what political reform means. Instead, reform has become a widely used mantra covering very different perspectives.

One such perspective is the liberal democratic outlook, which defines political reform as the process needed to establish secular, Western-style democratic republics or genuine constitutional monarchies. Exponents of this liberal perspective call on Arab rulers to submit to constitutional restrictions on their power, to the will of the people in free, fair, and regular elections, and to term limits. They also demand abrogating emergency laws and security courts, expanding human rights (especially rights for women), ending state control over media, lifting restrictions on political parties and civic organizations, establishing independent judiciaries, and respecting the rule of law. The breadth and assertiveness of this agenda reflect the degree to which liberal voices have been emboldened since September 11, as many of these demands, particularly those relating to the powers of Arab rulers, were previously too dangerous to express.

Advocates of the liberal agenda include intellectuals, journalists, human rights and democracy activists, members of secular opposition parties, and a tiny number of businessmen and progressive-minded government officials. Many were educated in the United States or Europe and have ties to Western political, academic, and business circles; some are former leftists who became disillusioned with Arab nationalism and socialism. The declaration issued in March 2004 by a group composed mainly of intellectuals, former diplomats, and businessmen at a conference held at the quasigovernmental Alexandria Library in Egypt exemplifies the liberal democratic perspective.[6] The Bush administration and the Western media heralded the declaration as a sign of the emergence of a genuine liberal democratic movement within Arab civil society. In fact, however, the Alexandria meeting illustrates the weakness of the liberal trend. The Egyptian government carefully screened all participants to exclude any genuine opposition figures or critics and filled the roster with individuals who lack connections to membership-based organizations that might serve as a mobilizing base for the declaration.

A second perspective on reform is the one held by moderate Islamists, a minority but important camp within the Islamist movement. Moderate Islamists echo some of the liberals' core reform demands, such as free elections, term limits, and empowered elected institutions. But they are adamant that political reform must accord with Islamic law and customs. It is difficult to know exactly what this means, given the existence of various schools of Islamic jurisprudence, each with its more liberal or fundamentalist interpretations. In general, however, those who insist that reform must conform to Islamic law tend to deemphasize individual rights, especially those for women and minorities, and to hold vague positions on the principle of rotation of power. More broadly, and of greater concern to supporters of liberal democracy, even moderate

Islamists envision political reform as a pathway to the creation of authentic Islamic states governed by religious law, not Western-style democracies ruled by secular laws. Instead of looking to the West for models, moderate Islamists share with the broader Islamist movement a determination to stem the penetration of Arab societies by Western secular values, economic domination, and political influence. They envision reform as a way to strengthen these societies against such corruption and "hegemony." The most detailed articulation of the moderate Islamic perspective to emerge from the current reform debate is found in the initiative published by the Egyptian Muslim Brotherhood in March 2004. The document includes a nineteen-point section on political reform and calls for a "republican, constitutional, parliamentary, democratic state in conformity with the principles of Islam" to replace the present Egyptian government.[7]

A third perspective is the modernization approach, advocated by many Arab regimes and their supporters in the government-linked intelligentsia and the private sector. Generally speaking, the modernization agenda features good governance reforms such as upgrading the judiciary, streamlining bureaucratic procedures, and fighting corruption. It also calls for increasing political participation, especially among women and youth, "activating" civil society (meaning development and welfare organizations, not politically oriented groups), expanding human rights education, and lifting some controls on the media. In addition to endorsing such steps, Egypt, Jordan, and Morocco have announced plans to upgrade legislation concerning political participation. The exact content of such reforms is not yet clear, but measures reportedly under consideration in Egypt include allowing opposition party representatives to sit on the committee that oversees party registration; in Morocco, imposing new restrictions on financing and establishment of religious or ethnic-based parties; and in Jordan, introducing mandatory voting and consolidating the country's many small parties into three large blocs of left, right, and center.

Advocates of the modernization perspective sometimes invoke the word *democracy*, but they portray it as a system that already exists in the Arab world and needs only some procedural improvements and greater infusions of popular participation to function properly. Thus, the modernizing perspective rejects the notion advanced by liberals that democracy would be a new, radically different system that would change the character of Arab states dramatically and in particular that would require rulers to submit to the will of the people. Instead, it emphasizes the need for gradual change carried out in accordance with the circumstances and culture of each country. The objective of modernizing reforms, then, is to develop more efficiently governed and economically successful versions of existing states, with their existing power structures. The Arab League's May 2004 declaration on reform and the June 2003 reform initiative of the Arab Business Council, a group composed of some of the region's wealthiest businessmen, both capture the gist of the modernization perspective.[8]

A crosscutting theme among the three perspectives is the rejection of, or at best a very grudging attitude toward, the role of outsiders, especially the United States, in promoting reform. A small minority of supporters of the liberal perspective endorse U.S. involvement.[9] Most liberals, however, accept the value of Western institutions and practices but sharply reject any role for the United States. Moderate Islamists are almost universally deeply hostile to outside interference, particularly from the United States. Indeed, the first item in the Muslim Brotherhood's reform plan refers to the need to reject all foreign-generated reform plans as interference in Egyptian affairs. Proponents of the modernization agenda are divided on the issue of Western involvement. The governments of Egypt, Saudi Arabia, and Syria have made a point of rejecting outside recommendations on reform, criticizing the Broader Middle East and North Africa Initiative in particular as a Western attempt to impose change. Other governments are less harsh. They repeatedly state the need to pursue only indigenous plans for reform but are favorable to outside assistance if appropriate. Only the Jordanian government has directly welcomed U.S. support for reform, even creating a ministry of political development to coordinate foreign reform aid.

Reform in Practice

The lively, often quite far-reaching debates about reform in the Arab world are only palely reflected in the actual changes that have been introduced to date by Arab states. Most of the political reforms enacted in the past three years are piecemeal measures that fall into the "modernization" category. Furthermore, reforms have been introduced from the top, by governments acting on their own initiative rather than in response to specific demands from their citizens. Some governments, such as in Egypt and Saudi Arabia, have organized national dialogues on reform, but participants and topics discussed at such gatherings are tightly controlled. They are primarily public relations exercises and opportunities for carefully selected members of the elite to blow off steam. Attempts by citizens to petition their governments for change have met with mostly vague responses or with arrests and pressures on the petitioners to desist from further activities. Notably, the rulers of Lebanon, Libya, Syria, Tunisia, the United Arab Emirates, and Yemen have made general statements in support of reform but have not yet implemented any significant measures.

Since September 11, only in two countries, Bahrain and Qatar, have governments implemented reforms that seek to change the overall structure of the political system. In Bahrain, King Hamad bin Isa Al Khalifa continued his program, embarked on soon after his assuming power, of transforming his country into a constitutional monarchy and reducing long-running, sometimes violent tensions between members of the majority Shiite community and the ruling Sunni minority. In February 2002, following measures in 2000 and 2001 that repealed emergency laws, abolished special security courts, and granted amnesty to opposition activists, Hamad promulgated decrees that guarantee the right of association, speech, and participation for all Bahrainis and launched a process to restore the elected parliament, which had been suspended since 1975. Hamad also transformed Bahrain into a monarchy with himself as king and created an appointed upper house of parliament with full legislative powers. Bahrain held elections for municipal councils in May 2002 and for the lower house of parliament in October 2002—the first elections held in Bahrain in twenty-eight years.

Qatar has also carried out reforms that are significant when measured against its history as a state with no elected legislative bodies or constitutionally guaranteed rights. In April 2003, the country's first constitution was approved in a national referendum. The document, drafted by a committee of experts appointed by Emir Hamad bin Jassem Khalifa Al Thani, creates a parliament with thirty elected members (fifteen others are to be appointed by the emir) and with some legislative powers. The constitution also grants political and civil rights to men and women and enshrines a range of other freedoms.

These reforms have established needed participatory institutions and fostered a more open political climate in each country. Bahrain's case is a particular achievement, as reforms have revived political life frozen since the mid-1970s and greatly reduced strife. But as positive as these changes are, in neither country has the reform process led to a reduction of the powers of the leader or otherwise created a pathway for a democratically elected leadership. Each country's rulers and their families continue to govern and to control national wealth with essentially unchecked powers. Political parties remain illegal in both countries. Only time will tell whether either ruler intends eventually to divest himself of the power to govern, or whether he simply believes that the enactment of a constitution has already transformed the country into a constitutional monarchy.

No other government has attempted a restructuring of the political system, not even one that ensures the continuing power of the executive as in Bahrain and Qatar. In other countries, post–September 11 reforms have been more narrowly focused and cautious, even to the point of being cosmetic. These reforms have mostly been targeted at elections, women's rights, and human rights, more generally.

Algeria, Jordan, Morocco, and Yemen have revised their electoral laws and upgraded their electoral administration to make voter registration, balloting, vote counting, and the announcement of results more efficient and transparent. According to international observers, recent elections held in these countries were conducted more professionally than earlier contests and were marked by fewer cases of blatant government intimidation of voters or other obvious attempts to influence the outcome.

These improvements in electoral administration were not, however, accompanied by gains for opposition forces. On the contrary, with the exception of Morocco, in every national election held in the Arab world since September 11, ruling-party or progovernment candidates won by a wider margin, and opposition candidates had their poorest showings, since the introduction (or re-introduction, in some cases) of multiparty politics in the 1980s and 1990s.[10] Even in Morocco, where the Islamist Party of Justice and Development (PJD) became the third largest party represented in parliament after the 2002 elections, the top two parties essentially maintained their position, precluding any rotation of power. Across the region, though some parliamentarians have bravely challenged ruling regimes on sensitive issues, legislatures still lack the political and institutional capacity to shape policy and act as counterweights to the executive branch.

A second reform trend evident since 2001 is the enhancement of women's rights and measures to expand their presence in government. Many governments have enacted progressive "personal status" legislation—new laws pertaining to marriage and divorce, child custody, and inheritance that decrease traditional discrimination against women. Morocco has seen the most dramatic change in this regard. In January 2004 the parliament approved a major revision of the *Mudawwana* (personal status code) that significantly expanded women's rights in all these areas. Moroccan women's groups had been pressing for such a revision since the 1980s, as had King Muhammad VI since coming to power. But conservative Islamist forces had thwarted all attempts at reform, holding massive demonstrations that condemned the expansion of women's rights as anti-Islamic. The situation changed after the 2003 terrorist attacks in Casablanca, however, in which radical Islamic cells were implicated. All Islamist groups, including the relatively moderate PJD, were put on the defensive politically, afraid to challenge the palace directly. As a result, the king was able to push through the reforms, even winning the endorsement of the PJD.

Egypt has introduced more modest reforms pertaining to women's rights. In a 2002 landmark decision, the judiciary ruled that women could travel abroad without the permission of their husbands or fathers. In 2004, parliament passed legislation granting citizenship to children born to Egyptian mothers and foreign fathers. The Jordanian government has also tried to enact legislation to increase penalties for violence against women and to expand women's divorce and inheritance rights, but conservative members of the lower house of parliament have repeatedly blocked such reforms.

Algeria, Jordan, and Morocco introduced electoral quotas to increase the number of women in parliament. In Oman, the first full-suffrage elections took place in October 2003, a vote that was the culmination of a process begun in 1991 of gradually expanding enfranchisement to all Omani adults. Finally, across the region, relatively large numbers of women have been appointed to judicial, ministerial, and diplomatic positions in the past two years.

Welcome as these advances for Arab women are, they should not be confused with democratizing moves. As Marina Ottaway argues in chapter six of this volume, reforms that expand women's rights in the Middle East do not address fundamental blockages to democratic change. These include the overwhelming powers of Arab rulers, the absence or weakness of institutions to check those powers, and the denial of democratic rights to all citizens, male and female.

With regard to human rights reforms, many Arab governments have taken steps that signal a growing acceptance of human rights as a legitimate public policy issue. Morocco, which has shown the greatest inclination of any Arab country to improve its human rights record, took another step by forming the Equity and Reconciliation Commission in January 2004, an institution unique in the region. Its mandate is to produce a public report on state repression from 1956 to 1999 and to compensate the families of Moroccans who "disappeared" during these years. In another first, the Arab League at its May 2004 summit in Tunis approved revisions to the 1994 Arab Human Rights Charter that strengthen the rights to fair trial and political asylum, affirm prohibitions on torture, and endorse gender equality. Jordan and Egypt set up national human rights councils in 2002 and 2003, respectively. The purpose of the councils is to expand public awareness of human rights and to increase government compliance with international human rights conventions. In 2003 the Egyptian government also allowed the Egyptian Organization for Human Rights to register as a nongovernmental organization, after years of rejecting its requests. Even Saudi Arabia has made unprecedented gestures toward human rights, allowing Human Rights Watch and Amnesty International to visit the country for the first time in 2003 and establishing a quasigovernmental human rights group in 2004.

These steps have had little or no effect on systemic human rights problems across the Arab world. Emergency laws remain in place, including in Egypt where the government recently suppressed an attempt by members of the national human rights council to issue a recommendation that the twenty-three-year state of emergency be annulled. International human rights organizations report that human rights conditions in many countries have worsened.[11] One reason for this deterioration is that many Arab governments have undertaken broad antiterrorism actions after September 11, such as mass detentions and heightened surveillance of political activity. Morocco, where human rights conditions improved during the 1990s, has experienced a regression in civil liberties since the 2003 Casablanca bombings and the March 11, 2004, attacks in Madrid, which were blamed on Moroccan extremists. The closer counterterrorism relationship established by Algeria, Syria, and Yemen with Western intelligence services and the strengthening of long-established ties to those services by Egypt, Jordan, Morocco, Saudi Arabia, and Tunisia have done nothing to safeguard human rights. Repression of opposition to the Iraq war and to Israeli actions in the Palestinian territories has also negatively affected the human rights environment.

The Balance Sheet

The issue of political reform has so far generated more talk than actual democratizing change in the Arab world. The main reason is that reform is still closely controlled by authoritarian governments that, while eager to demonstrate to the international community that the Arab world is not as retrograde as it is often portrayed to be, feel under no immediate domestic pressure to introduce far-reaching reforms. For different reasons, neither advocates of liberal reform nor those who want to build Islamic states have been able to force governments to enact the changes they want.

Arab liberals, who are issuing the most pointed and extensive demands for democratic reform, are still weak and isolated. The increased attention that democracy enthusiasts outside the Middle East have paid to Arab liberals' activities in the past few years has magnified their significance in Western policy circles but has not increased their influence within the Arab world. Indeed, the attention paid to them by the Bush administration and by Western democracy advocates may isolate them even more within their own societies, where they are often denounced as too close to the United States. They remain a very elite group, repressed by regimes and operating primarily as individuals with no significant constituency. As a consequence, they are easily marginalized by Arab governments or, conversely, co-opted. Many end up working for reform within ruling parties, or concentrate their efforts on signing broad, regionwide reform manifestos. Many are less able, or less willing, to take an open stand on reform issues at home. Arab governments reinforce this caution by showing tolerance, or even approval, for regional meetings that issue general statements about democracy, while cracking down on domestic political activism that touches on specific issues of local concern, even when couched in the most polite form. For example, the Bahraini authorities arrested democracy activists for circulating a petition demanding constitutional reform, and the Saudi government is putting on trial prominent liberal reformers who called for a fully independent human rights commission.

The moderates within the Islamist camp who are calling for democratic reforms have gained prominence in the past three years, but their influence remains marginal within the Islamist movement. Their endorsements of democratic reform are directed as much to Western audiences as to their compatriots. They write about the need for democracy and issue statements to that effect, but there is no sign that democratic change has become a leading topic at Friday mosque sermons, a leading channel of mass communication throughout the Arab world. At the popular level, the dominant political theme preached by Islamists is still hostility toward U.S. policies and Western cultural influence. Moderate Islamists, furthermore, are as isolated outside Islamist circles as they are inside them. Arab governments do not trust them, fearing they are simply the more presentable face of a radical movement that wants to grab power as soon as there is a democratic opening. Most democrats also remain suspicious. Despite the Muslim Brotherhood's fledgling attempts to build bridges to secular opposition parties in Egypt, the polarization between the liberal and Islamist camps remains, precluding the emergence of broad coalitions for democratic change. Western countries, furthermore, are hardly rushing to embrace moderate Islamists as partners for their vision of transforming the Middle East. The United States in particular appears even more wary about the inclusion of moderate Islamist groups than it was before the September 11 attacks.

This leaves incumbent regimes in control of the reform agenda, at least for now. As a result, they introduce measures that they believe will benefit their image in the outside world and may buy them time domestically but that do not infringe on their own power and prerogatives. They shrewdly allow their citizens to talk about reform as a safety valve for discontent, as the expansion of red lines of political discourse in the past few years demonstrates. So far, Arab regimes have proven quite adept at balancing the need to demonstrate to the world—and to some extent to their own citizens—their willingness to change, without allowing the reform process to gather a momentum they will not be able to stop.

Whether the reform ferment will remain largely in the sphere of discourse, or spur the beginning of a wide-reaching political shift toward democracy, depends on numerous factors. One is the capacity of liberal reformers to attract the popular support they are now sorely lacking, by developing an appealing social agenda to accompany their abstract political demands. Another is the ability of moderate Islamists to forge alliances with secular opposition forces and to gain influence within Islamist circles. A third factor is the future trajectory of the war on terrorism and the outcome of the situations in Iraq and Palestine. All are currently fueling anti-American sentiment that complicates the reform agenda by tainting in the popular mind its most vigorous proponents as agents of U.S. plans to undermine Islam. Finally, the willingness of the United States and other Western countries to press for democratization, rather than to accept modernizing measures as a sign of democratic progress, will help determine the long-term significance of the current reform ferment.

Notes

This chapter was originally published as Carnegie Paper 52 (October 2004).

1. Saad Eddin Ibrahim, "An Open Door," *Wilson Quarterly*, vol. 28, no. 2 (Spring 2004): 36–46.

2. Fareed Zakaria, "The Good, the Bad, the Ugly," *Newsweek*, May 31, 2004.

3. Remarks by George W. Bush at the Air Force Academy Graduation, Colorado Springs, Colorado, June 2, 2004, available at http://www.whitehouse.gov/news/releases/2004/06/20040602.html.

4. This paper reviews recent developments in political reform across the Arab world, with the exception of the Palestinian territories and Iraq, which are special cases not considered here.

5. See, for example, Freedom House, *Freedom in the World 2000–2001* (New York: 2001).

6. "The March 2004 Alexandria Document on Reform Issues in the Arab World," Alexandria, Egypt, March 14, 2004, available at http://www.bibalex.gov.eg. Other recent liberal reform declarations include the "Sanaa Declaration on Democracy, Human Rights, and the Role of the International Criminal Court," Sanaa, Yemen, January 12, 2004; "Letter from the First Civic Forum to the Fourth Arab Summit" (also known as the Beirut Declaration on Reform), Beirut, Lebanon, March 22, 2004; "Doha Declaration on Democracy and Reform," Doha, Qatar, June 4, 2004; and "Priorities and Mechanisms for Reform in the Arab World," Cairo, Egypt, July 7, 2004.

7. "The Muslim Brotherhood Reform Initiative," March 2004, available in Arabic at http://www.afaqarabiyya.com, a web site affiliated with the Brotherhood.

8. For the Arab Business Council's reform platform, see http://www.weforum.org/pdf/ABC/ABC_Achievements.pdf. For the Tunis Declaration issued by the Arab League on May 23, 2004, see http://www.arabsummit.tn/en/tunis-declaration.htm. For illustrative modernization platforms drafted by Arab governments, see "Draft Government Plan for Political Reform in Jordan," Amman, Jordan, March 2004; "Memorandum on Reforms in Algeria" (Algiers, Algeria: Office of the Presidency of the People's Democratic Republic of Algeria, June 2004); and the "New Vision" reform program of Egypt's ruling National Democratic Party, Cairo, Egypt, September 2003, available at http://www.ndp.org.eg/aboutus/en/aboutus_2_1.htm.

9. See "Priorities and Mechanisms for Reform."

10. Between September 2001 and April 2004, Algeria, Bahrain, Jordan, Kuwait, Morocco, and Yemen held parliamentary elections, and Algeria held presidential elections.

11. See Human Rights Watch, *World Report: 2002* (New York: 2002), *World Report: 2003* (New York: 2003), and *World Report: 2004* (New York: 2004) and various country reports and press releases on Arab countries, 2001–2004. See also Middle East country reports issued by Amnesty International from 2002 to the present, especially "The Gulf and the Arabian Peninsula," June 22, 2004.

Part Two

No Easy Answers

5

Is Civil Society the Answer?

Amy Hawthorne

IN PARALLEL WITH ITS PROSECUTION of the war in Iraq, the Bush administration formulated a second, longer-term democracy-promotion track for the other countries of the region. On November 6, 2003, President George W. Bush delivered a major speech announcing this track. He declared that because "sixty years of Western nations excusing and accommodating the lack of freedom in the Middle East did nothing to make us safe," the United States had adopted a "new policy, a forward strategy of freedom in the Middle East"—to be pursued in countries including those with governments friendly to the United States.[1]

Bush's speech broke new ground because it was the first time that a U.S. president had publicly criticized some of America's Arab allies for their authoritarian ways and had mentioned democratization so explicitly as a leading objective of U.S. Middle East policy. The real test of a genuine shift in U.S. policy, however, will be whether Washington can translate lofty rhetoric into effective policies to support genuine democratic change.

This is an exceedingly difficult undertaking. For one thing, in sharp contrast to Washington's last high-profile, regionwide democracy-promotion initiative—to consolidate the new democracies of Eastern Europe and the former Soviet Union after the collapse of state socialist and communist rule there—the United States will pursue this second track of Middle East democracy promotion in countries that are not yet undergoing a transition away from authoritarian rule. Despite halting steps toward political reform in some Arab countries, no genuine

81

democratization process has unfolded. As several decades of experience in global democracy promotion have shown, outside assistance has the greatest impact where indigenous momentum for democratic change is evident.

Other obstacles to robust U.S. engagement with Middle East democracy are the United States' lack of credibility as a promoter of democracy in the region and widespread anti-Americanism. The fallout from the attacks of September 11, 2001, resentment over perceived American indifference to Palestinian suffering, and the unpopularity of the United States–led occupation of Iraq are strengthening these long-running currents in the Arab body politic. Further complicating the picture are the continuing reluctance of the United States to antagonize friendly Arab governments by pressing them on democracy and the related concern that calling for rapid political openings will empower forces hostile to the United States. The Bush administration's grand rhetoric on Middle East democracy notwithstanding, in practical terms U.S. officials appear hesitant to rock the boat in friendly Arab states.

All these factors have contributed to the idea of making aid for Arab civil society a leading element of a new U.S. democracy-promotion strategy for countries beyond Iraq. (Civil society also appeals to many European officials who are beginning to consider developing a more vigorous democracy-promotion policy for the Middle East.) Defining civil society and its role as a prodemocratic force is a matter of extensive scholarly debate. Reduced to its elemental meaning, *civil society* refers to the zone of voluntary associative life beyond family and clan affiliations but separate from the state and the market. Nonprofit organizations, religious organizations, labor unions, business associations, interest and advocacy groups, societies, clubs, and research institutions, as well as more informal political, social, and religious movements, are all part of civil society.[2]

Under the right conditions, civil society can contribute to the democratization of authoritarian regimes and can help to sustain a democratic system once it is established.[3] In the Philippines, Eastern European countries, South Africa, Serbia, and most recently Georgia, for example, citizens have used civil society organizations to carve out independent political space, to learn about democracy, to articulate a democratic alternative to the status quo, to spread this idea within society, and to mobilize millions of their fellow citizens against repressive regimes.

In democracies, civil society organizations provide forums for citizens to pursue shared interests—political, social, or spiritual—freely, collectively, and peacefully. Through involvement in civil society, citizens learn about fundamental democratic values of participation and collective action, and they disseminate these values within their communities. Civil society movements that represent citizen interests can shape both government policy and social attitudes. By constituting a sphere of citizen activity beyond the direct control of government, civil society can form a counterweight to state power.

Because the idea of civil society is closely associated in many Westerners' minds with "people power" movements to push out dictators and with the success of Western democracy, programs to "strengthen" civil society have become a standard part of the U.S. and European democracy-promotion tool kit around the world. Civil society seems particularly appealing as the solution to the challenge of promoting democracy in the Arab world. Arab nongovernmental organizations (NGOs) have grown in number and prominence in recent years. This proliferation is often interpreted as a sign of burgeoning independent civic activity—and perhaps as the source of peaceful democratic change, akin to the prodemocracy movements that emerged in Eastern Europe in the 1980s.

At the same time, there is an assumption that the zone of civil society is safely apolitical—that it is separate from the political sphere dominated by anti-American sentiment and divisive struggles. Perhaps civil society organizations will be more receptive to U.S. support than political forces, and such support will not bolster anti-American groups, the thinking goes. Perhaps by aiding civil society the United States can build bridges to the "silent majority" of Arab publics, convincing them that the United States is on their side. Finally, focusing on NGOs seems like a good way to support a gradual, citizen-generated transformation of politics in the region, thus avoiding the risk of calling for the immediate democratization of the political sphere, and sparing the United States the discomfort of applying heavy pressure on Arab regimes.

For all these reasons, strengthening civil society is frequently offered as the answer to the questions now pervasive in Washington: "How can the Arab world democratize, and what should the United States do to help democracy there?"

The United States, along with European countries, should make assistance for civil society groups part of any new strategy to encourage democratic change in the Middle East. But these countries should do so with some caution, recognizing that civil society is not the magic missing piece of the Arab democracy puzzle. Civil society in the Middle East, as elsewhere, could be a democratizing force but is not inherently one. Civil society organizations are not necessarily easier for outsiders to assist than other parts of the Arab political landscape. Those devising and implementing new initiatives for Middle East democracy promotion must develop a better understanding of the nature of Arab civil society, the record of past U.S. assistance to civil society, and the limitations of outside assistance—particularly from the United States—in altering deeply rooted political realities.

Arab Civil Society: The Lay of the Land

Before considering civil society's role as a force for Arab democratization, it is important to understand its history, its constituent parts, and the forms it takes throughout the region.

Generally speaking, there have been four main phases of civil society development in the Arab world. Before the European penetration of the region in the nineteenth and early twentieth centuries, civil society consisted mainly of community-based self-help groups, guilds, and religiously oriented charitable and educational institutions, these last funded by Islamic endowments known as *waqfs* (plural, *awqaf*). A second phase began during the period of European colonialism. "Modern" forms of associative life, such as professional associations, trade unions, secular charities, cultural clubs, and Islamist organizations such as the Muslim Brotherhood, emerged across the region. Many of these organizations were politically active in a way that earlier forms of civil society had not been, and they played an important role in nationalist struggles and in supporting pan-Arab causes.

After Arab countries gained independence, a restrictive third phase began. New regimes feared that pluralistic, independent associative life would undermine national unity—and threaten their own attempts to consolidate power. Thus independent civic activity was brought under tight state control as civil society organizations were transformed into state-dominated institutions or were repressed. Repression was especially harsh in the new Arab socialist republics. (In the case of the Palestinian territories, foreign occupation rather than nationalist governments was the source of repression.)

The fourth phase, which has seen a relative liberalization and diversification of the civil society sphere, began in the 1980s and continues to the present day. Several factors have contributed to this phase. The spread of Islamist movements has led to a proliferation of religiously affiliated groups active in civil society. Many Arab governments began to implement limited economic and political liberalization as a way of staying in power.[4] They allowed some new NGOs to form, and they expanded the operating space for existing groups. International influences also played a role. The rise of the global human rights and prodemocracy movements encouraged the formation of Arab human rights and democracy organizations. The dramatic increase in foreign aid channeled to NGOs encouraged the growth of these and other civil society groups.

In broad terms, Arab civil society today comprises five sectors. First, in most Arab countries, the Islamic sector—made up of a wide array of groups, associations, and movements whose common objective is upholding and propagating the faith of Islam—is the most active and widespread form of associative life. Islamic organizations provide charitable and social services such as medical care, education, employment assistance, tutoring, and matchmaking, as well as religious instruction and spiritual guidance. Some of these groups have been in existence for many decades; most are newer, being part of the Islamic resurgence.

Although Islamic organizations share the overarching goal of upholding and spreading the faith of Islam, groups in this sector have diverse forms and political orientations. Some Islamic organizations are offshoots of (and are funded by) state religious establishments, and they propagate mainstream religious doctrine through education and charity work. Other groups aim to operate independently. Some, such as ad hoc religious committees that raise funds for Palestinian victims of the Intifada, hope that distance from the bureaucracy will enhance their agility and effectiveness. Others include service organizations affiliated with political movements, such as the Muslim Brotherhood and Hamas, that oppose incumbent regimes. The more independent groups are generally funded through tithes (*zakat*) and other local donations and by foreign individuals, charities, and governments.[5] At the far margins of the

Islamic sector are radical clandestine movements, such as Egyptian Islamic Jihad and Al Qaeda, that employ terrorism and indoctrination to achieve their vision of a properly "Islamic" society.

The second sector of Arab civil society consists of nongovernmental service organizations, or what are often called service NGOs.[6] Typically, service NGOs are nonprofit groups that resemble Western nonprofit agencies in some respects. They deliver services such as loans, job training, educational assistance, and community development to the public to complement, or in some cases substitute for, government services.

The service-NGO sector has proliferated since the 1980s. Many Arab governments have come to accept the value of private initiative playing an expanded role in development. Many are also concerned about Islamic opposition movements' use of charitable organizations to gain grassroots support and therefore are eager for service NGOs to become an alternative source of services. Western donors are eager to aid private initiative, because it reflects their broader policy of supporting market-based economic reforms in the region. Donors often view service NGOs as more efficient recipients of their funds than Arab government bureaucracies.

Although many of the services provided by service NGOs resemble those offered by Islamic organizations, they do not share the Islamic sector's goal of propagating religion and transforming society toward greater Islamicization. Service NGOs tend to operate openly and according to government regulations.

The third sector includes membership-based professional organizations such as labor unions, professional syndicates (bar associations, doctors' and engineers' syndicates, and the like), and chambers of commerce. Their main purpose is to provide economic and social services for their members. Unions and professional syndicates are among the largest civil society organizations in many Arab countries.

In many countries, professional syndicates are the relatively more politically active organizations of civil society, even though they operate under tight government controls. Because of syndicates' long histories in nationalist politics and the weakness of Arab political parties, regimes are willing to allow syndicates to provide a space for controlled political activism. Opposition figures (usually Islamists and leftists) compete vigorously for positions on boards of directors. They use these highly visible positions to take stands against government policy, implement programs that will gain members' support for their cause, and mobilize public opinion. For instance, Jordanian syndicates have been that country's center of activism against the normalization of relations with Israel.

The fourth sector is composed of associations whose main purpose is to foster solidarity and companionship, and sometimes to provide services, among groups of friends, neighbors, relatives, and colleagues. This sector includes mutual aid societies that help migrants to Egypt's urban areas who hail from particular villages, artists' and writers' societies, and youth organizations. In the Gulf countries, the sector also includes *diwaniyyas*, which are regular private gatherings of relatives, friends, and colleagues that serve as forums for socializing, conducting business, and discussing politics (within limits).

The main distinctions between organizations in this fourth sector and service NGOs are in form and funding. In contrast to most service NGOs—which are set up much like Western nonprofit organizations and are typically closely regulated by a country's ministry of social affairs or ministry of the interior—groups in the fourth sector are often fluid and informally organized and have little interaction with government officials; most are self-funded and few would ever seek government or donor funding. Only a very few engage directly in politics, such as when Kuwaiti *diwaniyyas* back candidates in parliamentary elections. The vast majority are distinctly apolitical, instead being concerned with culture, social identity, and solidarity.

The fifth sector of Arab civil society is composed of prodemocracy associations. It is the sector that most outside democracy promoters and analysts usually think of as making up "Arab civil society." The organizations in this sector seek to promote democratic change by spreading democratic concepts among their fellow citizens and by pressing Arab governments to adhere to international democratic norms. They carry out democracy-education programs, often targeted at politically marginalized groups such as women and youth; they mobilize citizens to vote, run for office, and observe elections; they monitor governments' human rights practices and press for women's rights; they lobby for changes in laws and government practices and fight corruption; and they research political issues.

Of the five sectors of Arab civil society, the prodemocracy sector is the newest and the most fledgling. The region's first human rights organizations were founded in Tunisia and in the West Bank in the late 1970s. Human rights groups were established in Egypt and Morocco in the 1980s. By the 1990s, a small community of prodemocracy organizations existed in most parts of the Arab world. The expansion of this sector has been fueled by political reforms that loosened some controls on associative life, the influence of the international human rights movement on activists in the region, and the rise of Western aid for democracy promotion. A very tiny percentage of associative life takes place within the fifth sector, because the groups in this zone are significantly smaller in number and membership than the associations in the other four sectors.

The extent and nature of civil society within the Arab world exist along a spectrum. At one end of the spectrum are Oman, Libya, Qatar, Saudi Arabia, Syria, and the United Arab Emirates—all of which prohibit the establishment of independent citizen organizations and allow only state-run citizen organizations. In Syria, a handful of independent civic groups have sprung up during the slight thaw of the Bashar Al Assad regime, but they have been repressed by the authorities. Any independent civic activity in Libya, if it exists, takes place deep underground. In the aforementioned Gulf countries, what limited civil society exists revolves around *diwaniyyas*, semi-official Islamic charities, and quasi-official research institutes. Not only are other forms of associative life essentially illegal, but most people's lives revolve extensively around family and tribal ties. Furthermore, oil and gas wealth has reduced the need for service NGOs (and for the foreign aid that has helped them to proliferate).

At the other end of the spectrum are Algeria, Bahrain, Egypt, Jordan, Kuwait, Lebanon, Morocco, the Palestinian territories, Tunisia, and Yemen. Kuwait and Bahrain, which in contrast to other Gulf states have a history of elected parliaments and opposition politics, have a smattering of nongovernmental Islamic societies, professional associations, clubs, and prodemocracy groups. Tunisia's civil society is dominated by a very large service-NGO sector and a few labor unions and professional associations. Its handful of prodemocracy groups suffer continuous state harassment and have a precarious legal status. Tunisia's Islamic sector consists primarily of associations tied to the government because of Tunisia's history of state-enforced secularism, which intensified in the late 1980s and 1990s with the government's attempts to eradicate an incipient Islamic opposition movement, Al Nahda, and any other independent Islamic activity.

Algeria, Egypt, Jordan, and Yemen have some civil society activity across all five sectors. They have diverse and active Islamic sectors that include independent, opposition, and government-connected organizations. Egypt, Jordan, and Yemen, as relatively poor Arab countries that receive large amounts of foreign aid, have large service-NGO sectors. Professional associations, mutual aid societies and other clubs, and small numbers of prodemocracy groups also exist in these countries (Egypt and Yemen, with their large numbers of migrant workers, have many mutual aid societies, as does Jordan's sizable Palestinian community).

Morocco, Lebanon, and the Palestinian territories are at the farthest end of the civil society spectrum, with the most diverse and active civil societies in the region. In Morocco, this is due to a long history of political pluralism, along with the late King Hassan II's early decision to launch economic and political liberalization, a process that has not been interrupted by his successor, King Muhammad VI.[7] In Lebanon and the Palestinian territories, years of war and civil conflict have fostered a high degree of political pluralism, which expresses itself through associational life. Weakened central authority also necessitated citizens' self-help and decreased regimes' ability to fully control civil society. (In the Palestinian case, the unusually large amounts of international aid and the elite's high levels of education and their exposure to democratic practices in Israeli politics have also helped to foster a civil society that is the largest and most sophisticated in the Arab world.)

Civil Society: The Source of Democratization?

About a decade ago, scholars in the United States who studied the Middle East began to devote a great deal of attention to civil society's role as the source of Arab democratization. This academic interest has now subsided somewhat, but in the meantime enthusiasm for civil society has spread to the mainstream of policy makers, donors, democracy-aid providers, and journalists. These civil society enthusiasts interpret the proliferation of civil society organizations across the region as a harbinger of democratization "from below."

They envision civil society playing a democratizing role in a variety of ways. To some, the very proliferation of civil society organizations—no matter their type, agenda, or influence—builds the infrastructure of democracy, because in their view an active associational life is a precursor of democracy. The fact that Egypt now has roughly 14,000 registered NGOs, for example, is sometimes cited as a sign of the empowerment of that country's citizens. Others view specific sectors of civil society as forces for democratization. Not surprisingly, prodemocracy NGOs are thought to have the greatest potential to push governments toward democratization. As one specialist declared:

> A new era is emerging in Arab politics today, one in which the state will increasingly be forced to retreat before a vibrant civil society. . . . The mushrooming NGO movement is pressing governments to be accountable, to adhere to the rule of law, and to abide by broad principles of good government.[8]

Others locate the seeds of democratic change in the Islamic sector. In their view, the opposition and informal organizations in this sector represent a challenge to the moral and political authority of incumbent authoritarian regimes; their grassroots support gives them a popular appeal and a "vibrancy" that other sectors of civil society lack. Thus they must constitute a prodemocracy movement. "Democracy will find civil society allies . . . among Islamists who have spent much of the past decade building up the social and charitable institutions that meet all the criteria political scientists use to identify civil society," one expert recently predicted.[9]

Still other civil society advocates see great potential in the service-NGO sector, where involvement in community development is thought to build skills and foster democratic values and attitudes in individuals that will eventually spread to the broader society. "Service NGOs have an impact that goes well beyond service delivery," contended a paper issued by a contractor of the U.S. Agency for International Development (USAID). "They also enhance the prospects for democratization because they foster associational life, empower individuals, and provide them with the skills and attitudes" that are useful for democratization.[10]

Contrary to these optimistic predictions, civil society groups have not made a real dent in the Arab world's surprisingly durable authoritarianism. Many civil society groups manage to survive and sometimes even become rather active within the limited space regimes have granted them. But they have not been able to expand this space much or to affect the political game more broadly. The growth in the number of civil society organizations has not led to democratization. In fact, this proliferation is better understood as a product of top-down liberalization than as a cause of it.

Several factors have contributed to civil society's weakness as a democratizing force. State repression is perhaps the most obvious one. Although Arab regimes may be poor performers in many respects, they have been unusually successful in maintaining control and quashing dissent.[11] As described above, some governments simply outlaw independent civic activity altogether; and others permit it but impose severe restrictions. These include allowing registered NGOs, professional syndicates, Islamic organizations, and other groups to undertake only "social welfare" or "cultural" work and forbidding "political activities." They regularly intervene in labor and syndicates' activities.[12] They require that NGOs' charters, boards of directors, and meetings be approved by government officials, who can send a representative to any activity. All funding must be approved by the goverment. Across the region, ministries of the interior investigate NGOs' staffs and reject applications for registration on security grounds.[13] In Gaza, for instance, civil society organizations seeking to register must submit the life histories of their founding members to the Palestinian ministry of the interior.[14] In Jordan, all NGO volunteers must be vetted by the security services.[15] Many groups prefer to register and submit to these controls because without legal status, they are even more vulnerable to the whims of the state.[16] Regimes also skillfully use emergency laws, harassment by security forces, and arrests to isolate those who cross the line of "unacceptable" civic activity and to deter others who are contemplating it.

Another obvious factor is political culture. The level of independent civic participation across the Arab world remains extremely low. Most civil society organizations attract only a very small percentage of the population; truly active membership is even less. For example, the membership of most unions and professional associations, though numbering in the millions because many professions require people to join, is often dormant. Not only have decades of authoritarian rule bred widespread political apathy, but throughout the Arab world social, economic, and political life still revolves to a remarkable degree around the bonds of family, clan, or tribe. Thus a critical mass of voluntary citizen activity extending beyond these primary relationships—of the sort that would begin to shift political weight from the realm of state control to that of society and thus contribute to democratization—has yet to develop.

Of course, repression and political apathy are hallmarks of all authoritarian settings. Yet, in some such settings, civil society organizations have played a central role in popularizing the idea of democratic change and in mobilizing citizens to push for democratization.[17] Therefore, we must locate deeper reasons for Arab civil society's minimal democratizing influence to date.

As noted at the beginning of this chapter, civil society is best understood in neutral terms, as the zone of voluntary associative life beyond family and clan ties and separate from the market. The form and character of such associative life can differ considerably, depending on the context. In democracies, the vast majority of civil society organizations are indeed civil and prodemocratic, influenced by a free political atmosphere, the rule of law, and the prevailing social consensus in favor of democratic values. But civil society organizations are not inherently counterhegemonic or liberal; particularly in authoritarian environments, civil society can be dominated by apolitical, progovernment, or even illiberal groups that fulfill roles other than democratization. For civil society to play a democratizing role in such settings, a critical mass of organizations and movements must develop three key attributes: autonomy from the regime, a prodemocracy agenda, and the ability to build coalitions with other sectors of civil society (and other forces, such as political parties) to push for democratic change. Civil society in the Arab world has not yet acquired these attributes.

Sectors of civil society that could ostensibly be a platform for the development of a prodemocracy movement are not sufficiently autonomous to do so. The webs of control and co-optation are spun in various ways. Labor unions are essentially arms of the state, with their leadership appointed by the government. Professional associations sometimes have more independent leaderships, but their members, like union members, are largely state employees or depend on government goodwill for their economic survival. Chambers of commerce are dominated by businessmen and businesswomen who similarly rely on close economic and personal ties to government officials for their business success.

Many think tanks are not truly independent; they are staffed by private citizens but receive all their funding from the government. More nefariously, security services have infiltrated the prodemocracy sector, creating "nongovernmental" organizations to duplicate the work of and siphon donor funds from genuinely independent groups. Donors have difficulty distinguishing these front organizations from the real thing.[18] More commonly, regimes have neutralized groups whose activities are deemed too sensitive by applying a combination of sticks (the threat of repression) and carrots (funding and political protection). (The region is replete with stories of feisty civil society activists who quiet down after receiving generous government funding, a sinecure, or other perks.)

The service-NGO sector, which because of its size is sometimes viewed as a potential counterweight to state power, is in fact largely an extension of it. Many service NGOs were established by former state employees; current and former officials often serve on the boards of directors. Most registered service NGOs receive significant government funding. The Kuwaiti government, for example, gives all registered voluntary associations meeting space and annual subsidies.[19] Labor unions, chambers of commerce, and even professional associations whose leadership opposes some state policies rely on government ties to protect their economic interests. Such intertwining relationships make those civil society groups reluctant to take actions that could jeopardize their ties to the officials who facilitate their work. Similarly, there are complex relationships between some parts of the Islamic sector and Arab governments. In some cases, regimes have facilitated the creation of certain Islamic groups as a counterweight to secular opposition groups. Others are offshoots of the religious establishment and thus do not seek Arab governments' demise.

The fact that a critical mass of civil society organizations has not adopted a clear prodemocracy agenda that can mobilize large numbers of citizens is another important characteristic of civil society in Arab countries. The informal parts of civil society are generally not politically inclined; and their very informality would hinder their ability to organize politically. As for service NGOs, a few have conducted advocacy campaigns to improve government policy on issues on which they work (such as the environment or rural development). But the majority do not engage in broader political activities—especially anything involving direct opposition to incumbent regimes. Beyond the fact that most are financially and administratively linked to the state, their fundamental mission is not to challenge systems and institutions of politics. Rather, it is to provide the services and socioeconomic development necessary to maintain social stability.

Indeed, when Arab leaders boast of their countries' burgeoning civil societies, as they often do, they are referring to service NGOs and similar organizations that are carrying out their own national development agenda. Thus regimes view these groups as "partners," not adversaries. As Egyptian President Hosni Mubarak explained in a November 2003 speech, "In recognition by the society of the fact that national development requires conscious participation by all members, there emerged a new concept of voluntary work. The number of civil society organizations rose to more than 14,000, operating in a variety of development spheres. . . . They perform their role as an active partner to the sustainable development process."[20]

Even those service NGOs that do not buy into the official development agenda are usually reluctant to jeopardize their work by running afoul of the authorities. As a staff member of an Egyptian development organization explained, "We don't like the government, but to be able to do our vital work, we cannot get anywhere close to politics."[21] Similarly, the priorities of most unions, professional organizations, and mutual aid societies lie in serving their members, not in democratic activism. (This is the case even for Palestinian civil society, the region's most active. Since the outbreak of the Intifada in September 2000, most Palestinian groups have focused on delivering services to a population under siege and on struggling against the Israeli occupation.) Certainly, there are informal, grassroots groups that resist state power, but their very informality makes it hard for them to galvanize broader support. This is in contrast to service NGOs and community groups in South Africa, the Philippines, and many Latin American countries that had a double agenda of development and democratic political change and could mobilize their communities toward both ends.

Nor does the Islamic sector constitute a prodemocracy force. Religious forces' adoption of a vigorous prodemocracy agenda is often a critical element in civil society's ability to push for democratization, as has been demonstrated by the role of the Catholic Church in Latin America and in Eastern European democratization and of Christian organizations in South Korean democratization. In contrast, the Arab world's Islamic organizations are by and large at most ambivalent toward democracy.[22] In some Arab countries, a handful of liberal Islamists seek to demonstrate that democratic concepts are fully compatible with the tenets of Islam. But they are weak and lack popular following.[23] Those parts of the Islamic sector that are politically relevant, such as the Muslim Brotherhood, have not pushed for democracy in a comprehensive fashion. Some emphasize themes of justice, participation, and reform. But they hold vague or negative positions on other aspects of democracy, such as the rotation of power and minorities' and women's rights. Other Islamic groups avoid political issues altogether, preferring to transform society through social and spiritual change.

The sector of civil society that does have a clear democratic agenda—the prodemocracy sector—has very limited influence. There are high-caliber groups that bravely push the political envelope and sustain repeated harassment. But even the most impressive prodemocracy groups have trouble attracting more than a tiny number of supporters. Most prodemocracy groups that have tried to lobby government officials for policy change have done so using their personal connections to those officials, not by mobilizing popular support for their cause.

Repression is undoubtedly one reason for their ineffectiveness; precarious funding and weak management also play a role. But there are more fundamental reasons. In sharp contrast to Islamic organizations, which use religious channels to mobilize support, prodemocracy groups lack a popular network and tools, such as a sympathetic media, to spread a prodemocracy message. They have to fight the stigma that democracy and human rights are foreign—particularly Western—concepts. Exacerbating this challenge, prodemocracy NGOs are overwhelmingly the province of the secular, liberal elite. Their discourse (highly abstract) and activities (mainly workshops and reports) often seem alien to the real-life concerns of Arabs.

Finally, as is clear from the preceding analysis, civil society across the Arab world is deeply fragmented. The different sectors of civil society sometimes work side by side but can rarely coalesce in a sustained fashion. This hinders the ability of civil society to unite groups of citizens around common goals in a way that might generate pressure on regimes. Contrast this, for example, with the sustained civic action that brought together South Korean students, workers, Christian activists, and intellectuals to push for democracy in the years leading up to that country's transition.

In part, this polarization is due to regimes' skill in manipulating and dividing civil society. But it also reflects a deeper reality: There is today no unifying vision for social and political transformation among key civil society actors in Arab countries. In countries with deep social divisions, such as Lebanon, civil society is organized overwhelmingly along confessional lines, with groups serving primarily as patronage vehicles to protect community interests.[24] More often, the major divide falls between the two sectors of civil society most relevant for democratization, the Islamic sector (because of its grassroots support) and the prodemocracy sector. A deep polarization exists between those who want to use civil society organizations as the leading vehicle to Islamicize society and those who believe that (liberal) civil society is the only bulwark against such a transformation.

The experience of civil society in Algeria and Tunisia provides a vivid example of this phenomenon. In the late 1980s and early 1990s, many prodemocracy groups in these two countries initially sided with Islamic opposition groups to press for liberalization. A few years later, when the Algerian and Tunisian regimes felt threatened and undertook blanket repression against Islamists and other independent political forces, these same groups lent their support to the regimes. They feared the Islamists' illiberal agenda more than they feared a rollback of their civil liberties and the regimes' continuation in power. Lise Garon terms these tacit bargains "dangerous alliances" and identifies them as a key factor in stalled political liberalization in the Arab world.[25]

These characteristics of civil society are not necessarily permanent. Various developments could lead civil society groups to become more autonomous, more prodemocratic, and more coherent. Economic growth could provide independent resources for some organizations currently tied to regimes; conversely, severe economic decline could spark discontent.

The rise of truly charismatic leaders in the prodemocracy sector, their access to new avenues for mobilization (such as new media), or a sudden deterioration of human rights conditions (if such groups were widely seen as defenders of ordinary citizens' rights) could enhance the local prestige and appeal of this sector. A changing relationship between Islamist and liberal political forces (for example, the emergence of a liberal Islamist trend, or the Islamicization of the prodemocracy sector) could increase the prospect of coalitions across sectors.

Equally important is what occurs in the broader national arena. When civil society organizations have played a vigorous role in democratic political change, they have gained real influence only after higher-order developments have reshaped the environment in their favor. For example, the economic failure in Eastern Europe delegitimized regimes and enhanced the stature of civil society actors after years of being marginal actors, enabling them to popularize their ideas and mobilize wide support at last. Similarly, the massive economic collapse in Indonesia unleashed mass discontent and made President Suharto suddenly vulnerable. This transformed the environment to allow civil society groups and opposition parties to mobilize citizens in an unprecedented fashion.

In the Arab world, similar changes could include an economic breakdown, or success followed by decline; the rise of new regime elites sympathetic to democratic reform; a breakdown in the security structure; and political liberalization that allows more competitive elections, elected institutions with power to challenge the executive branch, or the lifting of restrictions on the media.

Aid for Civil Society: A Disappointing Record

American democracy promoters, along with their European counterparts, tend to have an understanding of civil society that is simultaneously too broad and too narrow. On the one hand, they frequently vest unrealistic hopes in civil society as a democratic and democratizing force. They envision that, bolstered by outside assistance, virtuous civil societies of democratic-minded, nonpartisan, peaceful citizens will erode authoritarian regimes. They often also expect these civil society groups to operate as they are thought to in the United States or Europe—that is, to act as a counterweight to state power and to "check" or otherwise influence government behavior—and they provide assistance to help them do so.

On the other hand, donors conceive of civil society quite narrowly, as comprising the organizations—nonprofit organizations and public interest groups—that seem to resemble those with which they are most familiar in their own countries and whose leaders speak English and are comfortable in international circles. Donors often downplay or ignore religious organizations, social movements, and other unfamiliar, non-NGO forms of associative life. They also fail to take into account the relationship of the different parts of civil society to citizens, governments, and one another.

This double-edged tendency has existed in U.S. democracy-promotion efforts in the Arab world as well, even though until recently the United States paid scant attention to the question of democracy there. In the early 1990s, near the end of the George H. W. Bush administration, the United States launched small-scale programs to aid democracy in the Middle East, adding to this assistance occasional rhetorical support for political reform at the diplomatic level. This approach continued during the administration of Bill Clinton, which increased democracy aid to the region largely to avoid being seen as excluding the Middle East from its global democracy-promotion agenda. "Aiding civil society" was the leading element of U.S. efforts. The majority of democracy aid for the Middle East from 1991 through 2001—about $150 million—went to projects classified as "civil society strengthening."[26] At the same time, these projects were targeted almost exclusively toward service NGOs and prodemocracy NGOs.[27]

Projects to assist service NGOs received the lion's share of the funding. These projects were large-budget, multiyear efforts that involved many dozens of service NGOs. In Egypt, USAID funded two consecutive projects to strengthen civil society, which cost $27 million and $40 million, respectively. In the West Bank and Gaza—where the United States had funded some Palestinian NGOs during the Israeli occupation—after the Palestinian Authority was created in 1994, the United States expanded this aid and categorized much of it as civil society strengthening. In 2000, USAID launched a $32 million project to support Palestinian NGOs (mostly service NGOs). In Lebanon, USAID spent several million dollars to assist community-based service NGOs during the 1990s.

Promoting democracy was not the only rationale for these projects. In Egypt, the United States believed that giving private groups an expanded role in development would advance its larger policy goal of economic liberalization. In the West Bank and Gaza, the United States hoped to generate popular support for the Oslo peace process by helping Palestinian NGOs improve living conditions under self-rule. (In addition, NGOs were a key instrument for channeling aid, because Congress had imposed a ban on direct U.S. funding of the Palestinian Authority.) In

Lebanon, the United States wanted to help local communities rebuild in the aftermath of civil war. Because government agencies were very weak, community-based organizations and NGOs were better aid partners. During the Clinton administration, political Islam became a factor, though not one that was openly acknowledged. Some U.S. officials saw service NGOs as a potential counterweight to the Islamic charities and other groups that were a major source of grassroots support for Islamist opposition movements, and these officials wanted to direct resources to such groups for this reason.

Service NGOs also fit well into the vision for Middle Eastern democracy that prevailed among U.S. officials in the 1990s, vague as it was. According to this vision, democratic change should occur incrementally, with a minimum of conflict that might threaten the stability of incumbent regimes friendly to Washington. The critical element in this very gradual democratization would not be the election of new leaderships, or even a reduction in authoritarian regimes' powers or further liberalization of the political sphere. Rather, it would be the reform of existing government institutions to make them work more efficiently and thus more "democratically," along with citizens' habituation to democratic values and practices. State and society should be prepared for a future democratic transition before any Arab leadership should be required to submit itself to the will of the people or significantly expand political space. Such preparation was considered essential for Arab countries with little or no experience with democracy.

Service NGOs would expose Arabs to a form of microdemocracy, the thinking went, by habituating them to the concepts of civic participation and decision making through taking part in nonthreatening local issues (while avoiding core issues of civil and political rights). This would build an understanding of and enthusiasm for democracy from the ground up, preparing citizens to make responsible decisions when, at some point in the future, they were given a larger role in influencing national policies.[28]

Service NGOs were also appealing because they were non-Islamist, and at the same time nonpolitical.[29] Thus they were less likely to pose a threat to regimes (or to U.S. interests in the region) in the way that other sectors of civil society might if they were empowered. If service NGOs demonstrated to governments that they were professional, nonpartisan organizations that had the community's best interests at heart, it was thought, governments would be more likely to see them as constructive forces, rather than as sources of opposition needing to be repressed. This realization would compel officials to grant more space to those sectors of civil society that acted responsibly (that is, that did not challenge the state's legitimacy).[30] This would somehow spur a broader dynamic in which governments would allow greater citizen input into decision making, leading, in some fashion, to democracy.[31] (Of course, putting the onus on civil society to generate change would also lessen the need to press friendly governments on political reform.)

Assistance programs sought to build service NGOs' capacity as vehicles for citizen participation and as partners with governments.[32] USAID provided technical assistance in accounting, staff development, management, fund raising, and program planning, as well as training in so-called democracy skills (the ability to encourage participation, network, aggregate citizen demands, and exercise oversight of government agencies).[33] In the late 1990s, USAID began to emphasize advocacy training for service NGOs. Advocacy was defined as a participatory but nonpolitical activity. As a report on assistance to Egyptian civil society explained, "Advocacy is defined as an action, rooted in a broad-based community need or interest, taken by NGOs to represent themselves and their constituency to public officials or the public in general. In the Egyptian case, *this is exclusive of religious and political interests*"[34] (emphasis added).

Prodemocracy groups were also included in the democratization vision, although they figured in it somewhat less prominently. The United States saw them, like service NGOs, as vehicles for microparticipation and as incubators of democratic values within society. Instead of being potential partners of governments, however, prodemocracy groups were considered enclaves of reform and benign opposition. Most U.S. aid to prodemocracy groups was in the form of small, short-term grants. (For many years, such grants came directly from U.S. embassies in the region in a very decentralized fashion. With the establishment in 1997 of the State Department's Middle East Democracy Fund, a regional small grants fund was created and additional funding was provided to USAID to assist prodemocracy groups.) Funding supported financial management and institutional development and projects in civic education, election observation, voter education, human rights monitoring, anticorruption efforts, and women's empowerment. As with service NGOs, in the late 1990s the United States put a special emphasis on advocacy training.[35]

Funding for prodemocracy organizations was much less than that channeled to service NGOs. Prodemocracy groups are fewer in number and smaller in size than most service NGOs, making large amounts of funding difficult to absorb. Also, some groups were excluded (or excluded themselves) from assistance because they were outspoken critics of Arab regimes close to the United States and of U.S. policies in the Middle East.

Although the impact of these programs was quite limited, the assistance they provided was clearly valuable in certain respects. U.S. assistance supported the vital work performed by many service NGOs. Support for beleaguered prodemocracy groups across the region helped to keep these groups alive and to maintain a political space, albeit a small one, for their work. With U.S. aid, some groups improved their professional capacities, and they conducted programs that helped to break down taboos on sensitive issues such as corruption and women's rights.

Where civil society assistance fell short was in contributing to a process of democratization. The tens of millions of dollars in aid did not generate popular demand for democracy, alter Arab governments' intolerance of independent citizen activism, or spur a broader dynamic of political change. Although it is certainly unrealistic to expect external assistance programs to decisively affect the political direction of any Arab society, U.S. civil society aid can nevertheless be seen as flawed in two fundamental respects.

First was the manner in which civil society assistance was implemented. Programs involving service NGOs tended to be overly bureaucratic and micromanaged. U.S. contractors served as "pass-through agencies" for USAID funds, assembling large staffs to disperse grants to NGOs and to provide technical assistance. The rationale for this top-heavy arrangement was that outside contractors were needed because USAID was too understaffed to oversee what sometimes amounted to tens of millions of dollars in NGO grants. The result, however, was to create a bureaucratic superstructure that was reminiscent of some of the restrictions Arab governments place on NGOs. To be considered for funding, NGOs had to submit detailed proposals; once approved, they had to undergo various training programs and meet strict accounting and reporting requirements. Although the need for the accountability of funds is understandable, such requirements were beyond the capacity of most groups.

Aid for prodemocracy groups often suffered from the opposite problem: too much informality. This assistance was typically for short-term, one-off projects, with little follow-up. Across the board, the evaluation of civil society projects was superficial, rarely getting past the question of how many activities were completed to probe the deeper issue of whether the assistance contributed to political change.

Many civil society assistance programs were also overly instrumental. That is, the United States often looked upon NGOs as instruments to advance its own agenda. The result was that too often civil society assistance was designed around a U.S. agenda of what issues NGOs should focus on and how. Financially strapped NGOs usually try to be responsive to such donor agendas in the hope of receiving funding, even when the recommended activities do not have much local resonance. This phenomenon is evident in the large numbers of Arab NGOs working on the environment and on women's issues, recent donor favorites, as well as in the launching of advocacy campaigns by service NGOs that have never before undertaken such activities. The line between donors' useful suggestion of new ideas and the imposition of an external agenda is a fine one. When the latter takes over, the result is programs that undermine the concept of civil society as a sphere where indigenous citizen groups pursue causes and activities of their own choosing.

The second and larger problem was that civil society aid was based on a flawed vision of civil society, its weaknesses, and its role in democratization. The U.S. conception of civil society equated the sectors it considered politically acceptable—service NGOs and certain prodemocracy groups—with civil society writ large. This had the effect of targeting assistance to the groups with the least political influence or the shallowest roots in the community and thus placing unrealistic expectations on them. In adopting such a narrow definition of civil society, assistance providers lacked a full understanding of how these groups fit into the broader sphere of civil society and why some citizens were more drawn to other forms of associative life. Narrowly targeted aid also missed the opportunity to help groups develop links to and build coalitions across sectors.

Assistance providers also misdiagnosed the reasons for civil society organizations' weaknesses as agents of democratic change. Too often, NGOs' lack of political influence was attributed mainly to their lack of professionalism—often meaning the ways in which they differed from

Western NGOs. Many NGOs do suffer from poor financial management and undemocratic internal practices, and many influential American NGOs are well managed. But there is no proven direct link between stellar accounting procedures and staff management and influence as an agent of democratic change in an authoritarian setting. More often, civil society groups derive political influence from charismatic leadership, activities and messages that appeal to a broad audience, deep community support, and the ability to mobilize diverse followers around their cause. As explained above, service NGOs were unlikely to become the vanguard of democratic change or lead governments to relax political controls on civil society, regardless of these groups' professionalism; prodemocracy groups struggled with the problem of isolation as much as they faced management challenges.

Nor did assistance adequately address the problem of many civil society groups' lack of autonomy. At the diplomatic level, the United States largely ignored or downplayed the restrictive legal frameworks and other repressive measures that profoundly shaped the environment for civil society. Out of a similar desire not to ruffle diplomatic feathers, U.S. officials sometimes allowed Arab governments to decide which NGOs should receive funding and what activities they could pursue. Such close interaction enabled government agencies to further penetrate and control civil society.[36]

Finally, expectations about how democratization would occur were unrealistic. Projects that encouraged closer NGO–government interaction and cooperation had no demonstrable effect on improving the environment for civil society. With regard to advocacy programs, encouraging NGOs with dubious popular support to press government officials for policy changes raises the question of on whose behalf they are advocating. This approach bypasses the role of political parties in representing constituency interests to government, a key element of a democratic process. Moreover, encouraging advocacy on issues that excluded "religious and political" interests had the effect of encouraging a buzz of activity around marginal issues while core issues of power, contestation, and identity were supposed to remain taboo. Real advocacy must at some point touch on these issues, sensitive as they are.

The hope that microparticipation in civil society groups would generate broader democratic reform was similarly unrealistic. Democratization requires, among other things, an opening at the higher level of political institutions, contestation for national office, and expanded political liberties. These changes cannot be brought about by small numbers of citizens working to improve neighborhood garbage collection. Participation in ground-level community activities is valuable for many reasons, but such participation gains political meaning only when it leads to genuine empowerment.

Conclusion: The New Push

As Washington looks for ways to translate grand ambitions to stimulate Middle East democratization into on-the-ground policies and aid programs, civil society is likely to receive ample attention.

Already, "civil society strengthening" is a visible component of the Middle East Partnership Initiative (MEPI), the State Department's new, several-hundred-million-dollar effort to promote reform in the Arab world beyond Iraq. In his December 2002 speech launching the initiative, Secretary of State Colin Powell declared that the United States would seek partnerships with "community leaders to close the freedom gap with projects to strengthen civil society" and would strengthen "the civic institutions that protect individual rights and provide opportunities for participation." MEPI's political reform "pillar," one of four categories under which the initiative's programs are organized, has "strengthening civil society" as one of its leading objectives. To date, MEPI has funded several civil society programs, and new programs are in the pipeline. Outside the MEPI framework, USAID's large, multiyear NGO assistance programs in Egypt and in the West Bank and Gaza are still under way.

In his January 2004 State of the Union address, President Bush proposed that Congress double the budget of the National Endowment for Democracy (NED) to support new initiatives in the Middle East. Although NED operates independently of the U.S. government, this proposed funding suggests the administration's interest in civil society because NED focuses heavily on aiding NGOs.

Civil society aid can be a valuable component of U.S. democracy promotion in the Middle East. But in this new phase, efforts to assist civil society should be free of three myths that have hampered previous efforts in this domain, and they should avoid the shortcomings of earlier programs.

Letting Go of Myths

The first myth is that democratization in authoritarian countries can occur without real politics and without conflict. The United States often seems to embrace a vision of civil society drawn from the "people power" model—citizens embracing democratic values and banding together to fight authoritarian rule. But at the same time, the United States is attracted to the idea of supporting civil society in the Middle East because it seems safely nonpolitical. The United States continues to be extremely apprehensive about real citizen mobilization in the Arab world and does not want civil society to play a mobilizing role. But in cases of democratic transitions where citizen movements emerged as an important democratic force, the decisive stages of such activism usually came not with microparticipation through NGOs but with mass politics of a conflictive nature, such as mobilization, protests, and demonstrations. Such politics are often accompanied by extensive unrest and violence (for example, many hundreds of Indonesians were killed in the 1998 protests that pushed Suharto from power). This is not to suggest that the United States should encourage unrest and violence, obviously, but rather to point out that fundamental political change is always destabilizing to a certain extent.

The second myth is that civil society activism can alone create a democratic opening. In every case where citizen activism emerged as an important force in political change, it could only do so after broader social, economic, or political changes created new conditions that enabled this to happen.

The third myth is that civil society consists of latent democratic forces simply awaiting activation by Western donors. As was discussed above, in the Middle East different parts of civil society play different roles, and only some sectors have the potential or inclination to push for democratic change. It is unlikely that donor assistance can change this.

The Way Forward

New efforts to aid civil society in Arab countries should:

- *Focus on assisting civil society organizations that could play a role in political change.* Assistance to service NGOs should be shifted to the category of economic development. These groups are not catalysts for political reform or democratization, but they deserve support because of their important role in development.

- *Avoid perpetuating the narrow focus on the "usual suspects."* U.S. officials and democracy-promotion organizations should make contact with as many parts of civil society as possible. This includes a broader range of prodemocracy groups, professional associations that are potentially important players in political liberalization, Islamic organizations, and informal civil society organizations. Such organizations may shun U.S. support or, in the case of informal groups, be ill equipped to absorb it. But opening channels of communication to new sectors of civil society will help the United States better understand the entire civil society sphere and improve assistance to those sectors with which it can cooperate.
- *Think more strategically about civil society assistance.* Donors should develop programs that address the deeper reasons for civil society organizations' weakness as agents of democratic change and provide assistance that addresses the issue of repressive legal frameworks. They should help prodemocracy NGOs make their discourse and activities resonate more at the grassroots level and help them reach new audiences (perhaps through new media). Donors also should support opportunities for cross-sector collaboration, making the encouragement of civil society autonomy a priority by avoiding programs that allow Arab governments to control civil society funding or activities or that otherwise perpetuate control of civil society. If Arab governments insist on such control as a condition of assistance, donors should postpone the program until the controls are lifted. Finally, donors should help NGOs develop strategies for raising community funds, to decrease reliance on government subsidies.
- *Think more broadly about assisting civil society.* In many Arab countries, legalizing new political parties, holding more competitive elections, or lifting press restrictions can stimulate political openings of which civil society organizations can take advantage, and which expand opportunities for civil society to engage with political society. Donors should therefore combine direct assistance to civil society groups with indirect activities such as po-

litical-party development and encouraging more competitive elections and greater media freedom.

- *Avoid cookie-cutter programs.* The nature of civil society differs significantly in Kuwait and Morocco, Jordan and the Palestinian territories, Egypt and Tunisia; aid programs should not look exactly the same in each.
- *Involve civil society organizations more extensively in needs assessments, program design, and evaluation.* In addition, donors should shift away from programs that focus inordinately on training NGOs to receive and manage donor funds for donor-conceived activities.
- *Reinforce themes of civil society assistance at the diplomatic level.* Donors should raise the issues of overly restrictive NGO laws, the harassment of human rights groups, and other factors in the repression of civil society activity with Arab governments on a regular basis.

The Real Challenge

Aiding civil society abroad is more difficult than it might seem. This is not only because civil society is likely to play a more modest role in democratization than is often expected. Improving assistance in the ways described above will require policy makers and aid providers to display a level of patience, flexibility, and knowledge of local history, language, and culture that is typically lacking in U.S. democracy assistance, especially when the pressure is on to demonstrate quick results to Congress. Furthermore, despite the hubris that permeates the current U.S. discourse about "transforming" the Middle East, the most important factors affecting civil society's democratizing potential in Arab countries (or in any country for that matter) are beyond outsiders' direct influence. U.S. assistance at best can play a modest positive role.

Effective civil society assistance requires a sense of genuine partnership and a vision for change that is shared by donors and civil society organizations. In this regard, the Middle East poses a profound challenge in that civil society assistance cannot be separated from the broader context of U.S. relations with the Arab world. Such relations, though never close, have only grown more volatile since Washington launched the new policy of promoting democracy in the region. Widespread opposition to U.S. policy in Iraq and the Palestinian territories may be fostering a solidarity previously lacking among polarized sectors of civil society. It remains to be seen whether this will spill over into the realm of domestic politics and lead to the forging of new coalitions for democratic change.

In the meantime, the anti-American tone of Arab political discourse and the security concerns across the region make it difficult for U.S. officials to reach out to new parts of civil society. This tension is also leading civil society groups—especially those with the most credibility—to steer clear of U.S. assistance for fear that accepting it will taint them irrecoverably. Exacerbating this situation are U.S. counterterrorism measures, which require extensive vetting of all NGOs that are potential recipients of U.S. funding.[37]

Thus until U.S.–Arab relations improve, U.S. attempts to reach out meaningfully to Arab civil society are likely to be complicated by the realities of regional politics as much as by the challenges of democracy promotion.

Notes

This chapter was originally published as Carnegie Paper 44 (March 2004).

1. "Remarks by the President at the 20th Anniversary of the National Endowment for Democracy," speech delivered on November 6, 2003, available at http://www.whitehouse.gov/news/releases/2003/11/20031106–3.html.

2. Political parties are not part of civil society. Parties' main objective is to capture and exercise political power through elected public office. Although some civil society groups may seek to influence the political process, gaining public office is not their objective. The media are also a sphere separate from civil society. The media's market-based character and role as a vehicle for public communication differ from civil society's voluntary character and role as a vehicle for citizen association and collective activity. However, political parties and independent media are often closely intertwined with civil society, in that civil society organizations can share their philosophy, political agenda, and membership.

3. See Gordon White, "Civil Society, Democratization, and Development (I): Clearing the Analytical Ground," *Democratization*, vol. 1, no. 3 (Autumn 1994): 375–90; Gordon White, "Civil Society, Democratization, and Development (II):

Two Country Cases," *Democratization*, vol. 2, no. 2 (Summer 1995): 56–84; Thomas Carothers, "Think Again: Civil Society," *Foreign Policy*, no. 117 (Winter 1999/2000): 18–29; Marina Ottaway and Thomas Carothers, eds., *Funding Virtue: Civil Society Aid and Democracy Promotion* (Washington, D.C.: Carnegie Endowment for International Peace, 2000); and Neera Chandhoke, "The 'Civil' and the 'Political' in Civil Society," *Democratization*, vol. 8, no. 2 (Summer 2001): 1–24.

4. For an analysis of Arab liberalization motivations and strategies, see chapter 2.

5. For a useful overview of the Islamic sector in Egypt, see Carrie Rosefsky Wickham, *Mobilizing Islam: Religion, Activism, and Political Change in Egypt* (New York: Columbia University Press, 2002).

6. For background on this sector, see Denis J. Sullivan, "NGOs and Development in the Arab World: The Critical Importance of a Strong Partnership Between Government and Civil Society," *Civil Society and Democratization in the Arab World*, vol. 9, no. 102 (June 2000): 1–18; and Sarah Ben Nefissa, *NGOs, Governments, and Development in the Arab World*, MOST Discussion Paper 46 (Paris: Management of Social Transformations Program, UN Educational, Scientific, and Cultural Organization, 2001), 1–35.

7. See Azzedine Layachi, *State, Society, and Democracy in Morocco: The Limits of Associative Life* (Washington, D.C.: Center for Contemporary Arab Studies, 1998).

8. Laith Kubba, "The Awakening of Civil Society," *Journal of Democracy*, vol. 11, no. 3 (July 2000): 85–86.

9. Noah Feldman, *After Jihad: America and the Struggle for Islamic Democracy* (New York: Farrar, Straus, and Giroux, 2003), 227.

10. Chemonics International for U.S. Agency for International Development, *Final Report: Democratic Institutions Support Project* (Washington, D.C.: Chemonics International, 1996), A-22. The Democratic Institutions Support (DIS) project was USAID's main attempt during the 1990s to develop a strategic framework for promoting democracy in the Arab world. The DIS project, which was implemented by Chemonics International, had a major influence on democracy assistance to the region during the administration of Bill Clinton.

11. Eva Bellin argues that "in the MENA [Middle East and North Africa] it is the stalwart will and capacity of the state's coercive apparatus to suppress any glimmers of democratic initiative that have extinguished the possibility of transition. Here is where the region's true exceptionalism lies." Eva Bellin, "The Robustness of Authoritarianism in the Middle East: Exceptionalism in Comparative Perspective," *Comparative Politics*, vol. 36, no. 2 (January 2004): 139–57.

12. For a description of the Egyptian government's measures to control professional associations, see Ninette S. Fahmy, "The Performance of the Muslim Brotherhood in the Egyptian Syndicates: An Alternative Formula for Reform," *Middle East Journal*, vol. 52, no. 4 (Autumn 1998): 551–62.

13. See Amani Kandil, *Civil Society in the Arab World: Private Voluntary Organizations* (Washington, D.C.: Civicus, 1995); Denis Sullivan, *Non-Governmental Organizations and Freedom of Association: Palestine and Egypt, a Comparative Analysis* (Jerusalem: Passia, 1995); and Quintan Wiktorowicz, "Civil Society as Social Control: State Power in Jordan," *Comparative Politics*, vol. 33, no. 1 (October 2000): 43–61.

14. The registration process for "charitable or civil society organizations" in Gaza, for instance, requires founding members to submit to the ministry of the interior their curriculum vitae detailing current and former political affiliations, countries to which they have traveled, the date and reason for any detentions, the names of three close friends, and a summary of main events in the lives of the members. See Ribhi Qatamish, *Registration of Charitable Associations and CSOs: A Study of Legal and Administrative Procedures* (Washington, D.C.: Chemonics International/Tamkeen West Bank and Gaza Civil Society and Democracy Strengthening Project, 2003), IV-2. Similar regulations are in force throughout the region.

15. See Quintan Wiktorowicz, "The Informal Islamic Philanthropy Sector: The Limits of Formal Charities and Prospects for Innovation in Jordan," paper presented at the "Adaptation, Creativity, and Dynamism in Contemporary Muslim Philanthropy" seminar, Center for Strategic and International Studies, Washington, D.C., October 10, 2003.

16. The implementation of even more restrictive NGO laws could drive some organizations to leave the voluntary sector and reregister as civil companies and consulting firms, a process that may be under way in Cairo. This could give organizations more leeway to operate for a time, but it could also change their character as voluntary organizations by making the profit motive more important to their work.

17. See Michael W. Foley, "Laying the Groundwork: The Struggle for Civil Society in El Salvador," *Journal of Interamerican Studies and World Affairs*, vol. 38, no. 1 (Spring 1996): 67–104; Mehran Kamrava and Frank O'Mora, "Civil Society and Democratization in Comparative Perspective: Latin America and the Middle East," *Third World Quarterly*, vol. 19, no. 5 (1998): 893–916; Valerie Bunce, "Rethinking Recent Democratization: Lessons from the Postcommunist Experience," *World Politics*, vol. 55 (January 2003): 167–92; White, "Civil Society, Democratization, and Development (II)," 56–84; Marina Ottaway, "Social Movements, Professionalization of Reform, and Democracy in Africa," in *Funding Virtue*, 77–104; and Mary Racelis, "New Visions and Strong Actions: Civil Society in the Philippines," in *Funding Virtue*, 159–87.

18. Julia Pitner, "NGOs' Dilemmas," *Middle East Report*, no. 214 (Spring 2000): 34–37; Nadia Khouri-Dagher, "Arab NGOs: The Difficulty of Being Independent,"

Sources, no. 124 (June 2000): 6–7; author's personal interviews with NGO officials in Cairo and Yemen, May 2001, and in the West Bank, February 2003.

19. Haya Al Mughni, *Women in Kuwait: The Politics of Gender* (London: Saqi Books, 2000), 37–9.

20. President Mubarak's Address to a Joint Session of the People's Assembly and the Shura Council, November 19, 2003, available at http://www.sis.gov.eg/online/html110/o191123v.htm.

21. Author's interview with Egyptian NGO official, Cairo, May 2001.

22. The question of Islamists' perspectives on democracy is complex. For synopses of the main issues, see Guilain Denoeux, "Analyzing Political Islam: Debating Key Concepts and Their Implications," paper prepared for the Asia and Near East Bureau and the Bureau for Democracy, Conflict, and Humanitarian Assistance, U.S. Agency for International Development, March 2002; Gilles Kepel, *Jihad: The Trail of Political Islam* (Cambridge, Mass.: Harvard University Press, 2002), 360–76; Gudrun Kramer, "Islamist Notions of Democracy," in *Political Islam: Essays from Middle East Report*, ed. Joel Beinin and Joe Stork (Berkeley: University of California Press, 1996), 71–82.

23. On the weakness of liberal Islamists, see Emmanuel Sivan, "The Struggle within Islam," *Survival*, vol. 45, no. 1 (Spring 2003): 25–44.

24. See Paul Kingston, "Patrons, Clients, and Civil Society: A Case Study of Environmental Politics in Postwar Lebanon," *Arab Studies Quarterly*, vol. 23, no. 1 (Winter 2001): 55–72.

25. Lise Garon, *Dangerous Alliances: Media, Civil Society, and Democratization in North Africa* (London: Zed Books, 2003).

26. The information and analysis in this section are based on the author's review of U.S. democracy-assistance strategies, reports, and other documents and interviews with U.S. officials, democracy-assistance organizations, and members of Arab civil society groups conducted from 2000 to 2003.

27. During the 1990s, the United States funded a few programs to support labor unions in several Middle Eastern countries, but these programs were classified as activities concerned with economic reform, not democracy promotion.

28. As an assessment of USAID's civil society programs explained: "People learn about democracy by practicing it. Civil society is empowered by people taking an active role in decisions on the management of community resources. Greater access to decision making fosters effective participation, thereby generating greater popular demand for participation. Participants will seek over time to ensure that the rules of the political game are fair and in doing so, will democratize their policies" (Chemonics International for U.S. Agency for International Development, *Final Report*, B-5).

29. An assessment of Moroccan civil society conducted for USAID recommended that the United States focus funding on service NGOs because "in the

wake of this [Islamist] threat to the legitimacy of states in the region, non-politically threatening NGOs in Morocco represent an attractive alternative" to more political democracy and human rights NGOs and to Islamic organizations (USAID, *Strengthening NGOs for Democratization and Sustainable Development in Morocco: An NGO Assessment*, USAID Document PN-ABY-781 [Washington, D.C.: USAID, 1996], iv).

30. The Chemonics report argued: "One strategy is to encourage NGOs not tied to radical opposition groups to provide local services, by granting NGOs greater freedom and more access to local decision making. In the political space thus provided, NGOs can expand memberships, fields of activities, and access to decision-making. . . . Negotiated transitions to democracy will begin . . . as government elites and emerging civil society leadership gradually increase interaction and build trust" (Chemonics International for U.S. Agency for International Development, *Final Report*, B-1–B-2).

31. As a USAID paper on assistance to service NGOs in Egypt explained, "While it is more simple to conclude that a transformation of [Egypt's] prevailing political culture is absolutely dependent on the prevailing political system and its practices, . . . one can also argue that changes in the political culture can happen at the society level, prior to its happening at the political leadership level. Through information exchange, exposure to other countries' and groups' experiences, and the provision of channels of participation—albeit local in nature—this can have a powerful effect on creating empowerment in communities that might induce a broader dynamic for change" (USAID Egypt, "The NGO Service Center Activity," unpublished paper, 2002, 1).

32. As USAID's strategic plan for Egypt for 1996 explained, "In addition to the constraints formally posed by restrictive laws, . . . civil society effectiveness is limited by . . . lack of vision, and weak organizational skills. . . . Many civil society organizations . . . lack administrative capabilities and techniques that could increase their effectiveness in voicing their special interests in the public arena and in carrying on a dialogue with government decision-makers" (USAID Egypt, *Strategic Plan: 1996–2001*, USAID Document PN-ACA-849 [Cairo: USAID Egypt, 1996], 30).

33. For an example of a standard civil society technical assistance program, see America's Development Foundation for USAID, *Final Report: Civil Society Capacity Building Program—West Bank and Gaza Strip*, USAID Cooperative Agreement 294-A-00–00–00053–00 (Alexandria, Va.: America's Development Foundation, 2002).

34. John P. Mason and Iman Youssef, *Final Evaluation: Egypt Private and Voluntary Development Project*, USAID Cooperative Agreement 263-A-00–92–00017–00 (Arlington, Va.: Development Associates, Inc., 1999), 8.

35. For an illustrative example of recommendations for advocacy training for prodemocracy groups, see USAID Morocco, *Addendum to the USAID Morocco Country Strategy Plan: 1999–2005*, USAID Document PD-ABT-383 (Rabat: 2000), 29–38.

36. As the Development Associates report on the Egyptian private voluntary organization development project noted, "The Ministry of Insurance and Social Affairs played a supportive role in approving [NGOs] for participation in the . . . project and in recommending prospective grantees" (Mason and Youssef, *Final Evaluation*, p. "e").

37. For example, new USAID guidelines issued on January 8, 2004, require all Palestinian NGOs receiving U.S. funding to sign a pledge "not to promote or engage in violence, terrorism, bigotry, or the destruction of any state." Nearly 100 Palestinian NGOs have refused to sign the pledge.

6

The Limits of Women's Rights

Marina Ottaway

THE U.S. GOVERNMENT has made the promotion of women's rights and the empowerment of women a central element of its new campaign to modernize and democratize the Arab world. The Middle East Partnership Initiative (MEPI), the major aid program through which the United States seeks to facilitate the transformation of the Arab world, makes women's rights one of its priorities. No official U.S. speech about reform in the Middle East fails to mention the cause of women's rights. And the issue of women is sure to be raised at meetings where Middle East affairs are discussed, regardless of the main purpose of the gathering.

The new U.S. focus on women's rights and the position of women in the Arab world in general received strong encouragement by the publication of the United Nations Development Program's *Arab Human Development Report 2002*. Signed by a number of prominent Arab intellectuals, the report drew a dismal picture of a region lagging behind the rest of the world because of major deficits in freedom, women's empowerment, and education. The report argued that the deficit in women's empowerment was not simply a problem of justice and equity, but a major cause of the Arab world's backwardness. "The utilization of Arab women's capabilities through political and economic participation remains the lowest in the world in quantitative terms, as evidenced by the very low share of women in parliaments, cabinets, and the work force, and in the trend toward the feminization of unemployment," the report explained. "Society as a whole suffers when a huge proportion of its productive potential is stifled. . . ."[1] The argument has since been

115

repeated by President George W. Bush and administration officials. "No society can succeed and prosper while denying basic rights to the women of their country," declared President Bush in a May 2003 commencement speech at the University of South Carolina. Secretary of State Colin Powell echoed the sentiment, arguing: "Until the countries of the Middle East unleash the abilities and potential of their women, they will not build a future of hope."[2]

Promotion of women's rights in the Middle East is an easy goal for the United States to announce. It lends itself to resounding rhetorical statements. It can be translated in practice into many concrete, small projects that are not seen as threatening by most Arab regimes and are even welcomed by them as a means to demonstrate their willingness to democratize and modernize. An improvement in the rights of women does not threaten the power of the incumbent authoritarian government in the same way as free elections or a free press would. Except in Saudi Arabia, Arab leaders and opposition political parties alike, including all but the most fundamentalist Islamic organizations, gladly embrace the rhetoric of women's rights. Many governments are even willing to take small concrete steps, such as appointing the occasional woman to a high, visible position, or introducing amendments to divorce or family laws. For the United States and other democracy-promoting countries, women's programs have the added advantage of being relatively cheap and easy to implement—for example, encouraging schooling for girls, financing women's nongovernmental organizations (NGOs), or providing training for women's candidates in countries where women can run for office. The popularity of the women's rights cause and its obvious intrinsic merit have unfortunately generated many facile assumptions and much confusion about the conditions of women in the Middle East and the problems they face; about the relationship between women's rights and democracy; and about what an outside intervenor like the United States can accomplish. This chapter seeks to clarify some of these issues. It fully accepts the dominant assumptions that the rights of Arab women are not sufficiently protected in the Arab world; that social norms preclude women from fully enjoying even their limited legal rights; that this holds back the entire society; and that the United States should be concerned about the problem and contribute to its solution. It cautions, however, against the assumption that by promoting women's rights the United States contributes to the democratization of the Arab world, and it calls for a clearer separation of programs promoting the rights of women and opportunities for them and those promoting democracy.

Women in the Arab World

There are many misperceptions in the United States about the problems faced by women in Arab countries. The dominant image prevailing in this country is that of veiled, homebound, uneducated women who need help to take the first steps toward emancipation. Those women undoubtedly exist in the Arab world. So do highly educated, professional women, quite emancipated in their own minds but still struggling against restrictive social values. Nowhere in the Arab world do women enjoy equal rights, let alone equal opportunities, with men. The situation, however, varies considerably from country to country. This is true whether one talks of political rights, civil rights, family law, access to education and jobs, or more generally, the restrictions imposed on women by social customs. Social class creates additional differences among women in some countries. These differences are not sufficiently acknowledged outside the Arab world. Even the *Arab Human Development Reports* tend to generalize about Arab women, despite the fact that the statistical tables they contain contradict such generalizations.

Of the sixteen countries located in the Middle East and North Africa, ten have signed, and nine have ratified, the Convention on All Forms of Discrimination against Women.[3] Even in those countries, however, women's political, educational, and especially personal rights vary greatly.

Political Rights

Arab countries severely curtail the political rights of all their citizens, men and women. Even when recognized on paper, they are rarely respected in practice. Here, I am only discussing the formal political rights of women. Only three Arab countries do not recognize the rights of women to vote and stand for elections. Two of the three states, Saudi Arabia and the United Arab Emirates (UAE), do not hold elections in the first place, leaving Kuwait as the only country that holds regular elections but excludes women.

Some Middle East states recognized the political rights of women relatively early—Syria in 1949, Lebanon in 1952, Egypt in 1956, and Tunisia in 1957. It is worth adding here that Turkey, a Muslim country in the Mediterranean basin, although of course not an Arab state, recognized women's right to vote in 1930 and their right to stand for elections in 1934, ahead of many European countries. Except for the Gulf countries, Arab nations recognized the political rights of women around the same time as most other developing countries.[4]

No comprehensive data are available about the extent to which women exercise the right to vote—and even less about whether they vote autonomously rather than following the directions of a man in the family. What is clear, however, is that few women stand for office even when they are allowed to do so by law and that few are appointed to ministerial positions. The presence of women in parliaments and ministerial positions ranges from none in most countries to a maximum of about 12 percent in a few cases. Governing remains an overwhelmingly male prerogative in Arab countries—but it is worth bearing in mind that this is true in most of the world. In the United States women occupy only 14 percent of the seats in the House of Representatives and 13 percent in the Senate. Women approach parity with men in political posts only in some Scandinavian countries.

Educational Rights

Access to education varies widely among Arab countries for both boys and girls. For example, among primary school age children, 98 percent attend school in Tunisia, but only 57 percent in Saudi Arabia. In most countries, more boys attend primary school than girls, but the difference is quite low in some countries—two percentage points in Tunisia and three in Algeria—but dramatic in others—44 percent of girls and 76 percent of boys are in primary school in Yemen, for example. In Bahrain, the UAE, and Qatar, more girls than boys attend primary school.

When it comes to secondary education, the enrollment rate for women is higher than for men in Algeria, Bahrain, Jordan, Kuwait, Lebanon, Qatar, Tunisia, and the UAE. In tertiary education, more women than men attend school in six countries.[5] In some cases, the difference is considerable: In Kuwait 13 percent of men and 30 percent of women are enrolled in tertiary education. Except in a few countries, thus, Arab women are no more education-deprived than Arab men.

Enrollment statistics do not tell the entire story, and more detailed data are difficult to acquire. For example, it is not clear whether the quality of girls' and boys' schools is comparable in all countries and at all grade levels. What is clear is that education does not open up the same employment opportunities for women as for men.

Personal Status and Family Law

In this area, women remain at a clear disadvantage throughout the Arab world. In most countries, it is practically impossible for women but quite easy for men to file for divorce. Polygamy is legal and socially accepted, although not widely practiced. Laws, and even more clearly social values, condone so-called honor killings. With few exceptions, such as Jordan, where the legal age for marriage was recently raised from 15 to 18, women can be married off by their parents at a very young age and without their consent. Progress in these areas is extremely slow, and there is much social resistance to the legal reforms introduced in some countries. A 2001 Egyptian law granting women the right to file for divorce led to many dire predictions of social disintegration, including in the more liberal press. In Morocco, King Mohammad VI's proposal to give women greater equality, including the right to divorce, sparked large demonstrations by Islamist groups. Pro-reform demonstrations also took place, but the opponents of equality far outnumbered the supporters.

Reforms of family status laws are likely to emerge as the major battleground for women in the Middle East. Such reforms are crucial to improving the conditions of women. New laws do not change social attitudes instantaneously; indeed, in some cases they make the conservative elements more combative, but in the long run they help create more opportunities for women. However, these reforms are politically and culturally sensitive, and involvement or, in the eyes of some, interference by the United States could create a serious backlash. Already, the more conservative Islamist organizations condemn U.S. efforts to promote greater social and political participation by women, claiming that it would eventually lead to social promiscuity and license as happened in the United States.

The difficulty of working on issues that directly affect the social position of women and their status within the family is enhanced by the differences between educated, emancipated urban women and uneducated ones, both rural and urban, which exist in most countries. It is easy for foreigners to communicate with the former, but by doing so they only reach a small and atypical segment of the population, which is not always in touch with the rest, nor necessarily sensitive to their problems and values.

In view of the above considerations, it is clear that overgeneralizations about the conditions of women in the Arab world, their rights, and their empowerment are dangerous. Such generalizations risk making U.S. assistance ineffective. The curtailing of political rights in the Arab world is not primarily a women's issue and should not be treated as if it were. Putting in place programs to get more women elected to powerless parliaments neither empowers women nor promotes democracy. Access to education remains a serious problem for women in some countries, but in others women are already better educated than men, and the real problem for them is the absence of opportunities to use their education and knowledge once they graduate. Educated urban women in North Africa or Egypt encounter problems that are quite similar to those women confronted everywhere until recently—the slow breakdown of the barrier separating women's and men's roles, traditions that curtail the freedom of women under the guise of protecting them, and men's resistance to the professional advancement of women. They know a lot better than outsiders what are the real problems they face and what they can do about them. Rural women in Yemen, deprived of access to education and any public role, face completely different problems and probably need more outside support. Thus, it is not sufficient to talk about promoting the position of women in the Arab world, or increasing educational opportunities for them. Different countries, and different groups of women, need different reforms, including some in which U.S. agencies should not meddle.

Women's Rights and Democracy

Support for women's rights in the Arab world is seen in the United States as part of the effort to promote democracy in the region. Yet, the relationship between women's rights and democracy is not simple. The idea that working for women's rights is an integral part of the struggle for democracy is in part a tautology and in part simply wrong. The statement is tautological in the sense that democracy entails equality for all citizens, thus promoting women's rights means promoting democracy. But democracy also entails creating institutions that are accountable to the citizens and curb one another's power through a system of checks and balances. The existence of such institutions does not depend on the rights of women. These institutions can thrive, and have thrived historically, even when women do not enjoy the same political and civil rights as men. Conversely, states that did not have accountable institutions or a system of checks and balances have recognized the equality of women, historically and even now. Socialist countries in particular emphasized that they promoted the equality of women better than Western countries, while in practice curtailing the political and civil rights of all citizens.

In countries that started developing democratic systems before World War II, democratic political institutions were established over a hundred years before the political rights of women were recognized or even before women's rights emerged as an issue. The United States and Great Britain started developing strong democratic institutions without the benefit of women's suffrage or even of universal male suffrage. Political participation in both countries was originally quite limited. Over the course of the nineteenth century, participation expanded to include the male population—at least the white male population in the United States. Resistance to women's participation continued unabated until 1918 in Great Britain and 1920 in the United States.

The battle for women's suffrage was quite difficult in both countries. Although in retrospect the outcome seems inevitable, it did not appear so at the time. Social values and customs prevented the recognition of equal rights for women, in the same way as they once prevented the recognition of equal rights of racial minorities in the United States. Once women became mobilized, however, the democratic nature of the political system made the outcome inevitable because only a degree of repression untenable in a democratic system could have stopped women from demanding equal rights. Despite widespread social prejudice against women's rights, democratic principles left no other choice. The inclusion of women was part and parcel of democratic consolidation, as was the inclusion of racial minorities in the United States forty years later. The existence of democratic institutions and of a democratic culture and tradition made the inclusion of women and ethnic minorities inevitable in the long run.

After World War II, and in some countries even earlier, the recognition of women's political and civil rights has become routine everywhere, including in countries that did not or do not embrace democracy. What has been historically a dramatic breakthrough toward democratic consolidations has turned almost everywhere into an idea to which almost all countries in the world pay homage, although in reality politics and governance remain a male prerogative almost everywhere. But recognition of women's rights has not automatically made political systems more pluralistic or more likely to develop democratic institutions.

This is quite clear in the Arab world today. Those Arab states that recognize some political rights of citizens—such as being able to elect legislative assemblies—also recognize the political rights of women. Kuwait, which does not recognize political rights for women, is a real anomaly in this regard. What keeps Arab countries from being democratic is not the exclusion of women, but the fact that elected institutions have very little power and impose no effective checks on monarchs who govern as well as rule and on presidents whose power base is in the security forces or a strong party.

The struggle for women's rights and the core struggle to achieve democracy—that is, to reduce the excessive and arbitrary power of the executive—must be seen as separate processes in the Arab world today. Progress toward democracy in the Arab world depends on the emergence of countervailing forces and organized groups that the government cannot ignore and that have to be accommodated in the political system. Simply including women in a hollow political process does nothing to create such countervailing forces. This does not mean that the promotion of equal rights for women has to wait until countervailing forces emerge or political institutions that curb the excessive power of the executive are put in place. Certainly, the two battles can be waged simultaneously. There should be no illusion, however, either that promoting women's rights will lead to democracy or that the emergence of institutions of checks and balances will automatically solve the problem of equality for women.

Policy Impact of Including Women

Although formally recognizing women's political and civil rights does not ensure the transformation of a nondemocratic country into a democratic one, there is some evidence that including women in the political process appears to have an impact on public policy. The empirical evidence on the impact of women's presence in legislatures and elected local councils is extremely sketchy, anecdotal, and generally partisan, because the studies are often conducted by researchers who want to demonstrate positive results. Still, the results are fairly consistent across regions and studies. In general, it appears that local councils and parliaments where at least 20 percent of the members are women are more likely to focus on issues that directly affect women (such as divorce or land ownership laws) or that affect the welfare of their families (such as the availability of clean water or schooling).[6] However, it is also clear that much of the progress made in improving the legal status of women in most countries has been made by male-dominated legislatures.

The number of women in policy-making positions remains low worldwide. For example, in early 2003, women represented less than 14 percent of the total in the U.S. Congress. The percentage of women parliamentarians was highest in Scandinavian countries, but even there women still constituted less than 40 percent of the total, with Sweden the only exception. Formal equality of rights does not translate easily into equal political roles for men and women even in the countries where women are most emancipated.[7]

Available evidence suggests that women only become an effective voice in legislatures when they are present in sufficient numbers to constitute a substantial bloc. This evidence has encouraged the launching of programs that seek to increase the number of women in elected positions. The 1995 UN Conference on Women, held in Beijing, adopted as a target that women should occupy 30 percent of parliamentary seats. By March 2000, twenty-one countries had imposed a quota of 20 or 30 percent for at least one house, and an additional country, Finland, has imposed a 50 percent quota.[8] Some Arab governments, including those of Jordan and Egypt, have made an effort to appoint more women to national legislatures and high-level government positions. The United States, which does not advocate a quota system, is nevertheless committed to increasing the presence of women in Middle East legislatures. For example, through the MEPI, the United States is providing training to female political candidates in the hope of increasing women's presence in the legislatures.

Opinions remain sharply divided about efforts to increase the presence of women in elective offices. To some, the low presence of women is an urgent problem to be tackled through the imposition of quotas and the adoption of special measures. To others, it is simply a symptom, a reflection of cultural values and social traditions that cannot be expected to change rapidly. The issue remains one of intense debate in part because the evidence is not particularly clear. Although there is no doubt that the countries where women enjoy the highest political presence are also the ones where women's rights receive the greatest recognition and respect, it is far from clear whether the former causes the latter or vice versa.

Women's Empowerment in the Middle East: A Greater Impact?

Increased participation by women in political life has hardly any impact on the functioning of political systems and, at best, a modest impact on policy. The removal of legal and social barriers that prevent women from enjoying access to education and jobs has a great deal of impact on the personal lives and income-earning capacity of women, and thus on their children. These are not negligible results, and they certainly justify efforts by the United States to promote rights for women as well as their advancement in the society. However, an expectation has developed that women's rights and empowerment in the Arab world will have a more far-reaching impact. As the *Arab Human Development Report 2002* stated, in order to participate fully in the world of the twenty-first century, Arab countries must tackle the deficit of women's empowerment.

Is there reason to believe that the promotion of women's rights, not only in theory but in practice, would have a greater impact in the Arab world than it has had elsewhere? Could promotion of women's rights shake these societies in a much more dramatic way than has been the case elsewhere? Is the extension of women's rights the beginning of a road to profound change in Arab countries, as the rhetoric suggests?

For the vast majority of Arab states, the answer is negative. In most countries, women already enjoy the same political rights, limited as they are, as men. Family status laws are improving slowly in a number of countries; and this process is likely to continue because this is an area where incumbent governments can demonstrate to the world their reforming zeal without undermining their power. Women are also becoming much better educated in most countries, even in the closed societies of the Gulf. It is true that social values are changing slowly and that the growth of Islamist movements in many countries is creating new obstacles for women. But in general a gradual process toward improving women's rights is under way.

The political systems of most Arab countries can incorporate such changes in the position of women without difficulty, because their political systems have a degree of flexibility. Although no Arab regimes can be considered democratic, many are semiauthoritarian, combining relatively democratic political institutions and some limited recognition of individual rights and personal freedom with an overly strong executive. Countries such as Egypt, Jordan, or Morocco, for example, have proven adept at maintaining a balance between authoritarianism and limited democratic freedoms, and they can undoubtedly absorb some changes in the position of women without much difficulty. Autocratic but secular countries—Syria, for example, and in the past Iraq—have no problem making concessions to women.

The question of whether the expansion of women's rights would have a different, more far-reaching effect in Arab nations than it had in the rest of the world thus can only be raised in relation to the countries of the Gulf, which are the most closed socially and politically. Even in these countries, however, the present trend is toward slow, cautious social and political reform. Bahrain, Kuwait, Oman, and Qatar are moving hesitantly in that direction, with the governments apparently in full control of the pace of change. Saudi Arabia has been very wary of embarking on any type of reform, social or political, although recent statements suggest that it may decide to follow the example of its neighbors.

In conclusion, there seems to be little reason to expect that improved rights for women in the Middle East would have a more dramatic political impact than similar reforms in the rest of the world.

Can the United States Make a Difference?

Despite the resounding regime change rhetoric of official speeches, the Bush administration is in reality taking a rather soft, indirect approach to promoting democracy in the region. Only the governments of Syria and Iran are being singled out for strong unambiguous criticism. The administration has taken a much more ambivalent, cautious position vis-à-vis Egypt and Saudi Arabia, the home countries of most of the September 11 hijackers, but also countries whose cooperation the United States still needs. In most other countries, the administration is taking a lenient attitude, praising highly any hint of political reform and refraining from criticizing glaring shortcomings.[9]

The major vehicle through which the administration is trying to promote this indirect approach to democratization via social transformation is the Middle East Partnership Initiative: a program developed during 2002 and officially launched at the end of the year. MEPI funds projects designed to foster educational, economic, and social reform. The promotion of women occupies a central place in the MEPI approach, with many projects targeting primarily women. Though classified as one initiative, MEPI is better understood as a series of independent activities rather than one organic whole. Women's programs are no exception. They include, for example, women's literacy programs in countries such as Morocco and Yemen, organizing conferences on women, training in business skills and microcredit programs for Palestinian women, training of female political candidates in several countries, training of advocates for women's rights, and programs on women's health. There are many more projects of this kind already under way and more yet are being planned as the funding for MEPI increases.[10] The initiative was funded at $29 million in FY2002 and $100 million in FY2003, with more expected for FY2004.

Can these discrete projects make a difference? The question needs to be considered from different angles. From the point of view of individual women reached by the projects, this assistance can have a positive effect, although in most cases not a dramatic one. On one hand, well-managed microcredit projects have been shown to help women, marginally increasing their revenue, an improvement that usually translates into better food for the family or school fees for the children. On the other hand, microloans do not usually change people's lives, but only make poverty less dire—not a negligible outcome. Similarly, literacy programs do not dramatically change the lives of women or create employment opportunities for them, but they do help bring them in touch with the modern world around them and affect their attitudes toward the education of their children, particularly girls. As is often the case with foreign assistance, some programs will prove to be poorly conceived and designed and will make little difference even at the level of individuals.

As contributions to the democratization of the region, programs of this kind are unlikely to make a difference. President Bush has declared that the United States "will consistently challenge the enemies of reform," but there is no challenge to the real opponents of democracy in MEPI's projects, particularly projects that target women.[11] Generally small and innocuous, the projects do not affect the distribution of power and do nothing to make it more difficult for governments to contain political liberalization and prevent the development of true opposition groups. The very concept of "partnership" with governments and civil society organizations on which MEPI is based precludes the enactment of programs that incumbent governments do not like. Instead, there is a real risk that authoritarian or semiauthoritarian governments may use MEPI projects as a means to bolster their reformist credentials without substantially increasing political, economic, or social space. In conclusion, it is difficult to see MEPI projects that focus on women as part, even a modest part, of a strategy of democracy promotion.

Conclusion

Advancing women's rights in the Arab world is an important goal, and the United States should continue to pursue it in the name of equity and justice. Improving the position of women might also have a favorable impact on economic growth, children's welfare, and fertility rates, as has been the case in other countries. There should be no illusion, however, that pressuring Arab governments to recognize the rights of women and undertaking projects to improve their lives addresses the most fundamental obstacles to democracy: the unchecked power of strong executives. Promoting democracy and promoting women's rights need to be recognized as tasks that require different approaches.

Whether and how the United States could contribute to the democratic transformation of the Middle East at present is an issue that goes beyond the scope of this chapter. It is clear, however, that it cannot do so through programs that advance the rights of women and opportunities for them. Confusing the advancement of women and the advancement of democracy is not only incorrect but also dangerous in the atmosphere of deep distrust of the United States that already exists in the Middle East. Conflating democracy and the advancement of women encourages liberal Arabs, who are already doubtful about the U.S. commitment to democracy, to become even more skeptical—the United States has chosen to teach girls to read instead of confronting autocratic governments. Conservative Arabs, who already tend to interpret the moral degeneration (in their eyes) of the West to be a result of democracy, worry even more when U.S. officials talk about democracy and trying to change the position of women in their societies. The identification of democracy and women's rights leads to sinister interpretations and unintended consequences in the Arab world. There is great need for the U.S. government not only to rethink the nexus of democracy and the promotion of women, but also to become more sensitive to the great gap that separates what U.S. officials say and what different Arab constituencies hear.

Notes

This chapter was originally published as Carnegie Paper 42 (February 2004).

1. United Nations Development Program (UNDP), *Arab Human Development Report 2002* (New York: Oxford University Press, 2002), 23.

2. Speech delivered at the Heritage Foundation, Washington, D.C., on December 12, 2002.

3. UNDP, *Arab Human Development Report 2002*, table 31. The report lists twenty-two countries, including the Comoros, Djibouti, Mauritania, Palestine, Somalia, and Sudan. This paper will exclude the above countries and only consider sixteen: Algeria, Bahrain, Egypt, Iraq, Jordan, Kuwait, Lebanon, Libya, Morocco, Oman, Qatar, Saudi Arabia, Syria, Tunisia, the United Arab Emirates, and Yemen.

4. UNDP, *Human Development Report 2003* (New York: Oxford University Press, 2003), table 27.

5. UNDP, *Arab Human Development Report 2003* (New York: Oxford University Press, 2003), tables A-2, A-3, and A-4.

6. Irene Tinker, "Quotas for Women in Elected Legislatures: Do They Really Empower Women?" unpublished paper presented to the International Center for Research on Women, Washington D.C., on October 23, 2003.

7. UNDP, *Human Development Report 2003*, table 27.

8. Tinker, "Quotas for Women"; see also International IDEA, "Global Database of Quotas for Women," available at http://www.idea.int/quota.

9. The speech delivered by President George W. Bush at the National Endowment for Democracy on November 6, 2003, offers a prime example of this approach.

10. Information on MEPI programs is available online at http://www.mepi.state.gov.

11. Speech delivered by President George W. Bush at Whitehall Palace, London, England, on November 19, 2003.

7

The Political-Economic Conundrum

Eva Bellin

FOR NEARLY TWO DECADES the Middle East and North Africa (MENA) has languished in economic stagnation and lassitude. At a time when the logic of market-driven reform and export-oriented growth has become nearly canonical worldwide, the MENA region has proven steadfastly unenthusiastic about reform, shutting itself out of the benefits of economic globalization and falling behind most other regions in economic development. At the same time, the region has distinguished itself by spurning another worldwide trend: democratization. As democracy has spread in Latin America, Central and Eastern Europe, Asia, and sub-Saharan Africa, the Middle East has remained largely authoritarian, experiencing at most only mild liberalizing political reforms. This dual resistance to world trends is intriguing and resurrects the question of the relationship between political and economic reform. Is this dual resistance to reform coincidental? And what does this resistance say about whether and how Western policy makers and aid practitioners should try to link or sequence their efforts to promote political and economic reform in the region?

Conventional wisdom in the development community has long held that economic and political reforms are directly linked. With regard to sequencing, the debate has been dominated by two schools: one prioritizing economic reform, the other political reform. Yet neither approach is useful as policy guidance. Although linkage between economic and political reform indeed exists (and in the Middle East resistance to both kinds of reform is intrinsically interwoven in the logic of many regimes), the relationship between the two is not deterministic, nor is any fixed sequencing warranted. The permissive linkage between economic and political reform suggests that neither is a precondition of the other. Further, if either democratization or economic reform is the stated policy goal, each must be pursued not as a means to the other but rather for its own sake and on its own terms.

Economic Decline

Economic decline has plagued the Middle East since the mid-1980s.[1] Once a global leader, outpacing all other regions save East Asia for most rapid output growth, the Middle East has turned into a global loser, falling behind nearly every other region in development over the past two decades. Overall growth rates have stagnated. In most countries of the region, gross national product (GNP) has barely kept pace with population growth, and in some, such as Saudi Arabia and Iran, per capita GNP has registered an absolute decline. Unemployment continues to climb. The jobless rate is officially estimated at 25 percent regionwide, and the failure of job creation to keep pace with demographic trends projects even higher levels of unemployment in the years ahead. Investment levels have declined. Fiscally strapped states have dramatically cut back on public investment, and the private sector has not stepped in sufficiently to pick up the slack. Capital flight is endemic. Middle East residents hold an estimated $100–500 billion in savings abroad, and the region has been unsuccessful in attracting foreign direct investment (FDI) in sectors other than tourism and petroleum. Productivity levels are down. Middle East products and labor have become progressively less competitive in the global market and this has spelled worsening trade imbalances, rising international indebtedness, and increased debt overhang. Finally, poverty remains a challenge. More than 30 percent of the population is estimated to live below the human poverty line despite the MENA's reputation for admirably extensive family-sponsored and state-sponsored safety nets.[2] Overall, the Middle East and North Africa is a region of deteriorating living standards and persistent economic anemia— a pale shadow of the promise it held in the 1960s and 1970s.

To some degree the economic contraction suffered by the Middle East over the past twenty years was triggered by the decline in public investment that followed the fall in oil prices in the mid-1980s. But equally detrimental have been both the failure of the private sector (both local and foreign) to invest in MENA countries and the declining *productivity* of investment in the region. Economists have arrived at a consensus to explain this double failure. They trace it primarily to the dual phenomenon of too much state and too inadequate a state in much of the region.

By "too much state" economists refer to the outsized role played by the state in managing the economy. In most Middle Eastern countries, the state continues to play an economic role in society comparable in scope to that found in communist regimes of bygone days.[3] The flagship of this state-dominated economy is an immense public sector, envisioned, first and foremost, as the engine of national growth but also assigned countless political tasks such as sopping up unemployment, evening out regional development, providing cheap manufactured goods to the masses, and delivering political patronage to important state cronies.[4] The contamination of the public sector's mission with political goals introduces substantial economic irrationality into the sector's operation and contributes to its chronic inefficiency and persistence as a loss-maker. Worse still, irrationality in the public sector introduces inefficiency and distortion throughout the economy, given its central role as national producer, employer, and allocator of resources. Labor is not priced at its scarcity value; locally produced inputs are of poor quality and overpriced; credit is distributed on political grounds; protection of the local market is prioritized at the expense of export-readiness; and building intra-industry linkages with foreign multinationals is often cast as imperialist heresy.

The economy's domination by a politically driven public sector has multiple negative repercussions for investment and growth. First, the price distortions and inefficiencies introduced by the public sector mean that most Middle Eastern economies hold little allure for FDI. In fact, the region has largely missed out on the growth in international capital flows of the past decade, attracting only 3 percent of FDI worldwide and less than 1 percent of total portfolio flows to developing countries.[5] Second, the disinterest of foreign investors in the region has compounded the inefficiency of local production and shut Middle East firms out of technical innovations because they are not integrated into intra-industry trade.[6] Third, the public sector's large size combined with its preferential access to state contracts and state credit has crowded out the local private sector and retarded the latter's development. In short, too much state has undermined important sources of investment, both foreign and local, as well as the productivity of investment in the region.

Of course the region's economic problems do not derive *only* from too much state. Also important are the policy choices that highly interventionist states make. For example, other highly interventionist states (notably the developmental states of East Asia) chose to prioritize export-readiness and trade-led growth over protection of the local market and were able to achieve spectacular economic results. By contrast, the interventionist states in the MENA region have chosen to prioritize protection of the local market over export-led growth, given their political concern to protect local jobs and cronies as well as their economic concern to protect revenues. This decision to spurn a strategy of export-led growth has spelled exceptionally low levels of integration into international trade flows for the MENA region, shutting it out of a major source of cost discipline and technological innovation.[7] Again, as the East Asian cases demonstrate, none of this is necessarily the consequence of having a large, interventionist state.

Other factors that have also undermined foreign investment and the productivity of investment in the MENA region include the region's exceptional level of interstate conflict as well as the persistent problem of Dutch disease.[8] The MENA's high level of interstate conflict creates a climate of insecurity that discourages foreigners from investing. The problem of Dutch disease spells the overpricing of labor as well as other nontradables, undercutting productivity and similarly creating a disincentive for foreigners to invest. Neither problem is a consequence of too much state, and correcting them requires other political remedies.

In addition to the problem of too much state, most countries in the region are also plagued by the problem of *too inadequate* a state. This refers to the institutional deficit that characterizes so many Middle East countries: the lack of an adequate regulatory and legal framework to guarantee property rights, enforce contracts, and reduce the transaction costs faced by the private sector investors. As it stands, most Middle East economies constitute difficult environments for investors to work in, characterized by extensive red tape, opacity, arbitrariness, and corruption, all with minimal legal redress. Little wonder that foreign capital has scant interest in investing in the region (outside of the petroleum and tourist enclaves) or that capital flight is endemic. Nor is it surprising that most migrant workers prefer to invest their hard-won remittances in nontradables such as real estate rather than in entrepreneurial ventures such as industry at rates much higher than that found in other regions.[9] Together, these trends deprive the region of important sources of productive investment and growth.

For many years the region's state-dominated economies, with all their attendant inefficiencies, were sustained by access to rent. Petroleum rents, gas rents, strategic rents (that is, foreign aid born of a country's strategic value to wealthy donors), and transit rents together constituted the great enablers of the region's exceptional etatism. The best evidence for this lay in the fact that access to rent, not official state ideology, proved to be the best predictor of the public sector's size in any given country. Even avowedly "liberal" regimes embraced etatist policies when they enjoyed a rent windfall. These rents, by prolonging inefficiency and postponing sustainable growth, constituted a quintessential "resource curse." They undermined national development to the point of paradox where many of the best-endowed countries possess the poorest developmental prospects and their less-advantaged neighbors command more promising futures thanks to their quicker embrace of reform. By the late 1990s, it had become evident to even the rent-rich countries that rents were unlikely to keep pace with population growth and that resource wealth alone could not deliver sufficient economic development and employment creation to sustain national well-being and social peace. The call for economic reform became widespread.

Economic Reform and Its Obstacles

The economic medicine prescribed for the region by the International Monetary Fund (IMF), World Bank, and other adherents of the Washington consensus mirrored the conventional economic wisdom offered elsewhere. From the early 1980s onward, Middle East states were advised to move on three tracks of economic reform: (1) stabilization (short-term measures designed to restrain government spending, contain inflation, reduce the government deficit, and close the balance-of-payments gap); (2) structural adjustment (longer-term measures aimed at liberalizing the economy through the elimination of price controls, withdrawal of subsidies, introduction of currency convertibility, general deregulation, and encouragement of free trade and FDI); and (3) privatization.[10]

At the same time, the states of the region were advised to carry out institutional reform (or, in some cases, institution *building*) for the sake of achieving "good governance." The objective was to build judicial and regulatory capacity as well as encourage transparency, predictability, and ultimately accountability in government conduct.

The region's response to this prescription was mixed. Most countries embraced some measures of stabilization, reducing government expenditures, lowering inflation, and imposing fiscal reform. Many undertook this reform at their own initiative so that even countries that prided themselves on excluding multilateral institutions such as the World Bank and the IMF from their policy deliberations (for example, Algeria, Iraq, Syria) had embarked on some stabilization by the early 1990s. And by the mid-1990s, even relatively wealthy countries such as Saudi Arabia were persuaded by the logic of stabilization, embracing macroeconomic austerity and subsidy cuts.

But the attitude toward structural adjustment and privatization was far less enthusiastic. Here the region showed significant variation. Only a few middle income countries (Egypt, Jordan, Morocco, and Tunisia) proved truly receptive to such reform, whereas the poorest (for example, Yemen, Sudan, Mauritania), the richest (for example, the Gulf Cooperation Council countries), and the remainder of middle income countries (for example, Algeria, Iran, Syria) largely spurned it. Even the relatively receptive reformers were late to embrace reform (compared with similarly positioned countries in other regions), and their pace of reform has remained slow. By the year 2000, the four reformers were still in the bottom two-thirds of countries in terms of cumulative liberalization since 1985.[11] Consequently, the region's performance has been poor, especially in the areas of trade liberalization, privatization, and institutional reform. Tariff barriers have remained high in much of the Middle East, strangling the possibility of trade-driven growth. Privatization has proceeded at a snail's pace, burdening the region with a huge and inefficient public sector that towers over that found in low and middle income countries elsewhere. Complex regulatory frameworks remain in place in most Middle East countries with little enhancement of the institutional means for redress, barring the development of transparency or accountability.

To some extent there are good economic reasons to "go slow" on many aspects of economic reform. For example, the path from economic reform to growth is by no means guaranteed. Factors such as slow regional growth, world economic recession, and trade barriers that protect the developed world's textiles and agriculture from competition with less-developed countries together weaken the linkage between trade liberalization and the delivery of growth for developing countries.

But the truth is that the lion's share of opposition to structural adjustment and privatization in the region has been driven not so much by economic rationality as by political logic.[12] Middle East regimes are loath to privatize public enterprises because these enterprises serve as key sources of state patronage (jobs for the masses, lucrative posts for political cronies) and so are crucial to the regime's strategy of building support at the mass and elite levels. Many groups who form the core constituencies of these regimes (for example, public sector workers, bureaucrats, army officers, crony capitalists) staunchly oppose economic reform, and embracing it would put the regimes' political foundation at risk. Beyond this, Middle East regimes are reluctant to liberalize trade because exposing national firms to the crush of foreign competition would likely spell massive firm failure and extensive job loss (a prospect not only economically harmful but also politically ruinous in a context where unemployment is already high). Middle East regimes also have little interest in relaxing regulatory frameworks because regulations constitute an important source of discretionary favor and political control. Similarly, the goals of building institutional accountability or transparency hold little appeal to political elites who know that institutional opaqueness and arbitrariness constitute important levers of power. In short, policies that seem economically irrational are crucial to the political logic of these regimes (providing patronage, sustaining coalitions, endowing discretionary power). As a result, few regimes are willing to undertake reform unless pressed by crisis; even then they are likely to hedge their bets and embrace, at best, only partial reform.

Political Reform a Precondition of Economic Reform?

The political foundation of the widespread resistance to economic reform in the Middle East suggests that to achieve economic reform in this region political reform must precede it. Only by altering the political logic that sustains these regimes, moving from a base built on the discretionary distribution of patronage to one grounded in the legitimacy that comes with procedural legality and political accountability, will political elites ever be persuaded to undertake economic reform. It is on the basis of this analysis that many argue that democracy must come prior to economic liberalization in the region.

This prescription taps into a rich debate on the proper sequencing of political and economic reform. Conventional wisdom has long oscillated between two very different views on this matter. From the 1970s through the early 1990s, the predominant position in the development community was that economic reform ought to precede political liberalization on the grounds that authoritarian regimes were better equipped to shepherd economic development and carry out economic reform. Democracies, they argued, are hostage to electoral pressures and so find it difficult to impose painful economic policies on their societies, especially when the costs of reform are concentrated and the benefits are diffuse. Under these conditions, potential beneficiaries face much more serious collective action problems in getting their preferences served than do potential losers.[13] In addition, the election cycle in democracies tends to introduce an element of myopia in the time horizons of policy makers, preventing the sustained pursuit of reform. If the benefits of reform are not to be realized until after the election cycle and the costs are experienced up front, elected officials have diminished incentive to reform.

By contrast, this school argues, authoritarian regimes are not dependent on elections. Being more insulated from popular opinion, they can afford to take the long view on policy decisions and are able to prescribe harsh economic medicine when economic rationality warrants it. This was the reasoning often cited by authoritarian leaders such as Singapore's Lee Kuan Yew, South Korea's Park Chung Hee, and Chile's Augusto Pinochet, who routinely rationalized the delay of democratization in their countries on developmental grounds. The outstanding economic success of a few authoritarian regimes such as Singapore, South Korea, and Chile provided empirical ballast for this argument, persuading many in the development community that authoritarian regimes are indeed better equipped to steer economic development and that democratization should follow, not precede, economic reform.

By the mid-1990s, however, conventional wisdom began to swing in another direction, driven in large part by the simple fact that some new democracies had in fact proven capable of carrying out economic reform.

One of the most fascinating findings of the 1990s was the postcommunist paradox: Among postcommunist countries, it was precisely the most democratic regimes that carried out the most comprehensive economic reform, whereas the more authoritarian regimes proved sluggish about reform. Frequent elections, shorter executive tenure, and greater chances of electoral revenge did not prevent postcommunist countries such as Poland from implementing radical reform programs, whereas countries such as the Ukraine and Belarus, led by executives with more secure tenure and more insulation from electoral pressures, proved much more resistant to reform.[14] Similarly, the experience of Latin America revealed that democracies in that region performed no worse than authoritarian regimes in terms of introducing stabilization programs or imposing austerity measures; if anything, democracies performed slightly better with respect to reform implementation.[15] Overall, democracies had proven fully capable of carrying out harsh economic reform, especially when impelled by economic crisis.[16]

The developmental advantage of authoritarian regimes was further discredited by the fact that the vast majority of authoritarian regimes had not proven to be developmentally virtuous like Park Chung Hee's South Korea but rather had turned out to be predatory and economically irrational. Authoritarian regimes were not necessarily insulated from special interests. To the contrary, many proved hostage to the particular interests of core constituencies (for example, crony capitalists, the military) that undermined economically rational policy making as much as, if not more than, popular election. For every Chile and South Korea, there was a Brazil or a Philippines whose authoritarian regime was incapable of carrying out effective economic reform because of penetration by special interests.[17] Beyond this, authoritarian regimes lacked the discipline of popular accountability that contained predation and irrationality in democracies. Without this discipline, predation could soar to outrageous levels as was evident in authoritarian regimes such as Mobutu's Zaire and Trujillo's Dominican Republic.

Given the economic success of democracies like Poland and the economic failure of authoritarian regimes like Zaire, the pendulum in the development community swung in the direction of championing democracy as the most propitious environment for economic reform and development. The tendency to see all good things going together, with democracy and economic reform proceeding hand in hand, was further driven by the development community's persuasion that good governance was essential to successful economic development and that accountable governments (that is, democracies rather than authoritarian regimes) had the more powerful incentive to deliver good governance in a consistent fashion.

But perhaps the wiser lesson to draw from the developmental experience of the past thirty years is that regime type is too blunt a variable to predict reform or developmental outcome and that no preconception about a correlation between the two is warranted. Both authoritarian and democratic regimes have their potential strengths and weaknesses with regard to their capacity to undertake reform and shepherd development. Authoritarian regimes may enjoy insulation from popular pressure, but democracies may enjoy deeper stores of legitimacy to carry out difficult policy programs. Democracies may be myopic, but authoritarian regimes may be predatory. Some authoritarian regimes may be extremely capable of delivering good governance (Singapore), whereas some democracies (Argentina) may not. Regime type, in the final analysis, is not determining. Empirical evidence suggests that differential success at economic reform is much better explained by other factors, such as institutional endowment (Is there an effective bureaucracy? Is the party system fragmented or polarized?), leadership, level of crisis, power of organized interests, international context, and a given country's international clout.[18]

For the Middle East, this suggests an important lesson about the sequencing of economic and political reform. Democratic transition is not a precondition of economic reform. Democratization (as far distant as that might seem for most Middle East countries) need not necessarily undermine the economic reform effort, especially if the newly elected leadership were committed to reform and if the general population had suffered sufficient economic crisis to be willing to try something new, even if painful. But transition to democracy is not obligatory. Many authoritarian regimes have embraced economic reform, especially those such as China, Singapore, and South Korea that came to identify their own political success and longevity with their country's economic growth and development. In the Middle East, one country, Tunisia, seems to have embraced this developmental logic without shedding its essentially authoritarian character. And while one might wish to encourage this regime to democratize for democracy's own sake, Tunisia's economic success does not seem to have required political liberalization nor to be leading to it.

But even if democratization is not a precondition for economic reform, some measure of political reform in most MENA countries *is* imperative if economic success is the goal. Authoritarian regimes in the MENA region must be persuaded to shift from a strategy of political survival based on discretionary patronage to a strategy based on successful developmentalism. Most must invest in the creation of effective, rationally organized state bureaucracies—a prerequisite for the successful execution of a developmental program. In addition, they must replace arbitrary and corrupt governance with predictable rule of law. Neither this shift in survival strategy nor the creation of an effective bureaucracy nor the establishment of rule of law requires the embrace of democracy (authoritarian regimes in South Korea and Chile achieved both), but they do require significant change from the current status quo. Such change depends on the rise of committed leaders with a vision for change. Historically, such leaders have emerged in contexts of combined crisis and hope (more on this below). The bottom line is that political change might indeed have to precede economic reform in the Middle East and North Africa, but this political change need not necessarily mean democratization.

Economic Reform a Precondition of Political Reform?

But if democracy is not a precondition of economic reform, is economic reform a precondition of democracy? Or, to put it more modestly, is economic liberalization likely to abet democratic transition in the MENA region?

In recent years political scientists have tended to discount economic variables when explaining countries' differential success at initiating democratic transition. Instead, they have emphasized "the autonomy of the political," concentrating on factors such as leadership, institutional endowment, and strategic choice to account for transition success and failure.[19] My own work on the persistence of authoritarianism in the MENA region concurs with this approach, arguing that political institutional variables (and especially the exceptional will and capacity of the coercive apparatus in many MENA states) constitute the primary reason for the region's failure to catch the third wave of democratic transition.[20] That said, economic conditions are not irrelevant. They are especially important in terms of shaping the coalitions and social forces mobilized for or against political reform.

Perhaps the best argument for the importance of economic reform as a stimulus to democratic transition lies in the advocacy thesis. Democracy does not spring, spontaneously and fully formed, from the brow of authoritarian rulers. Rather, it is the product of struggle that hangs on the efforts of committed advocates, determined to wrest power from elites who are equally determined not to share it. In the case of the early industrializing countries of Western Europe, the cause of democracy was most forcefully championed by the protagonists of capitalist industrialization (that is, private sector capital and the organized working class).[21] Capital and labor saw democratization as a means to force accountability and responsiveness on a state largely perceived as hostile to their interests. In later developing countries, however, these social forces have been discouraged from playing their "historic role" as the agents of democratization because they are often the beneficiaries of state sponsorship and discretionary patronage and consequently are anxious not to compromise their privileged status by undertaking troublesome political campaigns. In this context, economic reform might abet the cause of democracy by introducing more market mechanisms and curbing state discretionary powers. Such reform would wean key social forces from dependence on the state and free them to play their role as the agents of democratization.

But while this argument is logically plausible, it is not immediately persuasive for most countries in the Middle East. Nowhere in the region is the organized working class or private sector capital either large or exceptionally robust. Worse still, economic reform is likely to reduce their numbers (at least in the short term) thanks to the breakup of public enterprises and the closure of uncompetitive firms. Although labor and capital may be persuaded of the utility of democratization, their limited clout is likely to curb their capacity to deliver a democratic political outcome for some time.

Cultivating class advocates of democratization is not the most compelling link between economic reform and democratization in the MENA region. More important may be the role economic reform plays in cultivating economic growth. Economic growth is strongly correlated with the viability of democracy, once democracy has been instated. One of the most robust findings of twenty-five years of political research on democratization is that democracy, or more precisely, the *survival* of democracy, correlates strongly with per capita GNP. Once a country reaches the threshold of per capita GNP of $4,200, democracy has a better than even chance of surviving.[22] By $6,000, democracy is nearly invulnerable. In fact, throughout history not a single democracy has ever collapsed that has achieved a per capita GNP of $6,055.

This research does not mean to suggest simple economic determinism. Prosperity alone does not deliver democracy. In the MENA region, for example, it is the richest countries, namely, the oil kingdoms of the Gulf, which are the most notorious underachievers in terms of democracy. In fact, it is the phenomenal wealth of these countries, or at least the nature of their wealth, that has undermined the development of accountable government. But even beyond the oil-rich states, per capita GNP of $6,055 does not automatically spell democracy. A number of countries, including East Germany, Singapore, the Soviet Union, Spain, and Taiwan, have enjoyed relative prosperity for extensive periods without transitioning to democracy.[23] Statistical research does not suggest that prosperity will deliver democracy. Rather, it suggests that once democracy has been *initiated* (for any number of reasons), it is likely to survive and flourish so long as per capita GNP remains above the threshold mentioned. In addition, statistical research also finds a direct correlation between a country's per capita GNP and the quality of democracy it enjoys, at least in many regions of the world.

What explains the strong relationship between per capita GNP and democratic viability? The causal mechanisms suggested by the long outmoded "modernization" school still hold water.[24] Some attribute this linkage to the higher level of education found in wealthier countries, arguing that the vigor of democracy rises with per capita GNP because highly educated people are more likely to uphold democratic values. Others point to the role that wealth plays in "greasing the wheel" of conflict, a crucial asset for a political system whose hallmark is the nonviolent resolution of conflict. Still others emphasize the larger size of the middle class in wealthier countries, a class whose presumed political moderation is an asset for democracies. All these mechanisms are plausible, though statistical analysis has not substantiated any single one as universally determining.

Do we really need to jump to statistical analysis?

In the Middle East, however, there is a simple, commonsense reason to link economic growth with democratization and even with the initiation of democracy. One of the staunchest impediments to democratization in the region has been the spread of radicalism, and most notably Islamist radicalism, that has been linked to the embrace of violence and terror. This radicalism has obstructed democratization in at least two ways. First, it has discouraged the natural constituency for democratization—intellectuals, professionals, feminists, and the secular elite in general—from making common cause with populist forces to campaign for political opening because they fear the radicalism of the Islamists. Second, influential international powers such as the United States have refrained from pressuring authoritarian allies in the region to democratize for fear of unleashing the Islamist threat. Were this threat of radicalism reduced, the split between secular and Islamist forces might be closed, and great powers might feel more secure about persuading their Middle East allies to embrace democratic reform.

How would economic growth contribute to declining radicalism? Although the cause of Islamic radicalism cannot be reduced to simple economics, it seems plausible to argue that the pervasive unemployment, stagnating living standards, and general hopelessness found in much of the MENA region help to fuel its spread. Attacking these problems through economic growth would likely diminish the mass appeal of radical Islamists, unplug key motivations for violence and terror, and foster the political moderation that is essential to viable democracy.

This raises the question of whether economic reform would in fact deliver economic growth to the region. Economists are by no means unanimous on this matter. In the short run at least, economic reform almost inevitably leads to economic contraction and decline.[25] But even in the longer run, the results of implementing the Washington consensus are mixed and ambiguous, and there is no guaranteed "magic of the market."[26] This strategy is especially hobbled in the Middle East by the region's poor endowment of skilled labor and infrastructure and its lack of clear comparative advantage in sectors outside of petroleum, gas, and tourism. These weaknesses combined with the problems of poor regional growth and persistent protectionism in the developed world make integration into world trade less promising a growth strategy for the Middle East today than it was for the signal success cases of trade-led growth from Asia of the 1970s and 1980s.

Still, as economist Alan Richards has argued, private sector–led, export-oriented growth is the only arrow that economists have in their quiver today to promote economic development.[27] And clearly stasis is not an option for the Middle East given the region's rising levels of unemployment and declining living standards. The modest success enjoyed by Jordan, Morocco, Tunisia, and Turkey in reaping growth benefits from this strategy is somewhat encouraging, especially for the middle income countries in the region. Its relevance for desperately poor countries such as Yemen or Sudan that are bereft of basic infrastructure is more questionable, just as it is for relatively rich countries such as Saudi Arabia or Kuwait with their vastly overpriced and underskilled labor supply. But for all Middle East countries, some measure of economic reform seems necessary, even though it does not point a clear-cut path to rapid success. Growth is likely to be slow to moderate in the near term, and although this may diminish some of the unemployment and hopelessness that has fueled radicalism in the region, it is unlikely to erase these problems any time soon. This analysis suggests only a modest linkage between economic reform and democratization.

Toward a Context of Crisis and Hope

A number of conclusions may be drawn from this analysis. The dual resistance to economic and political reform that distinguishes the Middle East is by no means coincidental but rather is the product of the interwoven political and economic logic of the governing regimes. The political logic of authoritarian regimes in the region—and specifically their reliance on selective patronage to survive—creates strong political incentives to resist economic reform that would diminish the regimes' discretionary power. The economic logic of Middle East regimes, and their embrace of strategies that unfortunately deliver unemployment and despair, fuels radicalism in the region, which in turn dissuades local and foreign forces from championing political liberalization and thus sustains authoritarianism.

To break this deadlock, should political reform precede economic reform or vice versa? The experience of other regions suggests that democracy need not be an obstacle to economic reform. But neither is it a necessary precondition. Authoritarian regimes have successfully carried out economic reform in Asia and in Latin America so long as they have come to identify their own success and longevity with developmentalism—a not inconsiderable political conversion. Political change is thus a precondition of economic reform, but the needed change is not necessarily democratization.

Conversely, economic reform should not be viewed as a precondition of democracy in the MENA region. Or at least it should not be viewed as necessarily delivering democracy. Given the belated stage of industrialization in the region, economic reform is unlikely to unleash class advocates of democratization powerful enough to carry off a liberalizing agenda. And given the Middle East's human resource deficits (among other factors), economic reform is unlikely to deliver rapid growth to the region. Without rapid growth, Islamic radicalism in the region is unlikely to be tamed, and both domestic and international forces are unlikely to unite around a drive for democratic transition. Under these conditions, the linkage between economic reform and democratic transition is, at least for the short term, tenuous at best.

Given the economic stagnation and despair that has seized the region, and given the lack of alternative economic wisdom, it nevertheless seems wise to encourage regimes in the region to embrace some measure of economic liberalization. But how to persuade authoritarian incumbents to give up the economic and political logic that has sustained them thus far?

Experience elsewhere suggests that a dual context of crisis and hope constitutes the best condition for reform readiness. Deep economic crisis has persuaded even authoritarian elites to embrace reform. Plummeting living standards, mushrooming unemployment, and hyperinflation all erode the coalitions and political logic that supported them in the past and make clear that economic reform is unavoidable.[28] At the same time, the most thorough reform has been carried out by regimes where economic reform looked most promising. It is no surprise that the most dramatic reformers in Eastern Europe also happened to be the countries geographically closest to Western Europe. These countries could see the consumer wonders of Western Europe glimmering just across the horizon, and they were credibly hopeful that the bitter pill of reform might deliver the same prosperity to them.[29]

What are the policy implications of this analysis? The analysis suggests that the United States should do what it can to replicate this dual context of crisis and hope in the region. Regarding the crisis element, the *does it reduce that hope...*

United States should refuse bailouts of economically troubled Middle East countries, especially the middle income countries. Such bailouts only enable prolonged stagnation. Beyond refusing bailouts, however, there is little the United States can do about heightening the sense of economic crisis, especially in the current context of rising oil prices that permits many countries, even those with limited oil revenues such as Egypt and Syria, to limp along.

Regarding the second element, there *is* more the United States can do in terms of fostering credible hope. The key is to make the path from economic reform to economic growth and prosperity less uncertain. This is not a simple task. One of the principal obstacles is the developed world's own tariff barriers in areas such as textiles and agriculture. These are politically costly barriers to remove, but their reduction is essential if economic growth in the MENA is the goal. In addition, the United States might focus on developing a variety of incentives or supports to encourage more interindustry engagement with the region, perhaps through infrastructural or organizational supports. The U.S. Trade Representative's free trade initiative in the Middle East is an excellent step in this direction, and the successful conclusion of free trade agreements with Bahrain, Jordan, and Morocco are very positive steps as well. The best route is to start small and focus resources on those countries that have already begun on this path of their own accord such as Jordan, Morocco, and Tunisia. A few signal economic successes in those countries would constitute models of hope for other MENA countries. As such, they might spread a modest reform contagion.

But none of this will produce success overnight. Political and economic reform is not for the faint-hearted or short-sighted. That the two are complexly interwoven underlines the importance of resolve in seeing them through. But simplistic pairings of the two processes will not stand. Economic reform in the Middle East and North Africa will not deliver democracy. At best, it will deliver limited growth that may moderate the margins of Islamic radicalism. Nor will democracy necessarily deliver economic reform. Only leaders committed to change and motivated by their own calculation of crisis and hope will liberalize their economies. These leaders need not be democrats, nor will democratically elected leaders necessarily fit the bill.

In short, if democracy in the region is the goal, it must be pursued for its own sake, on its own (political) terms, and not as a means to an end of economic reform. Similarly, if economic reform in the region is the goal, it too must be pursued for its own sake and on its own terms. Economic and political reforms are indeed linked, but in ways that are complex and nondetermining. Other analyses that suggest a simpler relationship or a fixed sequencing cannot withstand empirical or analytic scrutiny.

Notes

This chapter was originally published as Carnegie Paper 53 (November 2004).

1. Alan Richards, "Economic Reform in the Middle East: The Challenge to Governance," in *The Future Security Environment in the Middle East*, ed. Nora Bensahel and Daniel Byman (Santa Monica, Calif.: RAND, 2004); John Page, "From Boom to Bust and Back? The Crisis of Growth in the Middle East and North Africa," in *Prospects for Middle Eastern and North African Economies: From Boom to Bust and Back?* ed. Nemat Shafik (New York: St. Martin's Press, 1998); Dipak Dasgupta, Jennifer Keller, and T. G. Srinivasan, "Reform and Elusive Growth in the Middle East—What Has Happened in the 1990s?" in *Trade Policy and Economic Integration in the Middle East and North Africa: Economic Boundaries in Flux,* ed. Hassan Hakimian and Jeffrey Nugent (New York: RoutledgeCurzon, 2003); Moez Doraid, "Human Development and Poverty in the Arab States" (New York: United Nations Development Program, March 2000), http://www.worldbank.org/mdf/mdf3/papers/labor/Doraid.pdf.

2. The Human Poverty Index is distinct from the Income Poverty Index. The Human Poverty Index measures deprivation in terms of shortened lives, illiteracy, and lack of basic services. The Income Poverty Index measures the percentage of people living below the $1-a-day poverty line. The two indexes do not always move together. See Doraid, "Human Development and Poverty," 8–9.

3. Clement Henry and Robert Springborg, *Globalization and the Politics of Development in the Middle East* (New York: Cambridge University Press, 2001), 6.

4. John Waterbury, *Exposed to Innumerable Delusions: Public Enterprises and State Power in Egypt, India, Mexico, and Turkey* (Cambridge, U.K.: Cambridge University Press, 1993).

5. Nemat Shafik, "Prospects for Middle Eastern and North African Economies: An Overview," in Shafik, *Prospects for Middle Eastern and North African Economies*, 3.

6. Henry and Springborg, *Globalization and the Politics of Development*, 42–46.

7. Page, "From Boom to Bust," 153.

8. "Dutch disease" refers to the "deindustrialization of a nation's economy that occurs when the discovery of a natural resource raises the value of the

nation's currency, making manufactured goods less competitive with other nations, increasing imports and decreasing exports. The term originated in Holland after the discovery of North Sea gas." Source: http://investorwords.com/1604/dutch_disease.html.

9. Page, "From Boom to Bust," 147.

10. Adam Przeworski, *Democracy and the Market* (New York: Cambridge University Press, 1991), 144.

11. Dasgupta, Keller, and Srinivasan, "Reform and Elusive Growth."

12. Henry and Springborg, *Globalization and the Politics of Development*, 15; Richards, "Economic Reform," 58–60.

13. Stephan Haggard and Robert Kaufman, *The Political Economy of Democratic Transitions* (Princeton, N.J.: Princeton University Press, 1994), 157.

14. Joel Hellman, "Winners Take All: The Politics of Partial Reform in Post-Communist Transitions," *World Politics*, vol. 50, no. 2 (January 1998): 205, 213.

15. Karen Remmer, "Democracy and Economic Crisis: The Latin American Experience," *World Politics*, vol. 42, no. 3 (April 1990): 318.

16. Stephan Haggard and Robert Kaufman, "Economic Adjustment and Prospects for Democracy," in *The Politics of Economic Adjustment*, ed. Stephan Haggard and Robert Kaufman (Princeton, N.J.: Princeton University Press, 1992), 31.

17. Haggard and Kaufman, "Economic Adjustment," 334.

18. Remmer, "Democracy and Economic Crisis," 316; Marcelo Cavarozzi, with Joan Nelson and Miguel Urrutia, "Economic and Political Transitions in Latin America: The Interplay between Democratization and Market Reforms," in *A Precarious Balance: Democracy and Economic Reforms in Latin America*, ed. Joan Nelson (San Francisco: ICS Press, 1994), 15; Jacek Kochanowicz, Kálmán Mizsei, and Joan Nelson, "The Transition in Bulgaria, Hungary, and Poland: An Overview," in *A Precarious Balance: Democracy and Economic Reforms in Eastern Europe*, ed. Joan Nelson (San Francisco: ICS Press, 1994), 17–23; Henry Bienen and Jeffrey Herbst, "The Relationship between Economic and Political Reform in Africa," *Comparative Politics*, vol. 29, no. 1 (October 1996): 20; Haggard and Kaufman, *The Political Economy*, 33–37, 151–52, 163.

19. Haggard and Kaufman, "Economic Adjustment," 320.

20. Eva Bellin, "The Robustness of Authoritarianism in the Middle East: Exceptionalism in Comparative Perspective," *Comparative Politics*, vol. 36, no. 2 (January 2004): 139–57.

21. Eva Bellin, "Contingent Democrats: Industrialists, Labor, and Democratization in Late-Developing Countries," *World Politics*, vol. 52, no. 2 (January 2000): 176.

22. Adam Przeworski, Michael Alvarez, Jose Cheibub, and Fernando Limongi, *Democracy and Development* (New York: Cambridge University Press, 2000).

23. Przeworski et al., *Democracy and Development*, 94.

24. Seymour Martin Lipset, "Some Social Requisites of Democracy," *American Political Science Review*, vol. 53, no. 1 (March 1959): 69–105; Axel Hadenius, *Democracy and Development* (New York: Cambridge University Press, 1992), 78.

25. Valerie Bunce, "Democratization and Economic Reform," *Annual Review of Political Science*, vol. 4: 47; Przeworski et al., *Democracy and the Market*, 136.

26. Haggard and Kaufman, *The Political Economy*, 315–17; Dasgupta, Keller, and Srinivasan, "Reform and Elusive Growth," 1.

27. Richards, "Economic Reform," 128.

28. Cavarozzi, "Economic and Political Transitions," 15; Kochanowicz, Miszei, and Nelson, "Transition in Bulgaria," 18; Waterbury, *Exposed to Innumerable Delusions*, 3; John Waterbury, "The State and Economic Transition in the Middle East and North Africa," in Shafik, *Prospects for Middle Eastern*, 163–64.

29. Kochanowicz, Miszei, and Nelson, "Transition in Bulgaria," 18.

8

The Missing Constituency
for Democratic Reform

Marina Ottaway

THE CENTRAL DILEMMA of democratic reform in Arab countries can be summed up simply. Presidents and kings remain too powerful, untrammeled by the limits imposed by effective parliaments and independent judiciaries. Countervailing institutions remain weak, if they exist at all, not only because constitutions and laws deliberately keep them that way, but also because they are not backed by organized citizens demanding political rights, participation, and government accountability. This does not mean that there is no desire for democracy on the part of Arab publics. Recent opinion surveys suggest that in the abstract there is strong support for more open political systems, increased protection of human rights, and broader personal liberties. However, the existence of a general, diffuse sense that democracy is a good thing is quite different from the existence of organized constituencies that provide a counterweight to the authoritarianism of incumbent governments. The demand, or better the desire, for democracy is present in the Arab world today; what is lacking is a supply of broad-based political organizations pushing for democracy—political parties, social movements, labor unions, large civic organizations. Unless such constituencies develop, the future of democracy remains extremely uncertain. In many countries, governments anxious to burnish their modern image will continue to introduce modest reforms. Until the governments face stronger pressure from organized citizens, however, they will not take steps to truly curb the power of the executive by strengthening checks and balances and allowing unfettered political participation.

Small constituencies for democratic change do exist in the Arab world. Many intellectuals have embraced the idea of democracy and popular participation and are speaking up with increasing openness on these issues. This is not a new development. Political elites who believe in political reform have long existed in the region. Arab intellectuals have been keenly aware of the need for change ever since the intensification of contacts with Europe in the nineteenth century drove home the extent to which the Arab world was stagnating. But until recently, intellectuals have been divided about what change was necessary to revitalize the region. Not all looked to democracy for salvation. Nationalism, both as the nationalism of one country or as pan-Arab nationalism, has been an important response to the challenge of change. Arab socialism has as well. In the last decade, however, the idea of democracy has come to occupy an increasingly large space, even if it is challenged by the upsurge of Islamist ideas.

The Arab debate about democracy, which was rife in the early part of the twentieth century but was later almost completely absent from political discourse, has been relaunched. The concept of liberal democracy now enjoys support from Arab intellectuals who rejected it in the 1960s and 1970s as a Western ideology unsuitable to Arab culture and countries. These intellectuals are disenchanted with their governments, want political reform, and, despite the growing anti-Western and particularly anti-American sentiments in the region, are ready to accept that democracy is a valid political system for the Arab world. The intellectual elite has come to see democratic reform as an absolute necessity not only to break the hold of authoritarian regimes, but also to revitalize Arab societies, opening up their economies and societies alike. Even Arab governments, under pressure from their citizens and foreign governments, feel they must echo this sentiment that the time for reform has come. The willingness to implement reform, however, is another matter.

The United Nations Development Program's *Arab Human Development Report* of 2002 and 2003, written by Arab intellectuals, contain an impassioned call for democratic change. So do other Arab manifestos, including one issued in March 2004 by a group of intellectuals meeting at the reborn Alexandria Library in Egypt. The sincerity of some of these calls can be questioned—many of the so-called reformers who signed the Alexandria statement are close to their governments, belong to ruling parties, or write for government-controlled newspapers. The conference itself was sponsored by the Egyptian government, which went to great lengths to advertise and distribute the final statement. Nevertheless, these calls for democracy are being issued with increasing frequency and are changing the nature of political discourse in Arab countries. But there are also clear signs that this newfound interest in democracy has so far not translated into an attempt to build popular constituencies for democratic change.

Political parties embracing democracy remain weak, their leaders isolated in downtown offices while Islamist organizations set up headquarters in lower-class sections of town. Prodemocracy intellectuals in general shun political parties and prefer to set up nongovernmental organizations (NGOs), often with foreign funding. These organizations can quickly generate visible activities such as conferences that receive attention abroad, but these groups are not necessarily able to speak to the general public in their own countries. As a result, the acceptance of democratic ideas by Arab publics revealed by opinion polls has not become the foundation for the rise of a new political force. Ideologically, the Arab street belongs much more to Islamist preachers than to democracy activists.

Not only have prodemocracy elites failed to build broad-based constituencies, they have tended to ignore the crucial issue of how constituencies could be developed. Advocates of democracy move in a small world, somewhat isolated from their own societies. They congregate in their NGOs and progressive think tanks and write commentaries for domestic and pan-Arab newspapers. They reach across borders to like-minded people in other Arab states but do not attempt to reach down into their own countries. This failure to reach out to the public is only partially explained by the difficulty of organizing in countries with illiberal regimes; it is also a function of the gulf that still separates the educated elite from the rest of the population in the Arab world. Whatever the causes of the problem, the consequences are clear: Because democratic elites do not have a popular constituency and do not seem able to formulate a plan to develop one, they argue with disturbing frequency that democracy in the Arab world can only come from the top. They imagine gradual reform by enlightened, modernizing political leaders—often expected to arise in the next generation. Democratic aspirations turn into a wait for deliverance.

Organizations with a broad base of support exist in the Arab world, but they remain ambivalent about democracy. They are not averse to mobilizing the population but are suspicious of free political participation in a competitive system that recognizes citizens' rights to make free choices. Islamist groups today, like the Nasserite, Baathist, or more broadly Arab nationalist parties of yesterday, have a large following in all Arab countries, and thus establish links between political elites and a popular base. Arab nationalist or socialist parties believed in mobilizing the population and forged a social compact based on welfare measures. They also thought that they were the best arbiters of what was good for the country or for the Arab world, thus that individual choices could not be allowed to trump those leading to the public good. In practice, this meant that these parties turned authoritarian in the name of the public good. Similarly, Islamist parties, even those that profess their commitment to democracy, still struggle to reconcile the concept of the citizen's right to make individual choices and the idea that there are God-given truths that human choices must not contradict. This is a classic tension faced by all parties rooted in religion, no matter what the religion is. Even when they profess to support democracy as many do, including at least some in the Muslim Brotherhood, most Islamists add a caveat—democracy is good as long as it does not lead to choices that go against the *Sharia*. Since Islamic law is not a code, but a collection of interpretations by different sects and different schools within the sects over centuries, respect for Islamic law can lead to democracy or to its rejection, depending on the interpretation chosen.

Breaking Out of the Holding Pattern

Democratic elites in the Arab world so far have proven incapable of building a following, and elites who do have a constituency are not committed to democracy. The major constituency-based organizations in the Arab world at this point are either ruling parties that build their following on patronage or Islamist parties that construct it on faith and ideological commitment. With democratic elites poorly embedded in society and embedded elites poorly committed to democracy, discussions of political reform in Arab countries are vigorous, but actual change is slow, largely orchestrated from the top, and carefully limited to prevent any real challenge to incumbent regimes. As far as reform is concerned, the Arab world is in a holding pattern.

The holding pattern could conceivably be broken from the top. One or more incumbent governments could embark on a serious process of political reform. This scenario, often portrayed as the most suitable and least dangerous path toward democracy in the Middle East, is not likely to unfold. True, reform in most countries is ultimately introduced from the top by an incumbent political elite. Fortunately, revolutions are rare and are often led and controlled by political elites. But reform from the top usually comes in response to political pressures that make it costly and dangerous for regimes to insist on maintaining the status quo. To be sure, there are leaders who introduce reform on their own initiative in order to implement their own vision of a better society, but such reforms usually aim at modernizing the country rather than at making it more democratic—China, Singapore, and Iran under the Shah offer examples of modernizing reforms introduced from the top, without any democratic opening. And even in conservative regimes some individuals favor reform. However, the split between reformists and hard-liners, as identified by studies of Latin America and Southern Europe as the key to successful democratic transformations, is much more likely to take place when a regime experiences pressure for change.

Conceivably, a split between reformists and hard-liners could also be brought about by external pressure. This is unlikely to happen in most Arab countries. Outsiders have little leverage on the most important Arab countries. Dependence on Saudi oil makes it impossible for the United States or Europe to put pressure for democratic reform on the Saudi regime while also depending on it to stabilize oil prices. Similarly, pressure on Egypt is always tempered by its recognition of the legitimacy of the state of Israel. U.S. and, more generally, Western interests in the Middle East are too complex for political reform to remain consistently a central part of the agenda. In countries where the West does not have burning national interests—for example, in Yemen—outside pressure can be more consistent. In the absence of organized domestic constituencies, however, governments are able to limit the change to symbolic steps that do not alter the nature of the regime.

Arab countries have much experience with reform from the top. With the exception of the Gulf states, which started the process of economic and political change late, most Arab countries have experienced successive phases of political reform. The issue of democracy has been on the political agenda repeatedly, and in some cases it has advanced substantially, only to be abandoned again. For instance, in Egypt, and to a lesser extent in Jordan, Syria, and Lebanon, democracy was a part of a nationalist project during the 1930s and 1940s, but died as an issue during the following two decades. Democracy was already on the agenda in Morocco in the 1960s, but it failed to advance beyond a cosmetic multipartyism until recently, and even now the prognosis is uncertain. Everywhere, the absence of organized constituencies bringing sustained pressure for democratic change has allowed the process of political reform to slow down or be reversed.

Democracy is unlikely to develop without sustained pressure by organized constituencies, but the existence of such pressure does not guarantee successful transformation. Popular constituencies with nondemocratic goals are a threat to democracy—they supported the rise of the Nazis in Germany, the fascists in Italy, and many populist leaders in Latin America, including Venezuela's current President Hugo Chávez. Furthermore, challenged regimes do not always respond by developing a strong reformist wing. On the contrary, they may unite to suppress the dissidents. Even when the response to pressure is reform, it may simply amount to a revamping of the institutions of control. A recent example of reform that strengthens the incumbent regime is offered by Egypt's ruling National Democratic Party (NDP). Following a poor showing by the party's vetted candidates for the National Assembly in 2000, the NDP undertook a major effort to reinvigorate its organization and strengthen its hold over the country.

The prospects for democracy in the Arab world depend on the growth of constituencies committed to furthering the democratic goal, ideally because they are truly committed to democracy, but at a minimum because they see democracy as a means to gain power and further their interests. No democracy-promotion effort from the outside will achieve much unless internal constituencies develop. The question is, how can constituencies able to support a sustained process of political reform develop in the region? This is a crucial issue for Arab activists as well as for foreign governments and NGOs seeking to promote political change.

Mass Constituencies for Democracy: A Conundrum

Little evidence supports the contention that the desire for liberal democracy is not only universal, but also strong enough for large numbers of people to work hard to achieve it. To be sure, in opinion polls people everywhere express a preference for respect of human rights—nobody likes the midnight knock on the door. They usually, although not universally, express a preference for a political system that gives them the right to choose among competing parties and candidates. When it comes to actively demanding democratic change, the situation changes. Liberal democracy is an ideology that appeals the most to intellectual elites and to people whose most basic needs for food, shelter, and security have been satisfied. Many studies have documented that Western-style, liberal democracy thrives most easily in countries with a large middle class and in those with rapidly improving economic conditions. Furthermore, with the notable exception of India, democratic systems implanted in poor countries have rarely lasted. The duration of the democratic experiment is directly related to the level of per capita income reached by the country, as Adam Przeworski's work shows.[1] Even in countries that appeared securely democratic, an economic crisis can weaken if not eliminate support for democracy. Venezuela is at present the most dramatic example of such crisis-induced democratic reversal, but there is mounting fear that economic difficulties in other Latin American countries threaten the democratic gains of the 1980s and 1990s.

This link between support for democracy and relative economic prosperity is not surprising. While democracy promises protection of rights and a political process that gives citizens a role in forming the government, it does not promise concrete policy outcomes. Protection of some rights—for example protection against arbitrary arrest—is important to everybody, but other rights—for example that of free speech—provide limited benefit to people struggling for material survival. Political participation can help redress socioeconomic grievances, but not necessarily quickly and certainly not inevitably. Some countries now include in their constitutions not only "first generation" political and civil rights, but also "second generation" economic and social rights, but they cannot deliver on the latter. The right to work and the right to safe housing are much more difficult to turn into reality than the right of assembly and the right to vote.

The abstract rights- and process-oriented character of democracy is in sharp contrast to the concrete promises made by some of the ideologies with which democracy has had to compete historically, particularly nationalism and socialism. Nationalism does not promise people the right to fight for the establishment of their own country; it promises them their own country. Socialism promises jobs and economic equality. These are concrete promises with a more direct, mass appeal with which the more abstract idea of democracy has historically had trouble competing. Furthermore, these ideologies tap into people's emotions, including resentment, much more easily than democracy.

Making Democracy Relevant

Yet, democracy does not always remain an elite ideology without mass support. In well-established democracies, habit, education from an early age, and to some extent national identity make democracy a broadly accepted ideology—believing in democracy is part of being American, and most Americans would say they believe in democracy even when in practice they accept nondemocratic values. The same is true in many other countries. But even in nondemocratic countries, democratic ideals can gain widespread support and become a catalyst for political mobilization. In Eastern European countries such as Poland and Czechoslovakia, democratic principles were an inspiration to the mass movements that toppled the incumbent regimes. The failure of democracy to develop a broader appeal in the Arab world is thus not an inevitable consequence of the nature of democracy, but a phenomenon that needs to be explained.

Several factors can make democracy into an ideology that attracts a mass following. When people have embraced other, more facilely popular ideologies with disastrous consequences—for example, the radical, expansionist nationalism of fascism and Nazism—disillusionment gives democracy mass appeal. Or democracy can be perceived as the only alternative to an existing, hated political system. In Eastern Europe, democracy was seen as the opposite of communism, in the same way that the United States was seen as the opposite of the Soviet Union. In Latin America in the 1980s, democracy won new support from populations tired of the conflict, instability, and poor governance that they had experienced for decades under populist regimes or military dictatorships. Other factors also facilitated the acceptance of democracy in these parts of the world, including a perception that democracy was part of their cultural background and long-standing political aspirations. In Eastern Europe, furthermore, the example of the more prosperous, stable, and democratic West was also a strong factor in creating support for democracy.

Democracy's mass appeal that develops when people become deeply dissatisfied with the existing leaders and political systems can be very short-lived or, in some cases, more apparent than real. The movement for democracy that developed in Serbia, leading to the overthrow of Slobodan Milosevic, has not led to a stable democratic system. The outcome of the recent transition in Georgia is still unpredictable. And it is already painfully clear that the prodemocracy movements that developed in many African countries during the 1990s, in Zambia or Senegal, for example, were in reality movements for change, rather than for democracy. The rejection of an unpopular regime should not be confused with a desire for democracy and even less with the existence of a political movement capable of supporting the demand for democratization over the long haul.

Long-lasting movements for democratic transformation have developed historically when the idea of democracy has become associated with ideologies with an immediate popular appeal. Nationalism and socialism in particular have contributed to the spread of democracy in some countries. And in some Catholic countries, religion helped the diffusion of the democratic ideal with the growth of Christian Democratic parties.

European nationalism in the nineteenth century had a democratic component. The political elite who led the fight for a state supposedly coterminous with a preexisting nation also upheld the ideals of political participation and equality of rights that underpin democracy. In the twentieth century, anticolonial nationalism, led by European-educated or at least European-influenced elites, also embraced some democratic ideals. Full acceptance of liberal democracy, however, was tempered by the desire of the ideologues of anticolonial movements to distance themselves from the West and to develop systems based on an indigenous culture and values. Additionally, the appeal of the Soviet model, particularly strong in the 1960s, and the unwillingness of the new political elite to accept checks on their power also limited the implementation of liberal democracy.

Nationalism did not lead directly and automatically to democracy. The Revolutionary War in the United States was not followed by democracy but by a republican form of government in which participation was originally extremely limited and expanded slowly, only including women in 1920 and providing full participation of African-Americans in the 1960s. European nationalism spawned democratic ideals in the late nineteenth century, but fascism and Nazism in the 1920s and 1930s halted the process of democratic transformation for twenty years. Anticolonial nationalism led directly to the rise of a democratic political system in India, but most former colonies quickly ditched their democratic constitutions, embraced some form of socialist ideology, and established authoritarian single-party systems or military regimes. In most of these countries, new efforts to bring about a democratic transformation did not resume until the 1980s and the 1990s. But in some countries and periods, including in Egypt in the 1920s as will be shown below, nationalism contributed to the spread of democracy.

Socialism also helped in the diffusion of democracy in many European countries by turning into social democracy. Socialist ideals of economic justice, the end of exploitation, and equality across social classes had an immediate appeal to people struggling under the difficult conditions of the early industrial revolution. Socialist parties originally believed political transformation could only come through revolution. But some socialist parties eventually decided to try other tactics until the right conditions for revolution arose. Turning to the ballot box, they pulled their followers into the democratic process, particularly once they started obtaining concrete results with the enactment of prolabor legislation and welfare state reforms. The fact that democratic participation brought about tangible results helped make democracy a valued ideal in itself, rather than simply a means to enact parts of the socialist agenda until the revolution unfolded. Except for die-hard, fringe political organizations, the goal of revolution receded further and further and eventually faded away. As in the case of nationalism, the democratic outcome of socialism was not inevitable. In countries where socialist parties did not accept the idea that the ballot box was a means to achieve their goals and turned instead to violence to achieve power and repression to maintain it, socialism became a major setback for democracy.

The growth of Christian Democratic parties in Catholic countries also helped gain support for democratic political systems. Christian Democratic parties started developing in the nineteenth century in opposition to, rather than with the support of, the church hierarchy. Like many fundamentalist Islamists today, the Catholic Church did not accept the separation of church and state or the legitimate existence of a political sphere subject to the will of the majority rather than divine law. It took a long time, as well as the loss of virtually all territory once governed directly by the church, for most Catholics, and above all for the church hierarchy, to reconcile themselves to the emergence of secular and democratic political systems. Christian Democratic parties played a very important role in gaining acceptance for democracy among the more tradition- and religion-bound segments of the population, because they reconciled the idea of individual participation and choice with a conservative program respectful of church doctrine.

Disillusionment with other political systems or pairing with popular ideologies or with religion helped transform democracy into an idea with mass political appeal in many countries. The downside of this method of diffusion is that democracy has often proven a somewhat fragile ideology, because many people expected too much from it or saw it as a means to an end. People who embrace democracy because they see it as the opposite of the status quo easily turn against democracy when it does not deliver. In Eastern Europe and the former Soviet Union, disenchantment with the lack of jobs and economic security that developed with the end of socialism has led to nostalgia for the socialist past on the part of some, particularly older people. In Latin America, significant segments of the public are turning against parties and leaders who profess democracy but deliver economic misery. In Venezuela, long considered a consolidated democracy, a deep economic crisis led voters to throw out the old parties that had embraced democracy for forty years and to turn instead to a populist leader. Although the case of Venezuela is the most extreme, economic crisis threatens support for democracy in other countries as well and could lead to a revival of populism or even socialist ideals.

Similarly, nationalism easily prevails over democracy if the two come into conflict. In the Balkans, nationalists were willing to embrace democratic processes as a means of gaining power, but they were not willing to give up their ethno-nationalist aspirations in order to recognize the equal rights of all population groups. Nationalists came to power through democratic elections in Croatia but did not behave democratically once they were in power, particularly where the rights of minorities were concerned. Even Slovenia, arguably the most democratic of all former Yugoslav republics, remains opposed to the return of minority group refugees.

Democratization in the Arab world, when it takes place, will undoubtedly follow its own path and will differ in different countries. It will not follow closely the experience of other countries and regions. Yet, certain fundamental historical lessons are highly relevant. One is that democratic transformations require political organizations with a mass political base. The second is that organizations with a mass political base are developed more easily not around abstract democratic ideals but around concrete demands or ideologies with a direct emotional appeal. It is thus important to consider the ideologies with popular appeal that exist, and existed, in the Arab world.

Mass Ideologies in the Arab World

The transformation of democracy into an ideal with mass appeal has so far not taken place in the Arab world. The reason is not found in the peculiarities of Arab or Islamic cultures, but in historical circumstances. First, after an auspicious beginning in the 1920s and 1930s, when nationalism helped spread democracy in Egypt and some other countries, mass ideologies in the Arab world have remained antidemocratic. Second, the presence of the state of Israel has perpetuated in the Arab world a suspicion of Western intentions and Western ideas, including democracy.

Like all countries that experienced colonialism, Arab states in the 1950s and 1960s were seeking to distance themselves from the West not only politically but also ideologically. Reluctance to embrace what were perceived as Western—rather than universal—values in the name of cultural identity was widespread in this period. In most parts of the world, opposition to Western values declined as people learned from experience that the home-developed alternatives were worse. Disenchantment set in in the Arab world as well, but reluctance to accept democracy was prolonged by the reality of the Arab–Israeli conflict and the Arab perception that Western countries, and in particular the United States, blindly supported Israel and were indifferent to the plight of the Palestinians.

In this climate of nationalist resentment, the United States' criticism of Arab governments, which has become more open since September 11, and its new agenda of democracy promotion in the Arab world have become another aggravating factor in the relations with Arab countries, rather than a bridge to Arab reformers. When the United States talks about the need to promote democracy in the Arab world, reform-minded Arabs appear to cringe rather than rejoice. They question why the same country that supports Israel, condones the injustice toward Palestinians, and has been tolerant of authoritarian Arab regimes now wants democracy. They bristle at the idea that the United States can contribute to reform in the Arab world. The invasion of Iraq has made the situation worse by giving pan-Arab nationalism a new boost and by heightening suspicions of real American intentions in the region. The end result is that even the most ardent supporters of democratic reform seek to distance themselves from the United States and to make clear that their democratic agenda is not the same as that of the United States. Far from being a beacon for democrats as it was in Eastern Europe, in the Arab world the United States is a complicating factor.

Nationalism has not always been an antidemocratic ideology in the Arab world. On the contrary, between the end of World War I and the 1952 Free Officers' coup, Egypt provided a very interesting example of how nationalism can popularize democratic ideas. Egypt did not become a model democracy in this period, far from it. The tensions among the British, the monarchy, and the Wafd party, which controlled the government throughout much of the period, led to constant uncertainty. Nevertheless, Egypt was governed by a party that was both committed to the ideals of democracy and quite popular because of its strong nationalist stance while pushing for Egyptian independence and later restricting British influence.

The Wafd, as the Arabic name indicates, started as a delegation of prominent Egyptians who journeyed to London in 1918, when the European powers were rearranging the Arab world, to plead for the restoration of complete independence for Egypt, then a British protectorate. The British refused to receive the delegation, and the rejection inflamed the sentiments of the Egyptian public, already chafing under British control. Massive protests and incidents the following year caused the British to reconsider their position and to restore Egyptian independence in 1922.

The Wafd was a quintessential liberal organization. It believed in democracy and in the market. It drew its support from the enlightened segment of the upper class, which sought to change and modernize the country, develop the economy (particularly the industrial sector), limit the power of the monarchy by subjecting it to a constitution, and promote political participation, although on the basis of limited suffrage.

Because of its role in the restoration of Egyptian independence, the Wafd enjoyed enormous popularity in the 1920s. However, its leaders did little to capitalize on this enthusiasm in order to build a strong organization. As a result, the support the Wafd received for its nationalist position was not leveraged into support for democracy. Without an organized constituency, the Wafd also remained more vulnerable to the machinations of the king and of the British.

The Wafd's popularity declined steadily from its high point immediately after the restoration of independence. Its nationalist credentials were somewhat tarnished by the fact that the Wafd governments agreed to the continuation of the British presence. Nevertheless, it remained the dominant party, in part for lack of viable alternatives, and won elections repeatedly despite the palace's attempts to manipulate the results. After losing power from 1937 to 1942, the Wafd made a comeback and even as late as 1950 managed to win 228 out of the 319 seats in the Council of Deputies.

Although the Wafd filled most of the political space in this period, it did not fill the ideological space. With the foundation of the Muslim Brotherhood in 1928, the Wafd message of Egyptian nationalism and democracy was challenged by a new message of renewal based on the tenets of Islam and thus pan-Arab in its vision. Also, during World War II, anti-British sentiments led some Egyptians to look favorably to the doctrines propagated by Britain's enemy, Germany.

After the 1952 Free Officers' coup, Gamal Abdel Nasser quickly filled the popular political space more convincingly than the Wafd ever had. Nasser had many cards to play to win support, and he played them all successfully until the day he died. He played the Egyptian nationalist card quickly by restoring Egyptian sovereignty over the Suez Canal. He played the pan-Arab card, paying a heavy material price for it but also enhancing his image in the entire region. He played the card of Arab socialism by carrying out land reform, investing in the development of state-controlled heavy industry, building the Aswan Dam, opening the universities to the children of the middle and lower middle class, and giving them government jobs when they graduated. The economic policy was essentially unsustainable, but it was popular with the Egyptian populace. One card Nasser did not play, however, was that of democracy.

The most significant ideological challenge Nasser encountered while in power came from the Muslim Brotherhood, whose religious message continued to resonate despite Nasser's popularity. Remarkably, there was no true democratic challenge in the Nasser period—the Wafd message simply disappeared with the organization. It is not surprising that, when Anwar Sadat replaced Nasser in 1971 and cast around for a means to fight the lingering popularity of Nasserism and establish his political identity, he turned to Islam. The 1970s marked the growth of Islamist movements in Egypt and in the rest of the Arab world. The ideological space, briefly occupied by the Wafd's nationalism early on, and then by Nasser's Arab socialism and pan-Arabism, started being filled by Islamic organizations. By contrast, Sadat's decision to restore a modicum of democracy to the country in the late 1970s did not lead to an upsurge of democratic enthusiasm. The New Wafd party, revived in 1978 when Sadat legalized multiparty competition, completely failed to capture popular support, as did other parties professing democracy. However, Islamist organizations, even if banned from political participation, continue to command a following. The Egyptian political space at this time is occupied by the governing National Democratic Party, with its strong apparatus of patronage and clientelism. The ideological space is to a large extent occupied by the Islamists.

The history of Egypt in the period discussed above is unique in many respects, but some of its elements are found elsewhere. Anticolonial nationalism had a democratic component in other countries as well. Nasserism inspired people well beyond Egypt's boundaries. The Baath parties of Syria and Iraq embraced the same ideas, as did the Front of National Liberation in Algeria. The countries of the Gulf, which started their economic and political development much later, did not experience these early democratic and Arab socialist trends. The more recent spread of Islamic ideologies, however, is as evident in the Gulf as it is in other parts of the Arab world. Today, Islamic movements have come to occupy an important part of the political space—the lack of free elections makes it impossible to know how important—and an even more significant part of the popular ideological space.

Building Constituencies for Democracy

Without broad-based constituencies, democracy in the Arab world will not progress very far. Governments will introduce some reforms as long as they can do so without undermining their own power and exposing themselves to real competition. Not surprisingly, governments are unlikely to give up substantial power unless they confront widespread demands for change. Intellectuals alone cannot exercise sufficient pressure.

How can broad-based democratic constituencies be developed in the Arab world today? Here, the lessons from other parts of the world appear relevant. Preaching democracy in the abstract is unlikely to attract a mass following. As in other parts of the world, constituencies for democracy will develop either because people feel that all other alternatives to an unacceptable status quo have been exhausted or because democracy is associated with less abstract, more emotionally satisfying ideas with an immediate popular appeal. In neither case are such constituencies likely to emerge spontaneously, without a serious organizing effort.

There is much dissatisfaction with incumbent governments in all Arab countries, but only intellectuals, not the general public, hold the perception that all alternatives other than democracy have been exhausted. The vision of a pure and virtuous Islamic state as the alternative to present corruption still has a strong hold on the imagination of many. Even the less than edifying examples of the Islamist regimes in Iran, Afghanistan, and the Sudan are dismissed by true believers as the result of an aberrant Islamism, rather than of a basic flaw in the Islamist state concept. While government repression and the absence of free and fair elections in most countries make it very difficult to know exactly how much support Islamist organizations have, it is clear that their appeal is not exhausted in most countries. In this context, it is important to watch closely political development in Algeria, which for ten years has seen the very worst of Islamist groups run amok, and in Iran, which has experienced firsthand that an Islamist government does not necessarily correspond to the ideal. In these two countries, people may indeed see democracy as the only alternative.

Can democracy still combine with other ideologies and gain purchase that way? Can any of the ideas that have held or hold sway over mass publics in the Arab world become conduits for a broad acceptance of democracy? At the height of post–Cold War enthusiasm, many analysts would have been skeptical of such a hypothesis, assuming that ideologies other than democracy were dead. After witnessing the rampant nationalism of the Balkans, the spread of Islamic ideologies in the Arab world, and the revival of populist and socialist ideas in Latin America, the notion that other ideologies are dead and democracy has triumphed has become untenable. The question is whether any of these ideologies could become the vehicle for transforming democracy from an elite to a mass movement in the Arab world.

The combination of nationalism and democracy that some Arab countries experienced in the past is unlikely to be repeated. Single-country nationalism is not a compelling ideology once the goal of independence is reached. Pan-Arab nationalism still exists both at the level of the leadership and at the popular level, and it will continue to do so until the Palestinian problem is settled and thus no longer feeds collective outrage on the part of the Arab public. At the popular level, this pan-Arab nationalism fed by outrage is a vehicle for extremism rather than for democracy and is more likely to encourage acts of terrorism than demands for elections. There is also a residue of pan-Arabism found at the elite level, for example, in the constant and usually unsuccessful attempts by the members of the Arab League to stake out common positions on important issues. Controlled by the incumbent governments, this elite pan-Arabism is not a vehicle for democracy either.

There is also a residue of socialism in some Arab countries, fed by a mixture of nostalgia and, most important, by difficult economic conditions. Nostalgia will undoubtedly recede with the change of generations, but the socioeconomic conditions that feed socialism—high unemployment rates, severe income inequality, a perception of injustice—are likely to worsen in many Arab countries. This suggests that a segment of the Arab population will remain open to the ideas of redressing social injustice and improving the conditions of the downtrodden, which are the backbone of socialism and populism. The right leadership could conceivably build this aspiration for a better material life into a demand for democratic political participation, giving rise to social democratic parties or movements that might advance both the cause of democracy and that of socioeconomic justice, as happened in Europe in the past. The likelihood of such development needs to be discussed for each country separately. In general, however, socialist parties are organizationally quite weak in the Arab world. Furthermore, socioeconomic discontent can have many manifestations besides social-democracy. Often, discontent leads people to embrace nondemocratic populist leaders. It can cause people to turn to violence. More important, in the Arab world conditions that could create support for socialism or social-democracy are also leading to support for Islamic organizations. Thus, although the widespread discontent based on socioeconomic problems could theoretically be mustered to build constituencies for political change and democratic participation, if there were a deliberate effort to do so, this is not happening and not likely to happen.

Islamist organizations are key to building constituencies for democracy in the Arab world today. Although these organizations are not intrinsically oriented toward democracy, they do occupy such an important part of the political space that it would be very difficult to build large democratic constituencies without them. The seemingly paradoxical idea that Islamist organizations could contribute to the spread of democracy should not be dismissed out of hand. First, there is no fundamental incompatibility between Islam and democracy. Theological arguments showing that the two bodies of ideas are compatible have been mustered for over a century by a variety of thinkers and are quite well known. More important, the leaders of many Islamist groups are now taking a stand against violence and in favor of participation in the democratic process—although they are often doing so under the duress of prolonged imprisonment. Many are willing to at least engage in a debate on democracy, although it is not always clear exactly what different exponents of Islamic ideologies mean by democracy. Moderate Islamic parties are already participating in the electoral process in some countries, for example, in Morocco, Algeria, and Jordan. Where they participate legally, Islamist parties have not swept to power and have contributed instead to the pluralism of the political system. But election results are difficult to interpret in the Arab world, where the process is invariably manipulated by the incumbent governments. It is thus difficult to predict what would happen if more Islamist organizations chose the electoral route and if elections were truly free and fair.

So far, many governments, like Egypt's, remain adamantly opposed to the participation of even moderate Islamists, and many Islamist organizations remain ambivalent about democracy. These problems are neither surprising nor unduly troubling—it took decades for Christian Democratic parties in Europe to really develop their identity and overcome the opposition of the Catholic establishment and the suspicion of other political parties. A democratic transformation of Islamist political parties is not impossible, but much has to change before Islamist groups fully contribute to a mass movement in support of democratic transformation.

Although the popular support enjoyed by Islamist organizations makes them key to the emergence of democratic constituencies, democracy cannot thrive without political parties that represent a variety of points of view and offer a variety of platforms. Other organizations thus must also change and build their own constituencies. Old, now sclerotic, socialist parties have to rethink what constitutes a progressive agenda in the twenty-first century, rather than hanging on to worn-out ideas. Prodemocracy intellectuals need to go beyond the debates and manifestos produced within the comfortable confines of liberal NGOs and be willing to venture into a much more complex world of organization building. The foreign NGOs and contractors that try to promote democracy in Arab countries need to reconsider whether the generous funding of civil society organizations is not slowing down reform by siphoning off potential leaders from broad-based political parties into small elite organizations. None of this will happen easily, and certainly not automatically. Particularly at a time when terrorism is a real problem, both in Arab countries and internationally, suspicion of Islamic groups is inevitably high. Arab governments, furthermore, are threatened not just by possible terrorists, but also by any political organization that can mobilize a large constituency, as Islamist groups have the potential of doing. Bringing any large constituency into the democratic process inherently threatens the incumbent government. No matter what its ideological basis, any organization with mass support can become itself undemocratic and dangerous.

Most Arab governments will resist the formation of broad-based organizations, no matter what their ideological stance, because large organizations are dangerous to the perpetuation of their powers. This is not a situation unique to the Arab world. Except in the few countries where the incumbent regime simply collapsed because of external circumstances, as in some Eastern European countries, democratic transformation has always been a conflictual, though not necessarily violent, process. That is why democracy-minded intellectuals operating in small NGOs and think tanks are extremely unlikely to bring about change unless they succeed in building larger constituencies. And these larger constituencies, if Arab countries are like all others, are unlikely to be built purely around the abstract ideals of democracy.

Notes

This chapter was originally published as Carnegie Paper 48 (July 2004).

1. Przeworski, Adam, Michael Alvarez, José Antonio Cheibub, and Fernando Limongi, "What Makes Democracies Endure?" *Journal of Democracy*, vol. 7, no. 1 (January 1996): 39–55.

Part Three

Policy Choices

9

The Problem of Credibility

Marina Ottaway

BEGINNING IN EARLY 2002, the George W. Bush administration started paying unaccustomed attention to the issue of democracy in the Middle East. This was a result of the conclusion reached by many U.S. officials in the wake of September 11, 2001, that the authoritarianism of most Arab regimes was breeding frustration in their countries, and this frustration encouraged the growth of terrorist organizations. The new wave of U.S. discussions about the need for democracy in the Middle East triggered a strong negative reaction by Arab commentators and journalists. Initially, very little of their writing dealt with the problem of democracy in the real sense—that is, with the issue of how Arab governments relate to their citizens now and how they should relate to their citizens in the future. Instead, Arab commentators treated democracy as a foreign policy issue, asking why the United States was suddenly discussing democracy in the Arab world and what true intentions it was trying to hide behind the smoke screen of democracy talk. More recently, however, the debate has broadened. A growing number of Arab analysts have started focusing on the problems of Arab political systems and acknowledging the need for reform. Even the more liberal commentators, however, continue to express hostility toward the United States while calling for democratic change. The debate in the Arab press reveals some of the obstacles that the United States faces as it attempts to define its new prodemocracy role in the Middle East.

The Arab press consistently questions U.S. intentions. Arab commentators lambasted the Bush administration for using the idea of democracy promotion as a code word for regime change. They reacted negatively in December 2002 when Secretary of State Colin Powell announced a conciliatory Middle East Partnership Initiative (MEPI) that envisaged democratization as a slow, gradual process that the United States would encourage by promoting economic development, education, rights for women, and the funding of civil society organizations. They reacted with outrage in February 2004, in unison with their governments, when a U.S. proposal to launch a Greater Middle East Initiative at the June G-8 summit was leaked to the Arab press.[1] That the United States was talking with the G-8 about Middle East reform before talking to Arab countries was seen as arrogant. That the Bush administration was borrowing ideas from the Arab-authored *Arab Human Development Report* to formulate its argument about the need for reform, thus suggesting an identity of views between Arab and U.S. analysts, was seen as outright insulting.

The consistently negative Arab response to the Bush administration's new emphasis on Middle East democracy indicates that the United States faces a fundamental problem of credibility as a promoter of democracy in the region. Deep suspicions of U.S. motives will not be easily allayed. Yet, for the United States to completely pull back from promoting democracy or, more broadly, political transitions in the Middle East would be a mistake. Most Arab countries have deeply troubled, even dysfunctional political systems.[2] All face serious challenges from Islamist movements. The democratic opposition tends to be quite weak, reducing the politics of many countries to a confrontation between nondemocratic regimes and an equally nondemocratic, often Islamist, opposition. This is not a situation that augurs well for stability in the region, nor for progress toward democracy and the respect of human rights. Although there is no direct correlation between lack of democracy and terrorism, particularly terrorism directed against foreign targets, the domestic political situation in many Middle East countries is cause for concern.

Undoubtedly segments of the Arab public want their governments to become more open. Many of the Arab analysts lambasting the Bush administration's newfound desire to promote democracy in the Middle East admit that their countries must become more democratic. However, they have done so in terms so vague as to suggest that their words are not likely to be followed by action—which is confirmed by the scarcity of prodemocracy agitation in the Arab world and by the fact that the little political reform that has taken place has been initiated from the top. External pressure thus remains important to keep a prodemocracy agenda alive. However, the United States is unlikely to be able to exert such pressure successfully unless it builds its credibility as a prodemocracy actor. The recent diatribes in the Arab press indicate clearly why the United States has so little credibility in Arab eyes and highlight the main issues it needs to address to become a credible partner in democracy promotion.

Reading the Arab Press

In considering the reaction of the Arab press to the Middle East policy of the Bush administration, it is important to keep in mind that the writers have been reacting to their perceptions of what that policy is, not necessarily to the reality of the policy. For example, the writers saw Powell's December 2002 speech as an indication of a change in U.S. policy leading to a more aggressive posture in the Middle East, rather than as a moderate alternative to a policy of regime change. They reacted accordingly. It is not surprising that Arab commentators at times misperceived U.S. policy. It has been quite difficult, even in Washington, to be sure what the policy is, given the conflicting points of view within the administration as well as the usual tension between political rhetoric and reality. I will not try in this chapter to clarify what the administration's policy is and how it has evolved over time. Instead, I will try to interpret what the Arab commentators believe the policy to be and how they have reacted to it. That their interpretation has not always been accurate is itself an indicator of distrust: They interpreted all policy statements in a way that would cast suspicion on the United States.

Another issue that needs to be clarified at the outset is what importance can be attached to the articles in the Arab press.[3] Do such articles represent anything more than the views of some discontented intellectuals? Do they reflect the policy of their governments? Do such articles have an impact on public opinion? Answering such questions for countries with repressive regimes is never easy, but there is enough information from disparate sources to conclude that this outpouring of articles hostile to the United States and to the Bush administration's talk of democracy promotion in the Middle East should not be dismissed as unrepresentative or inconsequential. Studies, including public opinion surveys, indicate that distrust of the United States and suspicion about its motives are widespread in Arab countries and have worsened substantially over the last few years.[4] Furthermore, there is no indication that the prospect of a U.S.-led democratic transformation of the region is eroding support for Islamist parties—they have done very well at the polls in countries that held elections recently. Nor is there any indication that the Bush administration's new line has caused an upsurge in the popularity of democratic parties.

The views expressed in the newspapers thus do not appear to be at odds with those of the public. Nor are they at odds with those of their governments, which have allowed the constant and at times rather savage criticism of U.S. policy to continue. The press is controlled to a greater or lesser extent in all Middle Eastern countries, and writers could not take a position that the government does not approve of on a regular, sustained basis.

It is also important to consider what this barrage of articles indicates about the attitudes of the intellectual elite to which these writers belong, an elite whose involvement will be crucial to any process of democratization. These writers are well educated and often have degrees from Western universities. They have all had some exposure to the West. Many have lived in the United States, were happy there, and like going back on visits. They are, in other words, the people who could be expected to have the greatest interest in and aspirations for democracy. Yet their suspicion of the United States leads them to concentrate first on what they perceive to be the hypocrisy and contradictions of U.S. policy, and only secondarily on the problems of their own political systems. In turn, these journalists and analysts are read by, and thus influence to an extent, the better educated segment of the population—the professionals and businessmen who also must embrace the cause of democracy if the change is to take place.

Searching for Hidden Agendas

U.S. policy in the Middle East has traditionally favored the stability of friendly regimes, no matter how autocratic, over the promotion of democratic change. This acceptance of friendly autocrats was based on several factors: security considerations, dependence on Arab oil, and the fact that the United States had little leverage to force reforms on regimes whose cooperation it needed to maintain peace in the region and to secure access to abundant and cheap oil. As a result, the democracy aid directed to the region—about $250 million during the 1990s—financed cautious projects, carefully designed to avoid angering or destabilizing incumbent regimes.

It was thus a shock to Arabs when the Bush administration in the months following September 11 suddenly identified the absence of democracy in the Middle East as a serious problem that threatened not only the freedom of Arabs but U.S. security as well. In many statements, administration officials linked terrorism to the frustrations engendered among Arabs by the absence of democracy in their countries. This interpretation of the causes of terrorism was taken as axiomatic, even though known Middle East terrorists were directing their efforts against the United States rather than their own governments, as could be expected from people angered by the absence of democracy at home.[5]

The Bush administration's new emphasis on the lack of democracy as a cause of terrorism, its criticism of Saudi Arabia and Egypt (the two countries from which most of the September 11 hijackers originated), and its growing insistence on the necessity of regime change in Iraq and Palestine convinced many Arabs that the United States was rejecting the long-standing view that its interests in the Middle East were best protected by the stability of friendly regimes, and that it intended to promote regime changes throughout the area. It also sent Arab commentators scrambling to uncover the hidden agenda behind the United States' new emphasis on democracy.

The issue of what officials in the Bush administration actually said, what they hinted at, what was stated by neoconservatives close to the administration but not officially part of it, and what Arabs heard is very confused. To the best of this writer's knowledge, administration officials never explicitly equated democracy promotion with regime change except in the case of Iraq and the Palestinian Authority. In those two cases, the position of the administration has been clear: The first step toward democracy in Iraq was the removal of Saddam Hussein from power, just as the first step toward genuine reform in the Palestinian territory was the sidelining of Yasser Arafat. However, President Bush and National Security Adviser Condoleezza Rice also stated on more than one occasion that change in Iraq would lead to a far-reaching transformation of the entire region. In an interview with the *Financial Times* that provoked widespread, angry responses in the Arab press, Rice declared that the United States was committed not only to the removal of Saddam Hussein but also to "the democratization or the march of freedom in the Muslim world."[6] The Arab press response was prompt and vicious. "She is ignoring," the Jordanian daily *Al Dustour* replied, "more than one and a half billion Muslims who suffer from American greed and oppression and from its cruel and visible war against Islam and Muslims," while the London-based *Al Hayat* lashed out against "Ayatollah Condoleezza and the Export of Democracy."[7]

The comments of neoconservatives close to the administration were even more sanguinary. "We should . . . be talking about using all our political, moral and military genius to support a vast democratic revolution to liberate all the people of the Middle East from tyranny," wrote Michael Ledeen, a scholar at the American Enterprise Institute.[8] Adding up the administration's explicit statements about regime change in Iraq and Palestine, its view of democracy's march in other countries, and the statements of the neoconservatives, Arab analysts concluded that the United States intended to launch a major program to replace the Arab regimes it does not like and to dictate to people in the region how they should choose their governments and whom they should choose to lead them.

Reacting to this interpretation of the Bush administration's policy, Arab commentators launched a series of diatribes against the United States and its views on Middle East democracy. Despite the incredibly large number of articles—it seems every self-respecting analyst had to contribute his or her comments on this issue—only three basic arguments were used: first, the U.S. call for democracy is a smoke screen to distract international public opinion from the real, hidden U.S. agendas in the region; second, the United States has no credibility when it talks about democracy promotion, because of its past record in the region and even domestically; and third, the United States has no right to interfere in the internal affairs of Arab countries (I will not elaborate on this last argument as it is common to discussions of democracy promotion in any region). None of the writers entertained the possibility that the Bush administration might actually be committed to democracy for its own sake. Most of them did not even seriously consider that the United States might be interested in democracy for instrumental reasons, namely to prevent terrorism, as officials of the Bush administration kept on repeating. Instead, they all looked for hidden agendas. "One only has to look at what is NOT mentioned to realize what all this must be about," wrote a particularly conspiracy-minded columnist.[9] Commentators also refused to entertain the possibility that Iraq might have weapons of mass destruction and therefore might constitute a real threat not only to the United States but also to Iraq's neighbors. A Jordanian writer, for example, noted that "It is natural for the United States and Britain to view Baghdad's acceptance of the return of inspectors as a tactical maneuver because their real goal goes beyond the return of inspectors. They know very well that Iraq is not capable of producing weapons of mass destruction."[10] And a former Jordanian senator wrote that "Bush and his Israeli chorus know that there is not an atom of truth in their allegations and statements, for Iraq's weapons have been destroyed and [the country] is still under a land, sea, and air blockade."[11]

The hidden agenda most commonly assumed by Arab writers was a U.S. decision to allow Israel to control the region and to give Prime Minister Ariel Sharon carte blanche in dealing with the Palestinian territories and the Intifada. "The first objective is to serve Israel and implement its Sharonist wish of striking off the map a pivotal Arab country, thus giving Israel full dominance over the Arab region for an indefinite period of time. . . . Hence the first thing that the alternative Iraqi government will do, either voluntarily or under coercion, is to recognize Israel and unconditionally exchange diplomatic representation with it. The rest of the Arab countries would fall like domino chips."[12]

Another supposed driver of U.S. policy was a determination to take control of Iraqi oil fields. "The claims of the American media, endlessly reiterated—concerning Iraq's alleged possession of weapons of mass destruction that pose threats to US interests, the need to replace the present dictatorship with a truly democratic order—are no more than colorful confetti, thrown with the intention of diverting attention away from Washington's real objective, which is no more, and no less, than to secure access to Iraqi oil, and to ensure that Saudi Arabia and other Gulf countries no longer produce organizations like Bin Laden's Al-Qaeda."[13]

Other commentators saw democracy promotion as a means to extend American hegemony by lowering resistance to U.S. policies: "Within this framework, the only logical explanation for the so-called US program for bolstering democracy in the Middle East is that it is merely a means of pressuring Arab and Islamic governments and regimes to become more cooperative with US policies on Palestine, Iraq, Sudan, Afghanistan and other areas where Washington is committing gross mistakes that worry everybody."[14]

The many contentions that the United States lacks credibility as a promoter of democracy in the Middle East revolved around two major themes, with a third issue being raised more rarely, but then with vicious undertones. First, and very central, was the contention that U.S. officials have no credibility when they call for respect for democracy and human rights because of a callous disregard for the rights of Palestinians. "The United States cannot claim today to be the champion of freedoms while it is waging 'vicious' wars against the Arabs in most of their countries, from Egypt to Saudi Arabia, and from Iraq to Yemen. . . . This superpower, which protects and sponsors Sharon's mass killings and systematic destruction of Palestinian life, cannot emerge as an 'angel' in Lebanon, calling for virtuous work and looking after the seeds of democracy!" argued a Lebanese writer.[15] And a Jordanian commentator asked rhetorically: "And what does Bush have to say about the so-called Israeli democracy, which has produced the worst kind of far-right, extremist government, led by General Ariel Sharon, who is committed to continued occupation, the demolition of more Palestinian houses, the expropriation of Palestinian land, the assassination of Palestinian activists, ethnic cleansing and all-out state terrorism?"[16]

The second factor Arab commentators cited as undermining U.S. credibility is the long-standing U.S. support for autocratic Arab regimes willing to accept U.S. policies in the area, maintain the status quo, and supply the United States with abundant and cheap oil. "The US is not the country that people of this region can rely upon to generate a foreign climate conducive to fostering and supporting a true process of democratization. The U.S. has a long record of supporting dictatorships and of plotting to overthrow democratically elected governments. Whenever the defense of democratic values has come into conflict with the defense of US interests, the latter always win out."[17] Others are more sarcastic: "Now we are being told that Saddam is not a democrat, is not nice at all really, is actually a tyrant who gasses his own people. How nice to hear this two decades after the event in Khalabje, from the very governments who supported him in his first Gulf War against Iran. It did not seem to bother them then, or at any time in the past two decades."[18]

At times, commentators have also attacked U.S. credibility in a third way, by turning their attention to the U.S. global human rights record and even its domestic policies. For example, commentators reacted to U.S. condemnation of the imprisonment of Egyptian political activist Saad Eddin Ibrahim by noting, "We wished the U.S. would have focused its attention rather on Palestine, the Democratic Republic of Congo, Afghanistan and many areas in Latin America where real human rights violations are rife, instead of digging for allegations about Egypt's breaching of human rights."[19] Occasional articles, sparked by remarks made by Condoleezza Rice, argued that a country treating its African-American citizens as the United States does should not preach democracy to others. "As for you, black Condoleezza Rice," wrote the Jordanian daily *Al Dustour* in an article with strong racist overtones, "swallow your tongue, remember your origins and stop talking about liberation and freedom. Have you not been taught by your cowboy masters that 'slaves' cannot liberate themselves, that they are not capable to capture the large Islamic world whose cultural roots are planted in the depths of history?"[20]

Scorning U.S. Initiatives

Because of its own internal divisions, the Bush administration has proceeded on different tracks in pursuing the issue of democracy in the Middle East. While some officials made belligerent statements giving the impression the United States would no longer cooperate with autocratic regimes, others, particularly in the State Department, worked quietly to develop a more conciliatory approach. Their efforts centered on mounting a public diplomacy campaign to influence Arab views of the United States, forging a new set of aid projects (what has become the MEPI), and crafting a multilateral project with G-8 countries (the Broader Middle East and North Africa Initiative). Despite their moderation, verging on the inconsequential, all these initiatives incurred the ire of Arab commentators.

The public diplomacy campaign was unveiled in late 2002, during the month of Ramadan. Its central component was a series of mini television documentaries entitled "Shared Values," produced at a cost of $15 million. The programs aimed to show that Arabs and, more generally, Muslims in the United States were free to live according to their values and pursue their religion but at the same time were accepted and well integrated into mainstream society. The series aired from October 28 to December 10 on pan-Arab television stations and in Indonesia, Kuwait, Malaysia, and Pakistan.[21] These documentaries were greeted with scorn by Arab commentators: "Once more, the Americans are tangled up in an absurd strategy. Their TV campaign to ameliorate their image does not help much, since the essential is absent," wrote the Tunisian paper *Le Quotidien* in a derisive article.[22]

The MEPI was officially announced, after much hesitation and several postponements, by Secretary of State Colin Powell in December 2002.[23] Funded initially at $29 million for the entire region (an additional $90 million was added later as FY2003 supplemental), with $7–8 million earmarked for women's rights and civil society support and the rest going to education and development programs, MEPI was an extension of the cautious democracy-promotion policy of the 1990s. The idea behind MEPI was most clearly outlined by Richard Haass, then head of the Office of Policy Planning at the State Department, shortly before Powell's official announcement. "Democracy," he declared on December 4, "takes time . . . Democracy rests on an informed and educated populace . . . women are vital to democracy . . . while it can be encouraged from outside, democracy is best built from within."[24]

There is nothing in MEPI to frighten incumbent regimes and make them fear that the Bush administration is out to overthrow them. The United States was not planning "to abandon longtime allies such as Egypt and Saudi Arabia because of their lack of democracy" but would offer "positive reinforcement for emerging reform trends," explained an administration official.[25] But if the goal of MEPI was to appease the anger against the United States that existed at all levels in the Arab world, it failed. The same Arab press that had been inveighing against what it had interpreted as an aggressively prodemocracy stance by the Bush administration was equally vehement in its criticism of MEPI. In a pithy summing up of the Arab press reaction to the initiative, the State Department's International Information Program wrote: "Arab media panned MEPI as a misguided effort to improve the US's image in the Arab world and gain legitimacy for a war against Iraq" and "critics dismissed MEPI as 'peanuts' compared to US military expenditures in the region."[26]

For most commentators, MEPI simply added insult to injury. First, the United States had threatened to intervene in the domestic affairs of

Arab countries and change their regimes; then it tried to smooth ruffled feathers by offering a sop. "The US has set aside no more than 30 million dollars to support freedom and support democracy in the Arab region. . . . This sum is not only too little; it also reflects the extent to which the ruling elite in Washington despises the Arabs, and the degree to which it has no serious intention of resisting dictatorships in the region," commented *Al Quds al Arabi*.[27] A writer in Qatar added wryly: "Allocating $29 million is not even enough to launch an advertising campaign in the United States for a local domestic product."[28]

Compared with the tens of billions the United States would spend on a war in Iraq, the sum devoted to democracy, development, and education was seen by Arab commentators as another sign that the United States only pretended to care about the transformation of the Arab world and that its real priorities lay elsewhere: "The United States has allocated $29 million for [MEPI], while the supposed war against Iraq will be costing it $100 billion dollars. . . . This is what falls within the frame of subduing the Arab world and controlling its capabilities to force it into accepting a new Middle East order."[29]

Other themes raised in the reaction to MEPI are familiar ones from the earlier critiques of the regime change approach. For example, some Arab commentators accused the United States of hypocrisy for claiming that it would help cure the democratic deficit when in reality it continued to support autocratic regimes. Many of these articles had a self-congratulatory "I told you so" tone, with the writers pointing out that they had been right all along in predicting that the United States would continue to support autocratic leaders. A second familiar theme concerned Palestine. An Egyptian columnist exemplified both ideas when he noted that "We regard the American initiative with suspicion. . . . What is the benefit for U.S. from establishment of democratic regimes in Arab and Islamic states? Has it not been the prime mover of dictatorships in the Middle East since [the] mid-1920s? . . . The United States should first achieve justice in Palestine and then we might believe its democratic intentions."[30] A Qatar University journalism professor presented another take on American hypocrisy: "[The United States] allocates $29 million to defend democracy and freedom, while it opens Guantanamo camps and allows killing and torture in Palestine."[31] And the paper *Al Khaleej* observed, "Suddenly, the U.S. wants 'good' for Arabs. Who will believe that after the long U.S. history of suppressing them, supporting their enemies, violating their rights, and encouraging every-thing negative in this region for decades? How will people believe in what Powell says, when Washington works to strengthen the Israeli sup-pression in Palestine . . .?"[32]

The premature leaking of information about the then-named Greater Middle East Initiative similarly triggered another wave of pointed criti-cism and conspiratorial speculation. "There is no difference between what was said by the British, French, Belgian and Dutch colonizers . . . and what the modern colonial empires are saying," stated Salah Eddin Hafez in *Al Ahram*, casting the idea of democracy promotion in a sinister light.[33] Writing in *Al Hayat* on March 8, 2004, Khalid Al Hroub went further. Remarking that the United States was willing to cooperate with the un-democratic regimes of Tunisia and Libya, he concluded, "Democratiza-tion for the US means surrendering armaments and fighting terrorism, and any other claims are mere talk."

The fact that the United States envisaged a broader Middle East com-prising not only the Arab countries, but the entire arc from Morocco to Pakistan, including Turkey and Israel, also triggered conspiratorial in-terpretations of U.S. policy: "The Bush administration's recently-announced plans for a Greater Middle East Initiative show that the U.S. seeks to reshape the entire Muslim world. The recent visit of Turkish Prime Minister Erdogan to Washington revealed that the administration sees Turkey as the model for political change in Muslim countries for three reasons: the Turkish elite's commitment to the secularization of society and the suppression of the role of religion in public life; the Turks' Western self-image; and Turkey's open relations with Israel." The writer also claimed that the initiative involved sending Turkish representatives throughout the region to encourage their model of Muslim democracy.[34]

New Voices on Democracy

Although Arab writers have had little good to say about the U.S. inten-tion—or pretense, as they see it—to promote democracy in the Middle East, since the beginning of the debate a few writers have been willing to go beyond the anti-American diatribe. "Is it enough to reject their democracy?" Salah Eddin Hafez asked in *Al Ahram*.[35] His answer, ech-oed by other articles, was that the problem of democracy in the Middle

East was pressing, and that it was up to Arabs themselves to address it if they did not want others to do so for them. Or, as Uraib Al Rantawi noted in Jordan's *Al Dustour*, "The need for political, economic, administrative, and fiscal reform in the Arab world is real, even if it is the Americans that tell us about it."[36]

Only a small number of writers was willing to raise this fundamental point in the initial phase of the debate, when analysts thought the United States equated democracy with regime change. Their number increased somewhat in response to the launching of MEPI. Powell and Haass had issued a direct challenge by asserting that democracy would ultimately have to come from the inside, with the United States partnering in the effort but not leading the process. Haass was particularly explicit: "Democratization is a process that is fundamentally driven by members of a society, by its citizens. . . . If the United States or anyone else tries to impose the trappings of democracy on a country, the result will be neither democratic nor durable. The only way democracy can take root is if it is homegrown."[37]

To some extent, the writers' focus on the shortcomings of U.S. policy rather than on those of their own governments can be attributed to the limited freedom enjoyed by Arab writers. They could criticize the United States with impunity, because their governments were also leery of the Bush administration's intentions, but they could not easily discuss how to bring about domestic change without challenging those governments. But the problem appeared to go further. Many of the writers were caught between a nationalism that pushed them to reject foreign pressure and the knowledge that, without pressure, those governments were not likely to change. Public opinion, one writer stated, was caught between "the fire of the governing regime and the fire of the hated American pressure."[38]

As the furor caused by the U.S. invasion of Iraq abated, more commentators turned their attention to the political shortcomings of their own countries. Although the leak of the U.S. Greater Middle East Initiative to the pan-Arab newspaper *Al Hayat* created a surge of criticism in the Arab press, some writers admitted that U.S. initiatives to push reform in the Arab world forced the issue of political reform on the Arab agenda "in an unprecedented and forceful way" and started asking whether and how "the threat of external plans for reform could push this process forward."[39]

Discussions about reform in the Arab press became not only more frequent, but more focused as well, with arguments increasingly addressing more specific issues. Writers have moved beyond the generic criticism of Arab regimes that always found its way into op-ed articles to analyze more concretely the faults of these regimes as well as the question of who could lead a democratic transformation. Articles on the role and impact of civil society have become more common. Writers outline the new strategies adopted by civil society organizations to influence decision making and pose questions about their leadership, goals, sources of funding, and activities.[40]

Another lively topic of debate has been the attitude to reform of Islamist movements. Although some question whether "Islamists truly have become democrats or whether they are simply embracing political participation as the last option to keep their movement politically relevant," others take a clear stance against Arab regimes who use the "threat" of Islamist groups coming to power as a scare tactic to avoid a democratic opening.[41]

The role of Arab intellectuals has also been debated by the Arab press. Daoud Kattab, a Palestinian journalist, criticized intellectuals who resist Bush's initiatives for reform in the region without providing an alternative vision for comprehensive reform.[42] Al Hayat's Muhammad Al Haddad went further on May 9, 2004, accusing intellectuals of engaging in meaningless debates about reform in order to divert attention from the core issues: "By focusing on the irrelevant question of whether reform should be driven internally or by external actors, these intellectuals failed to clarify which internal actors would be involved."

Arab opinion writers did not shy away from criticism of regional reform initiatives either. Joseph Samaha, writing in Lebanon's Al Safir on March 6, 2004, described the Arab League's proposals for a pan-Arab parliament and a court of justice as "absurd" because "Arab regimes lack a legitimate political framework for representing their people. . . . and there is no rule of law in any Arab country in the first place." In a piece in Egypt's Al Wafd on April 25, 2004, Egyptian intellectual Said Al Naggar criticized the widely acclaimed Alexandria statement on Arab reform for its vagueness and for its failure to be explicit about the necessity for rotation of power—an implicit criticism of Hosni Mubarak and his twenty-two-year tenure as president: "I have the impression that the authors of the document wanted to tackle the reform question in a diplomatic way that would not offend the authorities . . . and hope that the next conference on reform will be held in a more frank manner."

The growing willingness of intellectuals to discuss issues of reform and democracy as well as their continuing caution in doing so appear to be in line with the sentiments shared by Arab publics, who seem to support democratic reform but are not demanding it vocally. Recent studies of Arab public opinion that test the values commonly upheld by the population of Arab countries conclude that such values are not very different from American values, even in the political realm.[43]

And yet, Arab countries are not changing much politically. Even those often hailed as examples of successful reform, such as Morocco and Bahrain, are in reality modernized autocracies with a liberalized façade, and there is reason to doubt that they can simply evolve toward democracy without a sharp break with the present political structures.[44] The dominant political characteristic of the Middle East remains stagnation. The idea of a purely internal process of change, unsupported by external pressure, is not realistic. Democracy is not the inevitable outcome in the Arab world for the foreseeable future. There is need for sustained external pressure and encouragement. However, to be successful, pressure must come from credible sources. At present, the United States lacks credibility in the Arab world.

Building Credibility

Lack of credibility does not prevent the United States from trying to implement projects to encourage democratic change in the Arab world. In fact, the MEPI generated its first project even before Powell's announcement. In November 2002, the State Department invited a group of Arab women who had run or planned to run for office to observe the election process here and to get advice from American experts on how to run a campaign more effectively. Projects of this kind have multiplied rapidly since then, because they can be carried out even in the absence of trust. There will always be visitors willing to come to the United States, students interested in studying at American universities, intellectuals willing to participate in international conferences. But these are not programs that can make a significant difference in countries that are already open to the world. Tens of thousands of Arab students have graduated from

American universities over the years; hundreds of thousands have visited. A few hundred more visitors will not make much difference.

To play a more important role in the political transformation of the Middle East, the United States needs to establish its credibility as a prodemocracy actor. This will be difficult, but it is not impossible. The problem of credibility has been faced and solved elsewhere. For example, the United States had very low credibility in Latin America when it first started talking of democracy promotion in the 1980s, because in that region, too, it had historically chosen the stability of friendly autocratic regimes over the unpredictable outcome of political transitions. Sustained U.S. support for democratic change in the second half of the 1980s and throughout the 1990s slowly allayed suspicions about U.S. intentions. The same is happening in many African countries, because U.S. support for democratic change has become more consistent during the last decade.

One lesson of democracy-promotion efforts in other regions is that restoring credibility is a slow process that requires consistent policies and sustained efforts to promote political transitions. The reaction of the Arab press and the Arab public suggests that in the Middle East, the United States also faces a set of obstacles specific to the region.

First and foremost, it is clear that the United States cannot hope to be taken seriously when it talks of its commitment to democracy in the Arab world unless it renews its efforts to revive negotiations between Israel and the Palestinians, puts pressure on Israel to allow Palestinian elections to take place, and is prepared to deal with any Palestinian leader elected in a fair contest. The consistent way in which these issues were mentioned in the vast majority of the articles leaves no doubt about this.

A second crucial issue that emerges clearly from these articles concerns the exploitation of Iraqi oil. If the United States is perceived to be exploiting Iraqi oil for its own interests, or if it uses postinvasion control over the oil fields to dictate levels of production and to ensure that oil contracts go exclusively to U.S. companies, this will confirm the worst Arab suspicions that the talk of democracy and regime change was simply an oil grab.

A third issue affecting the credibility of U.S. commitment to democracy is how consistently the United States will deal with autocratic regimes in the future. The temptation is going to be strong to continue taking a tough position against regimes that contribute nothing to the security and well-being of the United States—Syria, for example—while tiptoeing around the shortcomings of oil-rich countries, particularly Saudi Arabia. And it is going to be very difficult for the United States to find a level of pressure that can be sustained across the region. Lack of consistency, however, will only reinforce cynicism about the true aims of the United States in the region.

A fourth issue, particularly important in establishing credibility with democrats in the region, is the way in which the United States reacts to the cautious, top-down political reforms that are being implemented by some Arab monarchies. Excessive praise of such changes—such as Secretary of State Powell's statement in his December 12 speech that "countries such as Bahrain, Qatar and Morocco have embarked on bold political reforms"—raises the question of whether the United States is committed to democracy or will settle for face-saving steps by autocratic regimes whose core power remains unchallenged.[45] However, denunciation of these changes as largely cosmetic will open the United States to accusations that it is trying to impose its democracy, rather than letting Arabs develop their own.

Finally, the United States will fail to gain credibility unless it invests much more money in the MEPI or similar projects. The disproportion between the ambitious vision outlined by Powell and Haass and the sum devoted to the task was greeted with anger and disdain—and with some reason. The commitment of large amounts of money does not guarantee success, but the commitment of $29 million across fifteen countries does guarantee that the impact will be negligible.

The Bush administration may well consider that it is not in the interest of the United States to address the issues outlined above. It should harbor no illusion, however, that it can avoid taking those steps and still become a credible promoter of Middle Eastern democracy.

Notes

An earlier version of this chapter was originally published as Carnegie Working Paper 35 (March 2003).

1. The "Partnership for Progress and a Common Future" with the region of the broader Middle East and North Africa, or Broader Middle East and North Africa Initiative as it has come to be known, was launched by the G-8 at its June 2004 summit at the insistence of the Bush administration.

2. See Daniel Brumberg, "Democratization in the Arab World? The Trap of Liberalized Autocracy," *Journal of Democracy* (October 2002): 56–68.

3. This discussion is based predominantly on extensive reading of the articles in two influential dailies (the Cairo-based *Al Ahram* and the London-based *Al Hayat*), on summaries of articles from the rest of the Arab world by the Foreign Broadcast Information Service, and on the reviews of the Arab press in the Foreign Media Reaction reports prepared by the U.S. State Department's International Information Program.

4. See Bruce Stokes and Mary McIntosh, "How They See Us," *National Journal* (December 21, 2002): 3720–26; "Talking with the Islamic World: Is the Message Getting Through?" transcripts of a three-part program at the Institute for the Study of Diplomacy, Georgetown University, Washington, D.C., February, March, and April 2002; available at http://cfdev.georgetown.edu/sfs/programs/isd/research_islamic.cfm. See in particular the transcript of the first session, "The U.S. Image in the Islamic World," February 19, 2002; also Daniel Brumberg, "Arab Public Opinion and US Foreign Policy: A Complex Encounter," testimony prepared for the Subcommittee on Government Reform of the Committee on Government Reform, U.S. House of Representatives, October 8, 2002.

5. See Thomas Carothers, "Promoting Democracy and Fighting Terror," *Foreign Affairs* (January/February 2003): 84–97.

6. Interview with Condoleezza Rice by James Harding and Richard Wolffe, *Financial Times*, September 23, 2002.

7. Quoted in "Reform in the Arab and Muslim World: Arab Press Reacts to National Security Advisor Condoleezza Rice's Statements on Democracy and Freedom," Special Dispatch Series no. 427, October 11 (Washington, D.C.: Middle East Media Research Institute, 2002), available at http://www.memri.org/reform.html.

8. *Wall Street Journal*, September 4, 2002.

9. Haim Bresheeth, "Countdown to Chaos: Arguments Full of Holes Can Hardly Hide the Truth, Which Is about Oil, Elections, and Finding a Scapegoat," *Al Ahram* (Cairo, Egypt), no. 603, September 12–18, 2002.

10. Tariq Masarwah, "Yes, It Is a Tactical Maneuver," *Amman Al Ra'y* (Amman, Jordan), September 18, 2002, FBIS Transcribed Text.

11. Husni Ayish, "The Post-Modern Hitler," *Amman Al Ra'y* (Amman, Jordan), October 1, 2002, FBIS Transcribed Text.

12. Ayish, "Post-Modern Hitler."

13. Salama A. Salama, "Oil and War," *Al Ahram* (Cairo, Egypt), no. 599, August 15–20, 2002.

14. Husayn Abd-al-Wahid, "Democracy and US Interests!" *Akhbar Al Yawm* (Cairo, Egypt), August 31, 2002, FBIS Transcribed Text.

15. Talal Salman, "The American 'Advice' Turns the Closure into Assassination," *Al Safir* (Beirut, Lebanon), September 9, 2002, FBIS Transcribed Text.

16. Fahd Fanek, "Who Wants Democracy in the Arab World," *Jordan Times* (Amman, Jordan), September 30, 2002, FBIS Transcribed Text.

17. Hassan Nafaa, "Democratic Reductionism: Hassan Nafaa Questions the Sincerity of Washington's Newly Espoused Belief That Democracy Is the Way Forward in the Arab World," *Al Ahram* (Cairo, Egypt), no. 597, August 1–7, 2002.

18. Bresheeth, "Countdown to Chaos."

19. *MENA* (Cairo, Egypt), August 15, 2002, FBIS Transcribed Text.

20. Quoted in "Reform in the Arab and Muslim World."

21. For details, see Richard Boucher, State Department Spokesman, "Public Diplomacy: Reaching Out to Islamic Countries (Excerpt from October 30 Press Briefing)" (Washington, D.C.: U.S. State Department, October 30, 2002), available at: http://www.state.gov/p/nea/rls/rm/14835.htm. See also the public diplomacy web site being maintained by the State Department and Council of American Muslims for Understanding at: http://www.opendialogue.com.

22. Quoted in U.S. Department of State, International Information Program, Foreign Media Reaction, "U.S. Image in the Islamic World: 'Policy' Is the Problem," November 26, 2002.

23. Colin Powell, "The U.S.-Middle East Partnership Initiative: Building Hope for the Years Ahead," speech delivered at the Heritage Foundation, Washington, D.C., December 12, 2002; available at http://www.state.gov/secretary/rm/2002/15920.htm.

24. Richard N. Haass, "Toward Greater Democracy in the Muslim World," speech delivered to the Council on Foreign Relations, Washington, D.C., December 4, 2002; available at http://www.state.gov/s/p/rem/15686.htm.

25. Cited in Barbara Slavin, "Arab Lawmakers Get Close-up View of Democracy," *USA Today*, December 12, 2002.

26. U.S. Department of State, International Information Program, Foreign Media Reaction, "Middle East Partnership Initiative (MEPI): Arab Press Wary," December 20, 2002.

27. Quoted in *Mideast Mirror*, November 18, 2002.

28. Abdul Kareem Hashish, *Al Raya* (Qatar), quoted in U.S. Department of State, "Middle East Partnership Initiative (MEPI): Arab Press Wary."

29. Awni Kaaki, *As Sharq* (Lebanon), quoted in U.S. Department of State, "Middle East Partnership Initiative (MEPI): Arab Press Wary."

30. Gamal Badawi, *Al Wafd* (Egypt), quoted in U.S. Department of State, "Middle East Partnership Initiative (MEPI): Arab Press Wary."

31. Ahmed Al Qadidi, *Al Bayan* (Dubai, United Arab Emirates), quoted in U.S. Department of State, "Middle East Partnership Initiative (MEPI): Arab Press Wary."

32. *Al Khaleej* (Sharjah, United Arab Emirates), quoted in U.S. Department of State, "Middle East Partnership Initiative (MEPI): Arab Press Wary."

33. Agence France-Presse, February 19, 2004.

34. Fahmi Howeidi, *Al Sharq Al Awsat*, February 11, 2004.

35. *Al Ahram*, December 4, 2002.

36. Uraib Al-Rantawi, *Al Dustour* (Jordan), quoted in U.S. Department of State, "Middle East Partnership Initiative (MEPI): Arab Press Wary."

37. Haass, "Toward Greater Democracy in the Muslim World."

38. *Al Ahram*, December 4, 2002.

39. Khaled Al Haroub, *Al Hayat*, May 2, 2004.

40. See, for example, Salah Al Din Al Jurshi, *Al Hayat*, May 18, 2004, and Karim Mruwwe, *Al Hayat*, May 29.

41. See, respectively, Abdullah Balkaziz, *Al Hayat*, February 10, 2004, and Birhan Ghalyun, *Al Jazeera.net*, December 31, 2003.

42. *Al Hayat*, April 11, 2004.

43. See Pippa Norris and Ronald Inglehart, "Islam and the West: Testing the 'Clash of Civilizations' Thesis," Harvard University, Kennedy School of Government Working Paper, May 6, 2002; James J. Zogby, *What Arabs Think: Values, Beliefs and Concerns* (Washington, D.C.: Zobgy International/Arab Thought Foundation, 2002); and Stokes and McIntosh, "How They See Us," 3720–26.

44. Brumberg, "Democratization in the Arab World?" 56–68; and see Marina Ottaway, "Egypt: Institutionalized Semi-Authoritarianism," in *Democracy Challenged: The Rise of Semi-Authoritarianism* (Washington, D.C.: Carnegie Endowment for International Peace, 2003), ch. 1, 31–50.

45. Powell, "The U.S.-Middle East Partnership Initiative."

10

Choosing a Strategy

Thomas Carothers

THE SEPTEMBER 11, 2001, terrorist attacks against the United States led George W. Bush's administration to reassess America's traditional acceptance of Arab autocracies as useful security partners and to engage more seriously than any previous administration with the issue of whether and how the United States can promote democracy in the Middle East. The administration's declarations and actions on democracy in the region during the 2002–2004 period followed two distinct lines, one hard and one soft. The hard line aimed at regime change in countries with governments hostile to the United States. The ouster of Saddam Hussein was primarily motivated by U.S. security concerns, but some administration officials and policy experts close to the administration were also attracted by the chance to try to create democracy in Iraq and to stimulate the destabilization (and, some hope, the democratization) of other hostile regimes in the region, notably in Iran and Syria. The soft line was directed at the Arab governments with which the United States has friendly relations. It sought to put the United States in the role of encouraging and facilitating gradual transitions to democracy in the region, through a combination of increased aid, especially democracy-related aid, and diplomatic engagement.

As the United States attempts to further develop this soft line into a workable strategy of fostering democratic change throughout the region, it confronts two major complications with regard to its own role (leaving aside the enormous difficulties inherent in trying to promote democracy in a region rife with so many formidable obstacles to such change). First, as Marina Ottaway explains in chapter nine of this volume, the United States lacks credibility as a prodemocratic actor. This stems from America's long-standing support for nondemocratic regimes in the region, Arab perceptions that Washington undervalues the rights of Palestinians, and various other factors. Second, there is the stubborn fact that the friendly Arab autocrats serve significant American economic and security interests, and it is not clear that more democratic successor regimes would be as helpful to the United States. Beyond these two issues, however, lies a critical question that has received inadequate attention: What would a gradualist strategy for democracy in the Arab world actually be in practice?

To date, the soft line lacks definition. As U.S. State Department and U.S. Agency for International Development (USAID) officials have searched for ways to step up U.S. efforts to promote democracy in the Middle East, they have tended to put forward many ideas. All of these various ideas are appealing to one group or another in the U.S. policy community but do not necessarily add up to a coherent strategy—promoting women's rights, bolstering civil society, revitalizing education, fostering good governance, strengthening the rule of law, supporting decentralization, and so forth.

Looking at this growing domain of activities and initiatives, it is possible to see several competing strategies at work. This chapter identifies and assesses these diverse strategies, examines the question of whether they constitute a coherent whole, and identifies the key choice concerning strategy that lies directly ahead.

Political Blockage

Before discussing the contending strategies, it is useful to review the basic political situation in the region. In a small number of Arab states—Libya, Saudi Arabia, Syria, Tunisia, and the United Arab Emirates—the level of political repression is so high that there are few entry points available to the United States for programs to promote democracy. The United States could exert diplomatic pressure for political reform in these countries, but unless Washington were to back up such actions with much more substantial forms of coercive leverage, these dictatorial regimes would be unlikely to loosen their hold on power. An exception might be

Saudi Arabia, where the United States, due to its long-standing close ties to the Saudi government, might have at hand some levers of real influence to encourage progress on the recently announced program of political reforms.

A majority of Arab states—Algeria, Bahrain, Egypt, Jordan, Kuwait, Lebanon, Morocco, Oman, Qatar, and Yemen—are not outright dictatorships but semiauthoritarian regimes or, as some analysts prefer, partially liberalized autocracies. U.S. (and European) efforts to promote democracy are primarily directed toward these countries. Their governments allow a certain amount of political space. In some of them, opposition parties are legal and compete in legislative elections, and independent civil society groups are allowed to exist. In others (that is, most of the Gulf states), neither parties nor independent nongovernmental organizations (NGOs) are allowed, but citizens nevertheless enjoy a limited degree of political freedom and there is some open political competition. In all of these semiauthoritarian countries, the central power holders—whether they are presidents or monarchs—remain outside the directly contested political space.

As Daniel Brumberg argues in chapter two of this volume, the political liberalization that these regimes have pursued is quite different from democratization, and it would be a mistake to assume any easy or natural path from liberalization to democratization. The regimes have engaged in limited, often sporadic political liberalization to relieve accumulated domestic political pressure and gain some reformist legitimacy. The reforms are a means of preserving their hold on power, not of creating democracy. The reforms are not aimed at creating a process that would lead to the leaders eventually having to risk giving up power to some elected alternative. As Brumberg notes, liberalization in the Arab world tends to go a certain distance and then get stuck, resulting in the widespread regional syndrome of political blockage, or what he calls the trap of liberalized autocracy.

The state of the political opposition in these countries is a key factor in the partial liberalization trap. In most of these countries, the opposition falls into two parts. One part, by far the weaker of the two, consists of political activists associated with nationalist or secular traditions who advocate some liberal political ideas and whom Westerners usually call "the democrats." In most of these countries, this part of the opposition is politically weak, is unable to unite in a single party or coalition, lacks a strong base among everyday citizens, and is constantly in danger of being co-opted by the government. The stronger part of the opposition consists of Islamist forces, of diverse degrees of fundamentalism or radicalism. They tend to be well organized, dedicated, and have a significant base in the citizenry due to their network of social programs in education, health, and other services.

The willingness of many of the Islamist forces to accept a democratic political framework as something more than just a means of gaining power is uncertain at best. Their ultimate goals are even more uncertain. Arab governments use this fact—sometimes legitimately, sometimes cynically—as a justification for not further opening the political system. In turn, the continued exclusion of many Islamist groups from the inner circles of power fuels their own political radicalism, creating a negative cycle of political action and reaction that only reinforces the basic political blockage.

A few of these semiauthoritarian Arab regimes, such as Bahrain, Morocco, and perhaps Yemen, are still moving ahead with liberalizing reforms. A few others, including Egypt and Jordan, have recently been drifting backward, although in the wake of the Iraq war they and others are making some new reformist signals, seeking to gain favor in Washington. Yet all are basically stuck in a political state several steps away from authoritarianism but still very far from democracy.

The Gradualist Scenario

At the core of any search for a strategy to promote democracy in the Middle East is the question of what transition scenario the promoters envisage. How are these semiauthoritarian regimes actually supposed to democratize? Despite all the recent talk about Washington's newfound desire to foster democracy in the region, there has been notably little real discussion of what the process of going from point A (blocked semiauthoritarianism) to point B (democracy) might look like.

Experience from other regions indicates that, very generally speaking, there are two paths from authoritarianism (or semiauthoritarianism) to democracy. On one path, a nondemocratic country may undergo a controlled, top-down process of iterative political change in which political space and contestation are progressively broadened to the point that democracy is achieved. On the other path, the accumulated failures of an authoritarian or semiauthoritarian regime may provoke a loss of political legitimacy, which leads to the regime being driven out of power (by spontaneous public demonstrations, an organized opposition movement, or disenchanted political elites) and to an attempt to create a democratic system to take the place of the discredited, ousted regime.

Given that many Western policy makers worry about what political forces might take over if Arab governments experienced regime collapse, the gradualist scenario is undoubtedly much more attractive to most. Presumably, it is the overall goal of most Western efforts to promote democracy in the region. It must be noted, however, that the collapse scenario has been much more common around the world than the gradual success scenario. Only a handful of countries—including Chile, Mexico, Taiwan, and South Korea (though in South Korea there was much assertive citizen activism along the way)—have managed to move to democracy through a top-down, gradualist process of political opening, in which the dictatorial regime gradually changed its stripes and left power through an electoral process. But dozens of countries in Asia, Eastern Europe, Latin America, the former Soviet Union, and sub-Saharan Africa have seen their attempted democratic transitions of the past twenty years initially defined by a crash—the crash of the incumbent dictatorial regime.

One principal characteristic of the successful gradualist transitions was that they were built on economic success. In each country, growth and development created an independent business sector and a growing middle class with an interest in and capacity to fight for a greater political say in their own affairs. The economic success also tended to moderate the opposition and undercut extremist alternatives, thereby giving the ruling elite the self-confidence to keep moving toward greater political openness.

Another critical feature of these transitions is that the process of political change was eminently political. That is to say, it did not consist only or even primarily of the step-by-step expansion of independent civil society and the technocratic reform of governing institutions. Elections were crucial to the process—not just local or legislative elections but also elections in which opposition parties were allowed to compete for the central positions of political power. In Mexico and Taiwan, elections were for years manipulated in favor of the ruling party. But over time, the elections were made fairer, and when the opposition eventually managed to win, the rulers respected the results.

On the basis of the record of experience, it is evident that although the gradualist scenario is clearly more attractive to most Western policy makers, it is difficult and has been only rarely achieved around the world. Nevertheless, the most likely alternative in the Arab world—semiauthoritarian regimes continuing to remain politically stagnant, breeding increasingly radical and empowered opposition forces, leading to eventual regime collapse and ensuing political turbulence—is unattractive enough that a gradualist strategy of promoting Arab democracy needs to be clearly identified and seriously pursued. So far, it appears that the U.S. government's efforts to promote gradualist transitions in the Arab world fit into one of three different strategies: focusing on economic reform, indirectly promoting democracy, or directly supporting democracy.

Focusing on Economic Reform

Some U.S. officials—especially specialists who have worked in or followed the region for many years—are wary of more direct political approaches and instead recommend an "economics-first" strategy. In this view, the core driver of positive political change is most likely to be economic progress. Such progress would help a truly independent private sector emerge and shrink the corporatist states that predominate in the region, which would in turn bolster a more independent, vital civil society and media as well as competing political elites less vulnerable to co-optation and less prone to base their appeal on the widespread sense of societal failure and frustration. Greater wealth would also spawn a larger, more independent middle class with access to more travel and education and a wider range of political ideas.

In this view, therefore, the United States should concentrate its proreform energies in the economic domain. The prescribed economic reforms are the standard market-oriented measures that the United States and the international financial institutions advocate around the world—more privatization, fiscal reform, banking reform, tax reform, investment liberalization, and so forth. In this vein, the Bush administration decided to make a major push on free trade agreements with Arab governments and articulated the vision of a U.S.–Middle East free trade area.

The economics-first approach has several significant points of attraction. The underlying rationale is solid—there is no question that economic success does tend to make democratization more likely. Moreover, such an approach does not put the United States in the awkward, and usually resented, position of having to exert political pressure on friendly Arab governments. Economic reform is a message that is somewhat more palatable to Arab elites, and it is a subject on which the United States, due to its own economic success, has some credibility—in contrast to the serious problem of credibility plaguing U.S. declarations regarding democracy. At the same time, it should be noted that Western pushes for structural adjustment and other neoliberal reforms have been controversial and unpopular in some Arab societies (especially in those without a cushion of oil production).

Yet this approach has several serious potential limitations beyond the frequent public unpopularity of the recommended economic reform measures. The United States has already been pressing many Arab governments for years or even decades (for example, Egypt) to carry out market reforms, with only very limited success. Some governments have made progress on macroeconomic reforms, such as reducing fiscal deficits, but almost all have fallen badly short on the necessary institutional and microeconomic reforms, such as banking reform, tax reform, and modernization of the state.

Carrying out such reforms would entail a major reshaping of the way Arab states operate and their relationship with their own societies. These states have failed to follow through on such reforms out of a lack of will to confront deeply entrenched, politically protected, antireformist interests and a lack of desire to give up the political levers of control that statist economic structures provide. Although the idea that economic change should precede political change is very appealing, the sticky fact remains that the lack of political reform and political accountability is precisely what undermines efforts to motivate Arab governments to undertake far-reaching economic structural reform.

Moreover, even if Arab governments actually implemented the full set of recommended market reforms, there is no guarantee that high growth and sustainable economic development would result. Many countries throughout the developing world have attempted to achieve the East Asian–style economic breakthroughs (which themselves were not really built on the kind of market reform prescriptions contained in the "Washington Consensus"). Very few have succeeded. South America is a sobering example of a region that in the 1990s accepted and implemented a significant number of the recommended market reforms yet has experienced only modest growth and is now facing political turmoil and decay rather than democratic consolidation.

Even if Arab governments actually did get serious about market reforms and those reforms led to growth and development, the positive political payoff might be at least decades away. In East Asia, the link between economic success and political change took twenty to thirty years to develop. Many observers concerned about the political viability of stagnant Arab regimes doubt that, given the rising demographic pressures and consequent political pressures, these regimes will be able to hold out that long.

Indirectly Promoting Democracy

The second identifiable U.S. strategy for stimulating gradualist Arab political transitions consists of promoting better governance and other state reforms as well as expanded and strengthened civil societies. These types of activities can be considered indirect promotion of democracy because they do not tackle the core processes of political contestation. Proponents of this strategy are primarily found in USAID (which began sponsoring such efforts in the region in the mid-1990s), the State Department (in the Bureau for Democracy, Human Rights, and Labor and the democracy promotion group in the Bureau for Near East Affairs), and some of the democracy promotion organizations that operate with U.S. funding. The main tool of this approach is assistance for reforming governance and developing civil society (typically sponsored by USAID and now also by the State Department under its Middle East Partnership Initiative. U.S. policy makers have increasingly tried in the past year or two to complement such aid with diplomatic pressure on Arab governments to take seriously the challenge of improving governance and to give a real place to an independent civil society.

The most common types of work on reforming governance and the state include

- strengthening the rule of law, especially through judicial reform;
- strengthening parliaments, through efforts to build better internal capacity and bolster constituency relations;

- reducing state corruption, through anticorruption commissions, legislative rationalization, and advocacy campaigns; and
- promoting decentralization, through training for local government officials and legislative actions to increase the authority of local governments.

Programs to expand civil society often consist of

- funding for NGOs devoted to public-interest advocacy, such as on human rights, the environment, and anticorruption;
- support for women's rights organizations;
- strengthening independent media; and
- underwriting formal and informal efforts to advance democratic civic education.

Such indirect aid for democracy in the Arab world has several attractive aspects. All of these types of work unquestionably touch on areas of Arab sociopolitical life that need improvement. They are a collection of what Western aid providers and policy makers tend to consider "good things" that they believe should have relevance in every region of the world. Moreover, these sorts of activities often find a narrow but real response in the host societies, heartening democracy promoters and persuading them of the value of their work. Even if there is blockage at the central political level, there may well be, for example, some judges interested in trying to improve judicial efficiency, some decent local politicians eager to learn how to better serve their constituents, or some NGO leaders with admirable talents and courage. And the democracy aid community has a well-established capacity to deliver this kind of assistance. If a U.S. embassy or USAID mission in a country wants to develop a broad portfolio of indirect aid for democracy, the mechanisms exist to do so fairly easily and quickly, provided sufficient funds are made available.

A further attraction—at least from the point of view of U.S. officials wary of stepping on the toes of friendly Arab governments—is that most of these kinds of democracy programs can be initiated (though not necessarily successfully completed) without irritating host governments. Most Arab governments are willing to tolerate these sorts of activities, within limits. They may hope that the governance programs will render the state more capable of solving citizens' problems and burnish their own legitimacy as reformist regimes, even as they drag their feet on the necessary institutional changes. They are less likely to be fond of the civil society activities but tend to put up with them, as long as such efforts are not too assertive, do not help Islamist groups, and generally give host governments some control over which groups receive the foreign support.

The nonthreatening nature of indirect aid for democracy is attractive to U.S. officials but also a sign of the central weakness of this approach. Valuable as this aid can be, there is a danger that U.S. policy makers eager to show that the United States is taking seriously the challenge of Middle Eastern democracy will expect too much from it. Efforts to improve governance and to broaden civil society work best in countries that are actually attempting to democratize—that is, where an authoritarian government has been replaced with a new elected government or else has made a decision to move seriously toward a real democratic process. These efforts are designed as ways to *further* democratic consolidation, *not* as fundamental drivers of democratization itself. They can certainly be attempted in countries engaged in limited political liberalization. But in such contexts, they are likely to fit within the boundaries of that political arrangement, perhaps widening the boundaries a bit but not altering the basic political equation. They may in fact help strengthen semiauthoritarian regimes by giving frustrated citizens the impression that important reforms are taking place, thereby bleeding off a certain amount of accumulated internal pressure for change.

To put it more bluntly, adaptable, long-surviving semiauthoritarian regimes such as those in Egypt, Jordan, and Morocco are masters at absorbing liberalizing reforms without really changing their core political structures. In such contexts, it is very possible that outside democracy promoters can work for years helping to increase judicial efficiency, augment the capacities of parliamentarians, train local mayors, nourish civic advocacy, foster greater women's rights, and promote more democratic civic education without contributing to a basic change of regime type.

Directly Supporting Democracy

Although limited liberalization in the Arab world has thus far stopped well short of real democratization, a bridge between liberalization and democratization is not inconceivable. Building such a bridge, however, requires governments to take some important steps:

- moving toward broad, consistent respect for political and civil rights;
- opening up the domain of political contestation to all political forces that agree to play by the democratic rules of the game;
- obeying the rules of fair political contestation (above all, ceasing to rig or otherwise manipulate elections); and
- reducing the reserved political space (that is, expanding the reach of political contestation to include the country's central political power holders).

If most or all of these bridge-building steps are being taken, a country is moving from liberalization to democracy. The third direct approach to promoting gradualist democratic transitions in the Arab world seeks to use a combination of aid for democracy and diplomatic engagement to push Arab governments to begin building such a bridge in their own societies. Only a relatively small number of persons within the U.S. policy community advocate such an approach, primarily persons within the democracy aid organizations (above all, within the two political party institutes). And only fairly small-scale activities have yet been supported in this vein, though at least in two countries, Morocco and Yemen, they have been under way for some time and arguably with at least some success.

The central element of the strategy for directly supporting democracy is to encourage and pressure Arab governments to strengthen and gradually broaden the processes of organized political contestation in their countries. The most immediate focus of such efforts is normally elections—undertaking activities to make elections more meaningful. Full-fledged support in this regard would consist of various interrelated measures:

- programs to strengthen political parties—to help parties and politicians develop basic organizational skills, improve their constituency relations, improve coalition building, and the like; and where opposition political parties are not yet permitted (as in the Gulf states), urging the government through diplomacy to take the step of allowing the formation of parties;

- aid to strengthen election administration entities and push hard on governments to give such entities greater political independence;
- support for domestic and international election monitoring (resistance to election monitoring is more widespread in the Arab world than any other region and remains an area of considerable potential development);
- aid for civic groups that work to improve electoral processes by organizing candidate forums, monitoring campaign fairness, educating citizens about elections, and promoting voter turnout;
- activities to increase women's political participation;
- giving more consistent, high-level diplomatic attention to Arab elections, including real criticism when elections fall short and a reduction of ritualistic praise for problematic electoral processes; and
- respecting the outcomes of elections, even if they are not to Washington's liking.

The United States could complement this heightened attention to elections with a broader, high-level push to encourage or pressure Arab leaders to give greater respect to human rights, especially such core political and civil rights as freedom of speech, freedom of association, and due process. Many Arabs have the impression, which seems at least partly accurate, that the U.S. government pushes hard on human rights when persons connected to the United States are mistreated but remains silent when Islamists or other nonfriends of the United States suffer persecution. Correcting this double standard would send an important positive signal to Arab governments and societies.

Another broader element of assistance in strengthening the processes of political contestation could be a more serious effort by the United States to encourage Arab governments to be more politically inclusive, above all with regard to Islamists. Policies vary in the region concerning the participation of Islamist parties or organizations in formal political life, but everywhere the issue is crucial to the broader challenge of widening political contestation. The U.S. government could have much more extensive, regularized contacts with Islamists, both to get to know them better and to help them understand U.S. policy more accurately.

Opening up such contacts would not mean that the United States is approving of or embracing those groups, merely that it is acknowledging that they are a part of the political landscape. And this would send an important message of inclusiveness to Arab governments. In Egypt, for example, the current U.S. approach of having only minimal official contact with the Muslim Brotherhood and other Islamist groups reinforces the Egyptian government's policy of trying to exclude them from political life.

The strategy of directly supporting democracy is based on the idea that if the existing weak, limited processes of political contestation can be gradually infused with the principles of fairness, inclusion, honesty, and openness, governments will begin to give more real authority and power to elected parliaments and local governments, and citizens will begin to put some stock in political processes and related institutions. This in turn could encourage Arab leaders over time to reduce the political power they keep outside the processes of political contestation (that is, their own executive power) and eventually to contemplate the actual democratization of the central state.

The main attraction of the direct democracy strategy is precisely its directness—it attempts to tackle the core question of how Arab states might actually move from limited liberalization to actual democratization, something the other two strategies do not really address. Of course, even if the United States did decide to commit itself to this more activist approach, its role would still just be that of an advocate and enabler. Direct though it may be, this strategy primarily consists of pushing Arab governments to face the potential dangers of indefinite partial liberalization, identifying a road out, and urging and helping them to move along that road.

The potential payoff of this third strategy is high, but so too are its potential drawbacks and risks. If the United States actually pushed Arab leaders hard to respect human rights, be more politically inclusive, and subject their own rule to the public's choice, it would produce paroxysms of resentment among political elites in the region and alienate longtime friends. It could jeopardize the beneficial cooperation that Washington receives from friendly Arab autocrats on antiterrorist matters, on efforts to resolve the Palestinian–Israeli conflict, and on supplying oil.

Some of this resentment might be mitigated by the fact that a stepped-up set of initiatives to directly aid democracy would likely be carried out by United States–based NGOs and would therefore be at least one step removed from direct U.S. governmental action. Yet even these NGOs are frequently viewed in aid-receiving countries as extensions of the U.S. government. And if such aid is to be effective, it must be backed up with significant U.S. government jawboning and pressure.

And of course the third strategy runs squarely into the deeper doubts of many in the U.S. government and elsewhere about both the possibility and desirability of any real democratization in the Middle East. Might not genuinely open political processes bring to power Islamists who would disavow democracy once in power and pursue policies inimical to U.S. security and economic interests? This question has of course animated debates over Arab political futures for many years, and the various arguments and counterarguments have been much rehearsed.

The core argument for the direct democracy strategy is that a gradual but purposeful expansion of the political space and contestation could strengthen moderates and weaken extremists on both sides of the political divide in Arab countries. According to this argument, even though this gradual process would be risky and difficult, such a frontal approach to promoting democracy in the Arab world would be less risky and problematic in the long run than letting countries continue to stagnate and fester politically.

The Real Choice

In theory, the three different strategies to encourage gradualist transitions to democracy in the Arab world can be seen as three parts of one integrated strategy. In any given Arab country, the United States could simultaneously promote economic reform, increase efforts to indirectly aid democracy by assisting in reforming the state and expanding civil society, and initiate efforts to directly strengthen and broaden the established processes of political contestation.

The unfolding pattern of U.S. efforts to promote democracy in the Middle East since the early 1990s might in fact be seen as precisely the achievement of such a threefold synthesis. In the early 1990s, when the U.S. government first gave serious thought to how it might promote positive political change in the Arab world, the economic reform strategy gained favor. Then, in the second half of the decade, the United States began funding a small but growing number of programs to improve governance and foster civil society. The indirect democracy approach got a big boost after September 11, 2001—the new U.S. interest in promoting democracy in the Arab world was translated into ambitious plans to significantly increase programs to indirectly aid democracy, with the Middle East Partnership Initiative as the flagship. And then, very gradually, the U.S. government has started to support some programs that directly promote democracy—only a trickle in the 1990s but more in the post–September 11 context.

In principle, the three different approaches can indeed function as mutually reinforcing parts of one integrated strategy. In practice, however, quickly smoothing over the differences among them and insisting that U.S. policy entails pursuing all three at once gives the impression of a consensus that in fact has not yet been achieved. U.S. policy with regard to promoting democracy in the Arab world is in flux. The government is giving greater, more serious attention to the question than at any previous time. But within the many parts of the government that concern themselves with the issue—the White House, State Department, USAID, the Defense Department, and the intelligence agencies—there are many different opinions and ideas and little real consensus.

Advocates of the economic reform approach are often skeptical of the whole idea that the United States should promote democracy in the Arab world. Economic reform is their choice because it puts the day of political reckoning comfortably far off in the future and seems the least risky approach. They are usually willing to tolerate indirect democracy aid programs because they figure that such activities are unlikely to make much difference and are also relatively low risk. But they are skeptical of or actively opposed to direct efforts to promote democracy. Enthusiasts of the indirect approach accept that economic reform can have complementary value but warn against relying solely on it. They are often wary of the direct approach but are usually not opposed to at least giving it a try in limited circumstances. Advocates of the direct approach are sometimes doubtful about the economic route, seeing it as a cover for little real engagement with democracy. But they are usually favorable to indirect programs, viewing them as a natural partner of direct methods.

The crucial line is that between the direct approach and the two others. The U.S. government will undoubtedly keep trying to press for economic reform in the Arab world. And the new wave of indirect democracy aid efforts will certainly go forward. Therefore, the key question of strategy is whether the United States will decide to try to mount a major effort to support a strategy to directly promote democracy throughout the region or instead stick to the economic reform and indirect approaches.

Of course, the strategy of directly promoting democracy is not an undifferentiated tool to be applied (or not) in every country. Some countries are more ripe for such efforts than others, and direct methods may take somewhat different forms depending on the context. Morocco and Yemen, for example, have made some real progress with multiparty competition (in part with the assistance of U.S. and European elections and party programs) and could clearly benefit from continued, and indeed expanded, work in this domain. Algeria, Egypt, and Jordan are potential candidates for such efforts, although the sensitivities of their ruling elites about issues of political inclusion and rights are extremely high. A few of the small Gulf states, notably Bahrain and Qatar, may present some opportunities in this domain, although they are still grappling with starting-point issues such as whether to allow political parties and independent civic groups.

For the U.S. government to genuinely commit itself to direct methods of promoting democracy would mean a significant change of course—away from decades of support for political stasis and from deep attachments to particular rulers. It would mean taking significant political risks and expending real political capital that up to now has been used in the service of economic and security interests. This is the key choice facing the United States with regard to promoting democracy in the Middle East. Until it is clearly decided one way or the other, the growing number of U.S. policy statements and aid initiatives in the domain will lack essential strategic definition.

An earlier version of this chapter was originally published as Carnegie Working Paper 39 (June 2003).

11

Integrating Democracy
into the U.S. Policy Agenda

Michele Dunne

BETWEEN 2002 AND 2004, the United States accorded new prominence to political and economic reform and democratization as policy goals in the Middle East. Continuing that trend and translating rhetoric into effective strategies both depend on whether reform and democratization become fully integrated into the U.S. policy agenda in the region. Can the United States promote change at the risk of instability in the region while it remains dependent on petroleum from Arab countries? Can it pursue Arab–Israeli peace and democratization at the same time? Can the United States still secure needed military and counterterrorism cooperation if it antagonizes friendly regimes by promoting democratization as well? Is it feasible for the United States to promote democratization effectively amid widespread grievances against the war in Iraq and serious questions about U.S. human rights practices there and in Afghanistan?

The answer to all those questions is affirmative. The United States can and should seek peace, reform, and security for the region simultaneously, while continuing to buy Arab oil. Doing so, however, will require strengthening nascent aspects of U.S. policy and adding new ones. The United States should pursue these various goals separately in the first instance, without preemptively sacrificing one part of the policy agenda for another. It should also be alert to ways in which the goals can reinforce one another. The United States will also have to recognize the limits of regional approaches, such as the Broader Middle East and North Africa Initiative, in the quest for reform and democratization. For reform to become fully integrated into the policy agenda, the United States

209

should formulate practical, specific approaches to each country in the region—including difficult but important countries such as Egypt and Saudi Arabia, as well as easier ones such as Bahrain and Morocco—in which effective diplomatic engagement with the host government and assistance programs complement each other.

Middle East Democracy Promotion before 2001

Over the last thirty years, U.S. interests in the Middle East have become more numerous and complex and now extend to the internal affairs of states in the region. Until the 1970s, the United States was interested primarily in access to petroleum, which required a stable security and political situation, and in making peace between the Arab states and Israel. In the 1980s, military and strategic cooperation became increasingly important to protect access to petroleum supplies and provide staging areas for U.S. military operations in Asia and Africa.

In the 1980s, the United States also focused increasingly on the need for economic growth as a crucial component of maintaining stability in Arab countries. Through its push for economic reform, the United States established the principle that Washington could and should engage with Arab governments about their internal affairs. The United States discussed with the governments of Egypt, Jordan, North African countries, and even Israel reform objectives aimed at dismantling and privatizing statist economic structures, facilitating trade and foreign investment (including through accession to the World Trade Organization), and generating employment. In the 1990s, the United States undertook several high-profile initiatives including the U.S.–Egypt Partnership for Economic Growth (otherwise known as the Gore–Mubarak Commission) established in 1994, the U.S.–North Africa Economic Partnership (USNAEP) launched in 1998, and amendment of the U.S.–Israel Free Trade Agreement (concluded in 1985) to include the West Bank, Gaza, and Qualifying Industrial Zones in Jordan in 1996. The Bill Clinton and George W. Bush administrations focused on international trade as the engine of growth and economic reform, concluding free trade agreements with Jordan in 2000, Morocco and Bahrain in 2004, and announcing in 2003 the intention to pursue a regionwide U.S.–Middle East Free Trade Area.

Promotion of political reform in the region began to creep onto the U.S. agenda in a modest way in the early 1990s, partly as a reflection of the post-1989 global policy of democracy promotion and partly in response to limited political openings in the Middle East in the late 1970s and 1980s. From 1991 to 2001, the United States spent about $250 million on democracy programs in the Middle East, mostly in Egypt and the Palestinian territories. The goal of political reform began to appear regularly on U.S. State Department and U.S. Agency for International Development (USAID) planning documents for the region.

Unlike economic reform, however, political reform almost never made it onto the agenda of high-level discussions with Arab governments during the 1990s. With few exceptions, U.S. officials commonly assumed that pressing hard for political reform in the Middle East would be destabilizing and potentially damaging to U.S. interests. The chaotic political opening that took place in Algeria, which led to a decade of civil war after the military-dominated government prevented Islamists from winning national elections in 1991, reinforced this impression. U.S. officials generally believed that if there were to be political reform in the region, it should be gradual and driven entirely by internal forces, primarily by the middle classes and elements of civil society that were expected to arise as a result of economic reform. By the end of the decade, however, a growing body of work by scholars and experts showed that not only had economic reform not led to political reform, but that the lack of political reform was impeding progress on economic reform as well.[1]

U.S. officials also assumed during the 1990s that pursuing political reform and democratization in Arab states would disrupt efforts at Arab–Israeli peacemaking, a major focus of U.S. diplomacy. The general attitude in the U.S. State Department and the White House at the time was that it was easier to cut deals with autocratic rulers than with unpredictable parliaments and electorates. Officials also believed that the ongoing Israeli–Palestinian conflict prevented Arab peoples and regimes from focusing on domestic reform. Most important, on a practical level, senior U.S. government officials consistently resisted raising internal political issues with Arab leaders, even when U.S. ambassadors in the field recommended they do so. Senior officials deleted the issue from meeting agendas because they did not want to irritate Arab leaders, possibly damaging the prospects of getting their cooperation on the specific issues of the day related to the peace process. The result was a disjointed approach in which the United States dedicated funding to democracy assistance programs aimed at gradual, indirect change but failed to support those programs through meaningful engagement with the governments in question.

Sacrificing Reform for Peace: The Cases of Palestine and Egypt

Egypt and the Palestinian Authority were two notable cases in the 1990s in which the United States implemented democracy assistance programs but failed to engage their governments seriously on relevant policy reforms. Egypt received democracy assistance because it had a large economic assistance package, a small percentage of which could easily be diverted to democracy programs, and the Palestinians because they appeared to be on the verge of founding a state as the result of negotiations with Israel. In both cases, U.S. officials considered Arab–Israeli peace to be a much higher policy priority than political reform and democratization and did little to work with governing authorities to press for policy changes related to the issues being worked on through assistance programs. In both cases, by 2000 the result was failure in securing meaningful progress toward democratization or the peace deal for which democratization had been sacrificed.

U.S. democracy assistance to the Palestinians began as a result of the September 1993 Oslo agreement, which provided for an elected legislative council in the territories under the control of the Palestinian Authority. From 1994 onward, the United States made major investments in West Bank and Gaza programs to strengthen civil society organizations, judicial institutions, the Palestinian Legislative Council, and other institutions of the Palestinian Authority. There were also smaller programs to support legislative and local elections in 1996, promote decentralization of local government, and support the development of independent media. In all, the United States spent roughly $100 million on such projects in the West Bank and Gaza between 1994 and 2002.

Despite a sizable assistance commitment to Palestinian democratization, however, the U.S. government did little to press Palestinian leader Yasser Arafat to allow the development of a transparent, accountable, and representative Palestinian Authority. In particular, once the 1996 presidential and legislative elections—which U.S. officials viewed as a successful referendum on the Oslo process and on Arafat's leadership—were over, policy attention to the democratization issue faded quickly. While democracy assistance programs continued, Arafat took fateful steps that stunted the development of Palestinian institutions and precluded the emergence of democratic life by refusing for nearly six years to sign a set of basic laws ratified by the elected Legislative Council in 1997, establishing multiple security and intelligence services, and permitting rampant corruption. Meanwhile, U.S. policy-maker engagement with Arafat until 2000 focused almost entirely on the conduct of negotiations with Israel and security matters.

Would serious engagement with and pressure on Arafat (whose financial lifeline the United States controlled in the mid-late 1990s) have compelled the Palestinian leader to permit the development of a more democratic Palestinian Authority? Would Palestinians have responded differently, less violently, to the collapse of negotiations in late 2000 if they had effective means for peaceful political expression? The answers are unknowable, but it is clear that the results of Arafat's unchecked authoritarianism and mismanagement have been tragic for Palestinians and Israelis.[2] The Palestinian case is one in which Arab–Israeli peace and democratization should have been—and still might be—mutually reinforcing policy efforts. So far, neither the pre-2000 strategy of promoting a negotiated solution without meaningful democratization nor the post-2000 strategy of pressing for political reform without offering adequate hope of a negotiated solution with Israel has succeeded.

The case of Egypt is certainly less tragic than that of the Palestinians, but there too the sacrifice of democratization as a policy goal to the priorities of Arab–Israeli peace produced unsatisfactory results. Military cooperation and economic reform absorbed any political capital left over after Arab–Israeli peace priorities. Throughout the 1990s, promotion of democratization appeared in State Department planning documents as a policy goal in Egypt, and USAID carried out an active program of democracy assistance funded at an average of over $20 million annually. Assistance programs centered on developing nongovernmental and civil society organizations, promoting decentralization of local government, modernizing the judiciary, and improving parliamentary information systems, with smaller programs on strengthening labor unions and promoting education on legal and human rights.

One of the largest single democracy programs in Egypt, the NGO Service Center, demonstrated the problems that result when there is inadequate policy support for sizable assistance projects. In 1999, after several years of difficult negotiations, the United States and Egypt agreed on the terms for a U.S.-funded NGO Service Center that would offer grants and training to nongovernmental organizations (NGOs). The U.S. Embassy in Cairo and USAID had agreed to unfavorable Egyptian government terms for the center, notably that a board headed by an Egyptian minister would approve the eligibility of all NGO applicants to receive grants, effectively excluding organizations that the government considered too critical or unfriendly. To refuse such terms would have meant a nasty and perhaps public confrontation with the Egyptian government, as well as pulling the plug on a project in which USAID had already invested several years of effort.

Adding insult to injury, in 2000 the Egyptian government passed a law regulating NGOs that was considered extremely restrictive by international standards. The law effectively prevented many NGOs from playing the sort of policy advocacy role for which the NGO Service Center was intended to train them.[3] The U.S. ambassador in Cairo had raised the NGO law quietly with a number of ministers, and the U.S. State Department spokesman even publicly criticized the law, to no avail. In the related cases of the NGO Service Center's terms and the NGO law, U.S. engagement never went high enough to make a difference, because until 2002 presidential-level communications were devoted almost exclusively to peace process and strategic issues, with some discussion of economic reform during the mid-1990s.[4]

The U.S. government spent $32.5 million on the NGO Service Center before a policy review in 2004 determined to end the project. Although the Egyptian NGOs who received grants from the center undoubtedly did good work in their communities with the funds and acquired the capability to advocate policy changes, the center could do nothing to help them obtain the opportunity to advocate policy changes within a restrictive Egyptian system. The fault lay not with the center or with USAID, neither of which could reasonably be expected to persuade the Egyptian government to deregulate the NGO domain. It lay with the senior officials who launched such a program but failed to back it up with serious, high-level engagement on the Egyptian government's laws and practices that prevent NGOs from playing an effective advocacy role.

In 1999 and 2000, the United States did not engage with Egypt on the need for political reform and instead reserved high-level attention and political capital for use primarily on Arab–Israeli peacemaking. Egypt's role in the 2000 Camp David talks, however, was hardly a helpful one. In contrast, Bush did raise the need for political reform explicitly and publicly after his April 2004 meeting with Egyptian President Hosni Mubarak, and the Egyptians played an important role in supporting Israel and the United States in talks about Gaza disengagement. The point here is not that raising political reform persuaded the Egyptians to cooperate on the peace process; in fact, one should avoid such cynical approaches. The point is rather that countries such as Egypt make decisions whether, how, and when to cooperate on Arab–Israeli peacemaking for their own reasons and not primarily to punish or reward the United States for what it is doing or not doing regarding political reform.

If regional peace and democratization can and should be addressed with Arab governments at the same time, what about concerns that freer expression and more political participation will make Arab leaders less able to make peace deals with Israel? While realistic, this concern needs to be kept in perspective. First, on the practical level, the Camp David experience in July 2000 shows the dangers inherent in attempting to press leaders to sign a deal without adequate development of a public consensus among Palestinians, Israelis, or other Arabs in favor of the deal. Second, on the policy level, the United States needs to show it has the courage of its convictions. It must be willing to put up with the inconvenient vicissitudes of democracy in the Arab world, just as it does in Israel or Turkey, in the name of a better future for the peoples of the region.

The Post-2001 Context

Through a series of speeches and other public remarks by the president, national security adviser, and secretary of state in 2003 and 2004, and then by highlighting the issue at the 2004 G-8, European Union, and North Atlantic Treaty Organization summits, the Bush administration put political reform and democratization on the agenda. President Bush also began to raise the subject in meetings and press conferences with Arab leaders, notably during visits by Presidents Mubarak and Zine Al Abidine Ben Ali of Tunisia in spring 2004. As one Bush administration official put it, "the old bargain of choosing stability over change is now off; we've opened the conversation about the need for change."[5] The question then becomes how to move beyond the conversation's opening, or, put another way, if the old bargain is off, what is the new bargain?

A strategic assumption of the Bush administration that complicated the new democracy promotion effort was the idea that regime change in Iraq was the key to stabilizing and transforming the region, at least in the short term. Not only did administration officials believe that eliminating Iraq as a military threat would reshuffle the strategic deck, but they also believed that establishing a democratic government in Iraq would provide the needed demonstration effect to catalyze change throughout the Middle East. As President Bush said at an April 13, 2004, press conference during which he was pressed to justify the war in Iraq: "A secure and free Iraq is an historic opportunity to change the world."

The Bush administration acknowledged by its actions (if not its words), however, that it could not rely on a quick Iraqi transition to democracy as the sole engine of regional change. Since 2002, several presidential speeches, the Middle East Partnership Initiative (MEPI) launched in December 2002, and initiatives with G-8 and European partners in June 2004 focused on promoting political, economic, and educational change, as well as women's rights. Although some questions remain about the advisability of such high-profile initiatives, still more questions focus on their viability, especially on the gap between the high-flown rhetoric and the relatively modest funds and program goals of the initiatives. Something is missing in the middle: a strategy that connects rhetoric to reality and shows a pathway to integrating democracy with other goals in the region.

Several practical problems impede development and implementation of such a strategy. Presidential enterprises such as the Broader Middle East and North Africa Initiative unveiled at the June 2004 G-8 summit have the advantage of drawing attention to a problem but the disadvantage of absorbing tremendous amounts of bureaucratic energy and funding without necessarily producing commensurate results. In addition, officials at the State Department and embassies overseas—who would have to put the meat on the bones of country strategies—are much better at dealing with crises and short-term problems than they are at pursuing long-term policy priorities or at seeing either challenges or opportunities out on the horizon. In fact, many are so overworked that they can barely see beyond the next congressional testimony or high-level visit for which they must prepare.

Finally, those designing assistance programs face the practical problem of needing to spend the funds allocated for democracy promotion, whether or not they are able to do so in a way that supports policy goals, which themselves remain poorly defined. USAID and MEPI have understandably chosen to work in areas such as civil society, local government, judicial reform, and women's rights that seemed the easiest and least sensitive. There has been little assessment of areas in which reform would be the most meaningful, which must be determined on an individual country basis, and few attempts to coordinate policy engagement and assistance programs with a view to making progress in those areas.

Components of a Regional Strategy

The first component of an integrated regional strategy would be to work on the two overarching issues of regional peace and internal reform at the same time and with equivalent amounts of energy. Regional peace and reform at times can reinforce each other. Palestinian reform is the clearest example, but one might also recall how Arab states' economic reforms in the mid-1990s led to expanded commercial ties with Israel. As a key part of securing regional peace, U.S. administrations will have to continue to devote enormous resources to stabilizing and rebuilding Iraq. At times, peace and reform can also conflict as policy goals in the short term, but each is too important to be postponed until a breakthrough on the other.

The United States can pursue peace and reform because governments in the region generally make decisions about whether or not to cooperate with U.S. peacemaking—or military or counterterrorism efforts—based on a calculation of their own interests rather than a desire to do the United States a favor. They will do so even if they are annoyed by U.S. calls for reform. The one exception to this would be an extreme case in which a government believed the United States was actively trying to undermine it or support its overthrow, situations in which the United States should not find itself with any regional ally.

An idea from the late Israeli prime minister Yitzhak Rabin (at that time, referring to peace and terrorism) would be good advice: Pursue peace as though there were no democratization, and pursue democratization as though there were no peace. In other words, the U.S. government should pursue reform and democratization as policy goals in the first instance without worrying excessively about tradeoffs with other goals. U.S. officials should ask themselves whether such tradeoffs are truly necessary or just a matter of avoiding inconvenience and confrontation. If reform and democratization have become real policy goals, U.S. officials must be willing to take some risks on their behalf.

As part of pursuing regional peace and reform as equally important goals, the United States should also continue to pursue democratization in Arab countries no matter what happens in Iraq. A democratized and prosperous Iraq would certainly have an important and positive influence, but that outcome is not yet certain and might be years away. At the same time, there is no reason for the U.S. government to adopt a defeatist attitude in the face of claims that the U.S. role in Iraq negates U.S. credibility in promoting democracy. In fact, although many Arab governments and reformers have rejected the U.S. government as the messenger of reform and democratization, the message itself has resonated broadly and provoked productive debates across the region about the nature of reforms needed.

The United States should also make reform a consideration in its military and counterterrorism relationships. Even before the recent press for democratization in the region, the United States faced a complicated set of legal and human rights issues regarding military or security assistance and sales of equipment. While observing those limitations, U.S. officials should become more alert to whether high-level military or security officials in Arab countries are supporting or undermining indigenous efforts at political and economic reform and make this an important factor in deliberations about what kinds of U.S. assistance are appropriate. In addition, the U.S. government should find ways to incorporate more engagement with and training of foreign military and security officers on subjects related to respect for human and civil rights into its cooperation and assistance programs.

Implementing an Integrated Regional Strategy

Formulating a strategy to promote reform and democratization as one of several core issues is a first step, but how can it be implemented on a day-to-day basis? First, it will be important to differentiate what can be accomplished regionally from what must be done country-by-country. Regionwide efforts such as the G-8's Broader Middle East and North Africa Initiative can help inject momentum into the overall movement toward reform. Such initiatives reinforce a developing international consensus that political and economic reforms are inevitable and desirable in the Middle East, emboldening long-silent proponents of reform throughout the region. Many such reformers—Islamists and leftists as well as liberals, and even some government officials—criticize U.S. and international reform initiatives as a way to assert patriotism and oppose aspects of U.S. policy. What is important, however, is that international initiatives help open up political space so that reformers may articulate their own ideas, which are far more relevant than whatever the United States or other foreign actors might propose.

The danger of such regionwide initiatives, however, is that they risk creating motion that substitutes for real progress. A presidential initiative adopted by the G-8 can divert and consume many financial and bureaucratic resources that might be more productively spent elsewhere. Even more important, U.S. officials and diplomats can fall (wittingly or unwittingly) into the trap of engaging with Arab governments primarily on whether or not those governments participate in activities related to the initiative (agreeing to attend or even host a ministerial meeting of the Forum for the Future, for example), rather than on whether the government in question is carrying out meaningful reforms at home. Most of the serious work of promoting political and economic reform can only be done privately and bilaterally. This is precisely the sort of difficult work that the United States is only now beginning to undertake.

In approaching the region, the United States should pursue reform and democratization with every country, although the specific issues to be raised, the modes of engagement with government and nongovernment actors, and the kinds of influence the United States can bring to bear will differ significantly from one country to another. Pursuing only softer targets (countries with governments already showing a propensity to reform, such as Morocco, or those with whom the United States shares a limited set of interests, such as Tunisia) while ignoring harder targets (close allies such as Saudi Arabia or Egypt) will only rob the policy of credibility and perpetuate the mistakes of the past. At the same time, the United States should be ready to focus effort on special opportunities to promote reform, such as leadership successions or crises, and not miss them as it did with the Palestinians in the 1990s.

If any reform strategy requires engaging with governments in the region, how can the United States do so effectively? First, there should be a commitment to raise relevant issues as needed at all levels of bilateral relationships, from routine meetings held by U.S. embassy second or third secretaries to meetings with heads of state. President Bush broke the ice with the presidents of Tunisia and Egypt in spring 2004, making public statements expressing expectation of reform that were phrased mildly and positively, following more robust private engagement at the working level. If leaders in the region hear concerns about democratization from U.S. ambassadors and their staffs but not from senior administration officials or members of Congress, they will not take the concerns seriously.

Second, U.S. officials need to continue working on striking the right balance between public and private statements on reform and democratization. On the one hand, public statements that are too harsh or make demands that are too specific provoke anticolonial reactions and put Arab governments into corners. On the other hand, a lack of public statements lets governments off the hook. Making reform and democratization a persistent theme in public remarks and phrasing it in a measured and open-minded way helps to put and keep the issue on the regional and international agenda. Most of the serious conversations with governments on contentious issues, however, will need to be conducted in private meetings.

Third, even more important than a written policy strategy is that there are senior officials with direct responsibility for the countries in question who have internalized the strategy and are constantly looking for ways to implement it. Assistant or deputy assistant secretaries of state for the Near East in Washington and ambassadors or deputy chiefs of mission in embassies overseas are best placed to do this. The checklists and talking points for important meetings, approval documents for major assistance programs, and so on—the practical tools by which opportunities to promote policy goals are seized or lost—pass through their hands. Assistant secretaries and ambassadors will need support from working-level officials, such as desk officers and political officers at embassies overseas, who are on top of developments and should be instructed to make strategizing to promote reform and democratization central to their work.

Steps toward Individual Country Strategies

If the United States needs to integrate reform and democratization on a regionwide basis, it is even more critical that it does so in terms of policy toward each country in the Middle East. Such an effort would begin with a realistic evaluation of the country's current situation regarding reform and democratization, including the sort of reforms most in demand by the population and the degree of will to reform on the part of the government. In a few cases (for example, Iraq and Palestine at present), the political situation may be unstable or in crisis, leaving open the possibility for a far-reaching transition. In most countries, there is an entrenched autocratic system; the government might have shown some willingness to modernize institutions or even to liberalize political and economic life to a limited extent, but not to democratize (that is, giving the people the right and ability to change their government). There are difficult questions for the United States to address here in terms of what its goals should be, because history has shown that liberalization does not necessarily lead to democratization.[6]

Once U.S. officials determine which reform steps would be most meaningful and feasible in the current context, they should continue with an inventory of important U.S. interests in the country (military/strategic, counterterrorism/law enforcement, political, economic, commercial) and a realistic—but not defeatist—assessment of the influence the United States possesses. It is important to see clearly the limitations of U.S. influence: Short of the use of military force, the United States generally cannot make things happen in other countries against the will of the host government. But U.S. officials often underestimate or overlook the influence the United States does possess and leave political capital unspent. It is not a matter of coercion, but of using U.S. influence, in coordination with other major donors or trading partners of the country if possible, to help shape the environment in which governments make decisions.

Understanding the kind of influence the United States possesses and how reform fits into the overall scheme of U.S. interests in the country,

U.S. officials can then design a program of policy approaches to the government and related assistance programs that addresses the areas where reform would be most meaningful. In doing so, they should avoid undertaking assistance programs in marginal areas simply to use up assistance funds. They should also bear in mind that not only should assistance programs support policy goals, but also policy may well need to support assistance programs at certain junctures (for example, when Arab government policies or practices thwart program success).

As country strategies are implemented and updated over time, it will be important for U.S. officials to think opportunistically as well as strategically and scan the horizon for opportunities for progress, new sources of leverage, and possible problems or complications. State Department officials, busy with the crisis of any given day or week, rarely do this, and USAID officials often plan and commit resources so far in advance that they lack flexibility. The two bureaucratic cultures need to find a middle way to plan strategically but maintain the ability to shift plans to accommodate new developments or take advantage of new opportunities. In addition, Congress needs to permit and support greater flexibility on the part of USAID and the State Department.

Sketch of a Country Strategy: Egypt

A country strategy for Egypt must start by acknowledging that there is currently no ongoing process of democratization in Egypt for the United States to assist. After waves of limited political liberalization in the 1970s and 1980s, the 1990s was a decade of contraction in political and civil liberties, due partly to the government's focus on defeating Islamic extremists. Since 2002, senior members of the Egyptian government and ruling National Democratic Party have expressed support for the idea of gradual and limited political liberalization but so far have taken no significant steps in that direction. A cabinet reshuffle in July 2004 that brought in respected economic technocrats suggested that Mubarak's primary emphasis would be on revitalizing economic reform. Egyptian reformers—Islamists and leftists as well as liberals—generally agree on the steps most needed to break the political logjam: freeing up political activity and expression, instituting direct election of the president, and amending the constitution to redistribute power from the executive to the legislative and judicial branches. Discussions about political reform are taking place not only in light of the new U.S. focus on the issue, but also in the context of a likely succession in the Egyptian presidency within the next few years.

In terms of interests, the United States depends on Egypt for assistance with military operations in the Middle East and Africa, diplomatic support in Israeli–Palestinian negotiations, and counterterrorism cooperation, but not for energy needs. The American–Egyptian relationship is close and mutually beneficial, though often troubled by disagreements over regional or domestic Egyptian issues, and the United States would keenly feel the loss (through instability or a break in relations) of Egypt as a regional ally. At the same time, in recent years there has been a growing sense in Washington that the Egyptian leadership's reluctance to liberalize the economy and polity has prevented the Egyptian people from attaining the prosperity needed to ensure long-term stability. Stagnation in domestic policies over the past twenty years has also eroded Egypt's ability to exert leadership in the region.

As the primary benefactor of the Egyptian regime for the last quarter century, the United States possesses a great deal of influence but also faces increasing resentment related to its policies in the region. It is also Egypt's second largest trading partner after the European Union. The United States has made a large and continuing investment in Egypt's stability and development (over $50 billion in military and economic assistance since 1977), and its military assistance program of $1.3 billion annually is critical to the modernization of the Egyptian armed forces. U.S. economic assistance has been declining gradually in absolute and real terms, projected to decline from approximately $800 million to $400 million during the 1999–2009 period, but still provides a needed supplement to the Egyptian government budget.[7] As part of economic assistance, democracy-related assistance has been funded at roughly $20 million annually since the early 1990s. Bilateral agreements reached in the 1970s give the Government of Egypt extensive control over the use of assistance, making it difficult to promote economic or political reform objectives that go beyond current Egyptian policies.

As discussed above, until recently the United States had democracy-related assistance programs but did not integrate democracy promotion into its policy goals and dialogue with the Egyptian government. Now the United States is adding promotion of political reform and

democratization to the existing policy agenda, which includes cooperation with the Egyptian government on Arab–Israeli peacemaking,
military cooperation, counterterrorism, and economic reform. Instead
of sacrificing political and economic reform in favor of the other goals,
as has been done in the past, the United States should assume that
Egyptian government officials are rational and will make decisions on
all issues based on their calculation of what is in Egypt's interest.

Considering the influence it possesses, the United States could in
theory sacrifice all other interests and press hard for a rapid and probably chaotic transition to democracy in Egypt. Considering the risks associated with instability in Egypt, however, a more realistic choice would
be to press for a significant opening of political competition, development of political and civil society organizations, and economic reform.
This would create a much freer atmosphere in which the Egyptian people
could—should they so choose—eventually press their government for
full democracy.

Just as critical as integrating political reform and democratization with
other policy goals would be integrating policy engagement with assistance programs. Assistance programs can be effective only as part of a
coherent policy strategy including active engagement with the Egyptian
government on the structural changes in law and practice that political
reform demands.

The United States must also consider whether to impose conditions
related to political reform on its assistance, a difficult proposition considering that the long-standing assistance program is linked to assistance to Israel. Efforts to impose economic conditions on parts of the
assistance programs have sometimes delayed delivery of assistance when
Egypt failed to meet agreed benchmarks, but Egypt has generally
outlasted the United States and gotten the funds in the end. Rather than
imposing political conditions on assistance, a better approach would be
working to ensure that U.S. democracy assistance funds are spent only
on programs that stand a real chance of promoting meaningful reform.

Specific suggestions for a strategy that integrates policy engagement
and assistance include:

- Concentrating in the policy dialogue and in programs on issues
  that Egyptians have identified as critical: lifting emergency laws,
  revising laws on forming political parties and regulating NGOs,

forming an independent electoral commission and monitoring bodies, and amending the constitution to provide for direct election of the president, term limits, and redistribution of power from the executive to legislative and judicial branches.

- Making major program commitments only in areas where the Egyptian government has demonstrated the will to reform, or in critical areas where the U.S. government is prepared to work hard on persuading the Egyptian government to open up.
- Retaining enough flexibility in the assistance program to be able to respond to opportunities or challenges that arise; that is, avoid committing all the funds to large, multiyear projects.
- Carving out funds that the U.S. government can disburse directly, with the Egyptian government agreeing only to general program guidelines.
- Seeking alternative destinations for funds should the U.S. and Egyptian governments be unable to agree on meaningful programs.

Finally, thinking opportunistically as well as realistically about the potential for reform in Egypt, it is important to focus on the fact that there are important political events unfolding now as Egyptians position themselves for a succession in the presidency. The United States cannot and should not try to force change in Egypt, and all decisions ultimately reside with Egyptians. The United States can, however, use its significant influence to help press for a freer, more liberal political environment in which Egyptians will make important choices about their country's future.

Conclusion

Returning to the questions posed at the outset, it has become clear since September 2001 that the appearance of stability in the Middle East produced by political oppression and economic stagnation was no more than an illusion and did not guarantee U.S. interests, including access to petroleum. The United States can promote regional peace and cooperation on security affairs while also promoting internal reform, because Arab governments will continue to cooperate with the United States when it is in their interests to do so, even if they are annoyed by calls for reform. The United States can and should promote reform in Arab countries no matter what happens in Iraq, because even if many Arabs reject the United States' moral authority as messenger of freedom, they accept the message that change is badly needed.

If the United States chooses to integrate political reform and democratization with existing policy goals in the Middle East along the lines described above, what results can it expect? Here it is important to recall that, even in the handful of countries in the region where the United States is influential, U.S. influence is generally indirect. Not only can the United States not force governments to change, but also it cannot control the pace or direction of change once it begins. In many cases, the sort of change and the ways it manifests itself may not suit U.S. tastes perfectly. The most obvious cases with which the United States will have to make its peace are the inclusion of nonviolent Islamists of various stripes in the political process and the role of the increasingly competitive (if not truly market-driven) and critical Arabic satellite media.

At present, the task for the United States is to find ways to seek regional peace, internal reform, and strategic cooperation at the same time, for the most part pursuing each independently but also looking for ways they can reinforce one another. In the future, the United States may face a region in which different points of view and grievances against U.S. policies are expressed more openly and have real consequences for government decision making. This would be a more complex scene, to be sure, but one that offered a better life for peoples of the region and a more healthy and transparent environment in which to promote U.S. interests.

Notes

This chapter was originally published as Carnegie Paper 50 (October 2004).

1. See, for example, Clement M. Henry and Robert Springborg, *Globalization and the Politics of Development in the Middle East* (Cambridge, U.K.: Cambridge University Press, 2001); and Eberhard Kienle, *A Grand Delusion: Democracy and Economic Reform in Egypt* (London: I. B. Tauris Publishers, 2001).

2. For an early diagnosis of the failure of Palestinian state building, see Glenn E. Robinson, *Building a Palestinian State: The Incomplete Revolution* (Bloomington: Indiana University Press, 1997).

3. Although the 2000 NGO law was overturned on procedural grounds, in 2002 the Egyptian government proceeded to pass an even more restrictive law that allows the minister of social affairs to dissolve any NGO without going to court.

4. In August 2002, President Bush wrote to President Mubarak to protest a state security court conviction of Egyptian–American sociologist Saad Eddin Ibrahim in a trumped-up embezzlement case. In April 2004, Bush raised the issue of political reform explicitly for the first time in a press conference following a meeting at Bush's Crawford ranch.

5. Author's conversation with White House official, June 2004.

6. See chapter 2.

7. For a discussion of the declining impact of economic assistance, see Edward S. Walker Jr., "American Economic Assistance Program to Egypt," testimony before the House of Representatives International Relations Committee, June 17, 2004; available at http://wwwa.house.gov/international_relations/fullhear.htm.

12

Europe's Uncertain Pursuit of Middle East Reform

Richard Youngs

DELIBERATION OF DEMOCRACY promotion in the Middle East intensified after the attacks of September 11, 2001, and has been further energized by the transatlantic debates that were progeny of the Iraqi conflict. More intense debate over support for political change in the Middle East has forced the United States and Europe into a closer exploration of each other's actual and intended approaches to democracy promotion in the region. The United States' proposed—and ultimately ill-fated—Greater Middle East Initiative was viewed skeptically by European governments; in part at the latter's behest the Broader Middle East and North Africa Initiative that was eventually agreed at the Sea Island G-8 summit in June 2004 enshrines a more cautious, partnership-based approach to political reform. This initiative commits the United States and Europeans to work together on a new political dialogue with governmental, social, and economic actors in the Middle East; engage in regular discussion and information sharing on democracy assistance; and cooperate on a range of private development, microcredit, and literacy projects.

Notwithstanding this prospective cooperation, the operational details of the Broader Middle East and North Africa Initiative so far remain vague, and transatlantic relations are still subject to evident tensions. Many in the United States bemoan European irresolution, but others acknowledge the need for U.S. policy to understand and harness the European Union's (EU's) more pervasive presence in much of the Middle East. Although Europeans express dismay at the George W. Bush administration's heavy-handed instrumentalism, they have also been forced to engage with new U.S. initiatives that appear to heed the EU's own pleas for a focus on the root causes of instability. With the United States and the EU eyeing each other over the parapets of their Iraqi-inspired wrangles, it is an opportune moment to delineate and critically assess how Europeans have developed their democracy-promotion policies in the Middle East.

This chapter outlines the way in which the EU introduced a limited and selective Middle Eastern democracy policy in the 1990s, catalogues some of the new initiatives introduced by both European governments and the EU collectively since the terrorist attacks of September 11, identifies the distinctive conceptual features of Europe's approach to political reform, and concludes by suggesting ways in which EU strategy in the Middle East should be strengthened. The chapter contends that Europe's determination to reinforce distinctiveness from the United States has been a source of strength but also an obstacle to tempering persistent insufficiencies in EU strategy. While enjoying both quantitative and qualitative advantages relative to U.S. efforts, European democracy policies in the Middle East require significant revision if they are to attain the sophisticated holistic gradualism to which they aspire.

Laying the Foundations: European Strategies in the 1990s

Piqued at what they see as the United States' recent conversion to democracy promotion in the Middle East, Europeans lay claim to a longer-standing reform discourse in many parts of the region.

Most notably, the Euro-Mediterranean Partnership (EMP, or Barcelona Process) created in 1995 formally enshrined a commitment to foster "political pluralism" in the Maghreb and Mashreq states (Morocco, Algeria, Tunisia, Egypt, Jordan, Lebanon, Syria, along with Israel and the Palestinian Authority). Formal dialogue on political reform commenced, new trade agreements incorporated sanction-triggering democracy clauses, and an EU democracy assistance budget was created for the region. In practice, European strategy, even in this part of the Middle East, was cautious during the late 1990s. Little coercive pressure for political change was exerted, as the EU adhered to a philosophy of gradualism that relied on notions of soft power, peer pressure, persuasion, and cooperative partnership. European governments were highly indulgent of limited signs of progress, for example, in Algeria, Jordan, and Morocco. No systematic dialogue was developed on democracy with Islamist opposition forces, and there was little correlation between aid flows and states' respective degrees of political openness. Egypt remained by far the largest recipient of European aid. Even in these EMP states, where the EU established a wide-ranging and firmly institutionalized partnership, democracy remained well down the list of priorities, with significantly more resources devoted to economic reform, drug eradication, the environment, and population control.

Outside the framework of the EMP, the focus on political change was more difficult to detect. EU relations with the Gulf Cooperation Council (GCC) were restricted to trade issues, and several EU member states dramatically increased their defense cooperation with the region's regimes. Exploratory efforts at establishing an EU–GCC human rights dialogue were firmly rebuffed, in particular by Saudi Arabia, and the Gulf attracted virtually no political aid work from European donors.

The EU's "critical dialogue" with Iran was acknowledged to have concerned itself with Iran's alleged development of nuclear weapons and support for international terrorism, as well as being dominated for long periods by the Rushdie *fatwa*. The focus on internal politics was negligible. The conditions set by the EU for upgrading relations with Iran related to the country's external actions and not democratic reform. The EU's rapprochement with President Khatami after 1997 reflected a confidence that Iran's hybrid theocratic-democratic mix could be capable of resolving strategic difficulties. Indeed, as European governments sought to encourage reform through Khatami, the concern was to make progress on specific human rights issues—the use of stoning being a particular European focus—without pushing for systemic "regime change."

The two cases in which democracy promotion was even more obviously subjugated to other concerns were Iraq and the Palestinian territories. As has since been amply demonstrated, debates on Iraq were concerned almost entirely with the weapons of mass destruction (WMD) issue. A well-known range of views was evident among European governments on the right mix of containment versus engagement in the commonly agreed need to tackle Iraq's presumed weapons development program. But common to the range of these perspectives was the relegation of democracy promotion to something of an afterthought. In terms of concrete policy, little was done pertinent to internal political change. Most conspicuously, European states declined to offer direct support for

Iraqi democracy movements; indeed, several governments became increasingly skeptical of the democratic credentials of many of these groups. Senior EU officials have acknowledged a complete lack of debate during this period within the EU's common foreign and security policy on Iraq's possible democratization.

In the Palestinian territories, the EU provided the largest slice of funds for setting up the new quasistate institutions of the Palestinian Authority. In doing so they backed an executive-dominated institutional structure that enabled Yasser Arafat to prevail more easily over those elements of Palestinian civil society hostile to the peace process. After the Oslo Accords, aid was diverted from civil society organizations toward the new Palestinian security apparatus; repression and nepotism were overlooked; and the postponement of elections toward the end of the decade elicited little critical reaction from European governments.

In the case of Turkey during the 1990s, a degree of political openness and prospective accession to the EU lent European influence a qualitative difference compared with elsewhere in the Middle East, but here too doubts remained over Europe's commitment to supporting democracy. The EU insisted that the decision to exclude Turkey from its list of applicant countries in 1997 was motivated by a genuine desire to defend efforts to deepen Turkey's democratic process in the wake of the army's ousting of Prime Minister Erbakan and the subsequent banning of the Islamist Refah party. Once accession negotiations commenced after the Helsinki European Council of December 1999, European governments were firm in seeking to use this new purchase to press Turkey to strengthen civilian control over the army, and they increased spending on human rights, democracy, and governance initiatives. The EU's high-profile focus on Kurdish rights in Turkey has long been one of the most prominent features of its foreign policy and a point of difference with U.S. policy. At the same time, however, because Turkey's accession remained a distant prospect, critics charged European states with manipulating democratic entry conditions as a means of indefinitely delaying the entry of a Muslim state into the EU.

Across the Middle East, the hesitancy of European democracy strategy was reflected in the nature of incipient democracy assistance programs. Some political aid projects were started, but these were of limited magnitude and nearly entirely of the "softer" type of democracy assistance. The Middle East received just under €10 million per year between 1996 and 1999 from the European Commission's new democracy budget, but the region remained conspicuously absent from most governments' political aid profiles. The British, German, Danish, Swedish, and Dutch governments supported only a handful of human rights projects, totaling no more than €1–2 million a year. European governments declined to create formal "Middle East democracy" funds, classifying aid only in terms of more broadly defined "governance" categories. European democracy assistance at this juncture was directed mainly at reforming states in Eastern Europe, Latin America, and sub-Saharan Africa. Notwithstanding such caution and imprecision, the overall level of European reform-related funding still compared favorably with the $15 million spent annually by the United States on democracy aid in the Middle East between 1991 and 2001.[1]

Those political aid projects that were funded invariably related only indirectly to democracy. They were aimed, for example, at small business development, environmental and service delivery associations, or cooperation in the cultural sphere. France provided the largest official aid allocations for human rights in the Middle East, but the largest slice of its human rights budgets in practice went to cultural projects, overwhelmingly with tenuous political aspects. Where the EU met resistance to democracy assistance projects, political conditionality provisions were not invoked and the critical political content of many projects was consequently diluted. In the region's most closed societies, European governments did little more than fund European-based NGOs to develop an information-gathering and monitoring role. Barely measurable amounts of political aid went to Iran, Libya, Saudi Arabia, or Syria. Generous support for security forces—in particular in Algeria and the Gulf states—was oriented toward capacity building and incorporated few measures relevant to increasing democratic civilian oversight of security operations. None of this is to suggest that conditions were propitious to democracy aid creating major breakthroughs in the Middle East, but the limitations of EU programs militated against even more modest positive impact.

European Responses to 9/11

Against this background, the lessons that Europeans drew from the attacks of September 11 exhibited elements of striking commonality with

U.S. policy reassessments. European ministers and policy makers have regularly asserted a link between terrorism and political repression. British Prime Minister Tony Blair has argued on many occasions that security can best be achieved by "spreading our values." European Commissioner Chris Patten has opined that "fostering human rights should become an integral part of the fight against terrorism."[2] The new European security strategy, agreed upon in December 2003, concludes that "the best protection of our security is a world of well-governed democratic states."[3] Recently, German Foreign Minister Joschka Fischer has argued that "security is a broader concept in this fight against terrorism: social and cultural modernization, as well as democracy . . . are of almost greater importance [than traditional security issues]."[4] Although in characteristically more elliptical fashion, the then French Foreign Minister Dominique de Villepin also asserted something of the same logic, in acknowledging that security thinking could "no longer be explained by a series of alliances."[5]

And efforts to revitalize a policy of democracy promotion can indeed be witnessed through a number of new initiatives introduced by national governments. In Germany, a Task Force for Dialogue with the Islamic World was set up within Joschka Fischer's office; a €1 million Anti-Terror Package identified support for governance reform as a top priority; overall aid to the Middle East and North Africa increased 20 percent after 2002; and work on a new strategy for democracy assistance was commissioned with a view to injecting political aid with greater strategic thrust in the hitherto uncharted area of the Middle East. By 2004 France had increased its democracy and governance spending to 10 percent of its overall aid in the Middle East and North Africa, primarily through an enhanced *zone de solidarité prioritaire* program that included Algeria, Lebanon, Morocco, the Palestinian Territories, Tunisia, and Yemen.

In the United Kingdom, the Foreign Office elaborated a new Arab reform strategy and established a number of programs, including a reform-oriented fund for engaging with the Islamic world. An additional £7 million was made available for the Middle East under a new cross-Whitehall conflict prevention fund, with governance, security sector reform, and "engagement with political movements" outlined as priority areas. The Danish government has introduced a similar initiative on Arab reform, with €15 million a year available for new projects currently being identified; the effort has initially focused on more reformist states, but also targets Saudi Arabia and Syria. Sweden likewise moved for the first time to begin political work in the Middle East through a new 2003 Middle East and North Africa (MENA) regional program, which included an annual €5 million allocation to governance and democracy—approximately 13 percent of the Swedish investment in political aid. The Dutch government expanded eligibility for its human rights programs to non–LDC (least developed country) states, in large part to include Arab states.

At the EU level, new initiatives have been developed within the framework of the EMP. New EU guidelines for democracy and human rights promotion were established in 2003, which commit the EU to elaborating national plans for human rights to be agreed with EMP Arab states, in consultation with local civil societies. Agreement to a national plan will qualify the government in question for a "political premium" increase in aid. This idea was pushed most enthusiastically by the British, Dutch, and Danish governments; particularly significant was that the initially ambivalent French and Spanish governments did eventually support the guidelines. Separately, further sets of political benchmarks have been built into the EU's new Wider Europe initiative, aimed at reenergizing strategy toward Europe's postenlargement periphery. Aiming to widen the pool of resources available for political reform, in December 2003 the European Commission for the first time allocated €1 million to human rights projects (in Jordan) from its mainstream development budget. Most recently, the Commission agreed in December 2003 to a new paper on Europe's relations with the Arab world which commits the EU to ploughing increased resources into assisting Middle East political reform.[6]

Although much EU-level activity has been focused on the EMP, a more political dimension was also introduced into engagement with Iran. The offer of a new trade and cooperation agreement was linked to political dialogue in a tighter and higher profile than was originally proposed, and in December 2002, a regular EU–Iran human rights dialogue commenced. Tentative proposals were put forward for initiating an EU political aid profile in Iran; a number of European states—notably, the United Kingdom and Germany—developed judicial reform programs for Iran; and parliamentary exchanges between the European Parliament and the Iranian parliament began.

The focus on Palestinian "institutional reform" intensified after the start of the second Intifada, which was seen as provoked in part by Palestinian Authority corruption. The Palestinian territories have been by far the main destination for European political aid in the Middle East and are the one place where all donors have run comprehensive packages of governance aid. After September 2000, the EU channeled €10 million a month to support the Palestinian Authority's budget; it used these funds to ratchet up conditionality on greater judicial independence, increased financial reporting provisions, a freeze on hiring to the authority, and the transfer of funds to a single account monitored by the International Monetary Fund. Despite fears expressed by some European states that a national vote would be destabilizing, the EU did press for new Palestinian elections and imposed conditions relating to the independence of the National Electoral Commission. Pressure was exerted on Palestinian leader Yasser Arafat to widen the political space available to nongovernmental organizations (NGOs) receiving European funds. New projects were funded that aimed at strengthening an independent media along with human rights training courses for security services under the umbrella of the EU Special Advisor's Office in Ramallah.

The EU pressed for the creation of a formal EU–GCC human rights dialogue, politicizing diplomacy with the Gulf region to an unprecedented degree. Although the approach toward Saudi Arabia has been extremely cautious, some degree of European criticism of human rights abuses has been heard for the first time; and all EU donors now stress in similar terms their desire to identify and support "agents of change" in the kingdom. Several European governments have offered support for the (partly) competitive municipal elections proposed by the ruling family. At the same time, Yemen has become a prominent political aid destination for European donors, with new projects prioritizing judicial reform and parliamentary training. Denmark has initiated a partnering initiative with the Yemeni parliament, the United Kingdom is increasing its governance work in the country fivefold by 2005, and Germany has embarked on a program of democratic awareness-raising with Yemeni civil society.

Remaining something of a case apart, discussion in Turkey has been dominated by debates over the setting of a date for accession negotiations. The compromise eventually reached—to assess Turkey's preparedness in December 2004—has been judged in various ways: as a rein-

forced commitment to supporting Turkish democracy, as a new willingness to circumvent democracy criteria in preference to an alliance-
deepening logic, and as further prevarication using the democracy
requirement to serve a logic of exclusion. Assessing European democracy-promotion policy toward Turkey is subject to the confusing sleights
of multiple diplomatic smoke and mirrors. A whole series of issues—
Cyprus, bilateral Greek–Turkish tensions, the EU's own internal reforms,
the relationship between the European Security and Defense Policy
(ESDP) and the North Atlantic Treaty Organization (NATO)—have
dragged debates over democracy into their orbit. Perhaps less noticed
than this high politics, political aid support on the ground in Turkey has
significantly increased. An additional €250 million package for 2004–
2005 was targeted overwhelmingly toward political and administration
reform, and a revised accession partnership agreed upon in 2003 linked
aid more tightly to a set of detailed stipulations over reform. It is certainly the case that as Prime Minister Recep Tayyip Erdogan's efforts to
deepen democracy fused with the prime minister's lead role in cajoling
army hard-liners into more flexible positions on both ESDP and Cyprus,
direct European self-interest tipped the scales in favor of firmer support
for a deepening of Turkish democracy.

A European Third Way?

Such trends and initiatives suggest heightened concern with Middle East
reform. At the same time, it is significant that Europeans assert a guiding philosophy that they perceive to be qualitatively distinct from that
of the United States—a difference compounded by but extending beyond the ideological tenor of the Bush administration. The European
approach might be likened to a desired "third way" between regime
change and undimmed support for autocrats; one focused on gradual,
step-by-step political reform. This has expressed itself through a number of characteristics.

First, in the general presentation of their aims, European policies have
been couched in discourse very different from that guiding current
U.S. strategy. Europeans have most commonly eschewed a directly instrumental presentation of democracy's virtues, advocating political reform as part of a general process of social and economic modernization.

European states have in this sense gone to great lengths to distance their discourse on "the spread of liberal values" from U.S. language on "regime change." Europeans visibly wince at the directness of some U.S. statements—for example, the suggestion that anti-Americanism can be reduced to autocratic manipulation of popular sentiment and thus spirited away by democratic freedom.[7] Even as they assert their desire to see political opening in the Middle East, European policy makers invariably show greater relish in adumbrating the *dangers* of precipitate political change.

An express desire to avoid the language of "democracy promotion" is often apparent. German aims are defined as "the transformation of particular sectors," rather than democratization. The United Kingdom's new Arab reform strategy targets "the rule of law" rather than democracy. In discussions on the EU's new security strategy, a commanding majority of member states insisted on objectives in the Middle East being defined as an increase in "pluralism," not democracy. One European diplomat responsible for devising his government's new Middle East reform policy suggests that a "neutral cover" has been sought for gaining access to influence the broad direction of political change in the region, admonishing what he judges to be the United States' fixation with the end result of regime change. Another policy maker likens the European approach to reform to "crossing the stream by feeling the stones on the riverbed."

Second, the notion of "partnership" is strikingly prominent in the way that European governments and the Brussels institutions frame their new reform policies. Famed for its proclivity to "positive engagement," the EU is unsurprisingly not converting wholesale to strongly coercive strategy in pursuit of political change. Some more critical pressure has been exerted in relation to specific cases, such as Egypt's restrictive 1999 NGO law or Tunisia's frustration of a number of European aid projects (indeed, relations with Tunisia have become stormy enough for some assistance to be held back). But overt punitive conditionality remains anathema to most European states. Even the northern "like-minded" states judge talk of conditionality as "too pushy." Although Spain has always been one of the states most reluctant to contemplate coercive measures, new Prime Minister Zapatero is committing himself to returning to an even more strongly "traditional" approach of convivial alliance building in the Middle East. Any European-level measure that could be deemed interventionist is studiously avoided. Language in the EU's draft security strategy suggesting that the EU would intervene to "defend democracy" was removed at the behest of member states. Europeans are united in opposing the notion of certain states—Iran, Libya, and Syria—being excluded from the United States' new proposed initiatives in the region. Indeed, European engagement with these states aimed at counterproliferation has—almost openly—been bought at the cost of diminished leverage over political reform.

Few European statements on Arab reform fail to reassure that there will be no question of "imposing change from outside," of "dictating" change, or of "prescribing" any "template" for moving to democracy. Indeed, the common usage of these same stock phrases has been remarkable. European statements nominally concerned with democracy and human rights are in practice most notably replete with references to the "shared historical experiences," the "common cultural heritage," and the "deep sense of partnership" that are said to exist between the EU and the Middle East. Any reference to the EU's suspension clause is invariably accompanied by a reassurance that the latter's purpose is not punitive but "positive." One European government deliberately changed the language in its new Middle East policy initiative from "reform" to "partnership." The severest European complaint of the U.S. Greater Middle East Initiative was that it was drawn up without consultation with either governments or civil society in the Middle East.

In his first speech dedicated specifically to Middle East reform, British Foreign Secretary Jack Straw proposed developing a "network of friendships" around democratic reform, involving both governments and civil society.[8] Indicative of the French approach, Dominique de Villepin proposed a noncoercive, multilateral human rights corps for the Muslim world.[9] One senior French diplomat expressed his government's concern that change had been seen too much in terms of circumventing regimes through the civil society dimension rather than negotiating gradual change from within the elite. In a key statement of French policy aims in February 2004, de Villepin argued that political reform efforts must "start from the needs of Middle Eastern states themselves" and cautioned that "we need to associate [Middle Eastern states] as much as possible in our thinking in a genuine partnership." His suggested strategy was structured around political dialogue, especially with the Arab League; agreement on nonintervention; and a disassociation of democracy from Western self-interest.[10]

In new EU recommendations for national human rights plans and democracy assistance projects, the emphasis is firmly on using the EU's broader partnerships to match such political measures *with* authoritarian regimes. The proposed human rights plans are an offer, not a stipulation; so far, only Morocco and Jordan have shown interest. A key feature of recent European policy is the attempt to harness the United Nations Development Program's two *Arab Human Development Reports* and the Sana'a Declaration as "internal" proreform statements. There is, for instance, talk of supporting an Arab-run fund backing reform projects pursuant to the Sana'a Declaration. The tendency to caution is compounded by the situating of many new reform initiatives within chancelleries' Middle East departments—staffed, of course, by those most sympathetic to the notion of Arab specificities.

A third feature of EU gradualism is seen in the limited amounts of new democracy aid. The surfeit of new action plans, papers, and initiatives is not yet translating itself into significant increases in democracy-promotion support. The beefing-up of democracy aid budgets is slow and pitifully modest in scale. Certainly, democracy aid remains negligible compared with the funding of immigration controls, antiterrorist cooperation, law enforcement measures, and security cooperation with nondemocratic regimes across the Middle East. The speed at which the EU's "justice and home affairs" instruments are expanding throws into even sharper relief the procrastination that sees European governments only now—nearly three years after 9/11—beginning to initiate political aid profiles in the Middle East.

Funding for the Middle East from the European Commission–managed European Initiative for Democracy and Human Rights was actually halved to €7 million between 2001 and 2003—with a modest €4.5 million increase proposed for 2004–2007. In the year after September 11, the EU gave over twenty times more money for the preservation of historical sites in the Middle East than for democracy building. Only Algeria, Tunisia, and the West Bank were included in the commission's new list of recipient countries, with Morocco's exclusion attracting particular attention. Dominant constituencies in the European Commission and the European Parliament have resisted any diversion of funds away from the EU's African (Cotonou Convention) partners into the Middle East.

The Middle East remains underrepresented in most member states' political aid budgets. With its focus on the poorest developing countries, the United Kingdom continues to draw aid away from the MENA region, winding down bilateral programs in Egypt and Jordan. Discordant with post–September 11 rhetoric linking terrorism to Middle Eastern underdevelopment, the United Kingdom's development ministry laments that the region is still "over-aided."[11] The Foreign and Commonwealth Office's (FCO) Human Rights Fund had, by 2003, supported only twenty-three projects in the Middle East, out of a total of several hundred, while the new fund for Arab reform totaled only £4 million by 2004—compared, for example, with the extra £15 million released immediately to counterterrorist agencies after the Madrid bombings. A new "democracy unit" within the FCO's human rights policy department has thus far developed no role in relation to the Middle East reform agenda.

The Dutch have initiated only a handful of modest governance projects in Yemen and Egypt. Norway funds no political aid projects outside the Palestinian territories. Spain has formal bilateral programs incorporating governance elements only in Morocco, Tunisia, and the Palestinian territories. The European donors with the broadest profile in the region are in fact the Swiss Development Agency and the German Stiftungen (party foundations). In 2004, Germany's development ministry allocated a sizable €78 million—about one-tenth of its bilateral aid to MENA—to "democracy and governance" projects in the Middle East and North Africa but recognized that this category contained primarily technical cooperation.

Fourth, European distinctiveness also expresses itself in a preference for indirect forms of reform support. European donors have declined to support the kind of direct democracy propaganda pursued by the United States inter alia through funded radio stations. They have given negligible support to prominent exiles, opposing the notion of "picking winners" among reformers in the Middle East. Overall European aid to the Arab world is well in excess of U.S. assistance; just European Commission aid to the EMP states tops €1 billion a year. But, while the United States explicitly apportions nearly a third of its relatively small Middle East Partnership Initiative (MEPI) budget for democracy assistance, the vast majority of European governments still do not compile single "democracy" aid budgets. The guiding logic is almost one of wanting "to do democracy promotion" without actually saying it is being done—a situation many European officials judge to be the inverse of U.S. intentions.

European funding priorities stress human rights more than democracy. The aim is tangibly to advance particular "islands" of basic human rights far more than broader systemic reform. In 2002, 70 percent of European Initiative for Democracy and Human Rights (EIDHR) spending went to basic human rights categories—the death penalty, torture, minorities and racism, international justice, and impunity—and only 30 percent to democracy and the rule of law.[12] Indeed, the EIDHR is managed by national government representatives on the Human Rights Committee, which fights to retain the primacy of traditional human rights projects over the broader democracy agenda. Democracy assistance in more politicized spheres—elections, parties, parliaments, and civil-military relations—continues to account for a lower share of political aid in the Middle East than elsewhere. Although in other regions donor nations are increasingly seeking to link civil society work to parties and parliaments, this new focus remains largely absent in the Middle East. Nearly all parliamentary work takes the form of training for actual or would-be women parliamentarians. The EU's new guidelines for democracy promotion in the Mediterranean recognize the need for a broader focus, going beyond standard human rights legislation to include work on elections and other more political issues; in practice, little has been done beyond this statement of intent. While the new security dialogue now has a more prominent "security sector reform" brief, policy makers acknowledge that this still appears almost indistinguishable from traditional defense diplomacy and is doing little to check militaries' political power in the Middle East.

European "reform" support is oriented notably toward cultural, education, development, and governance projects. Germany's €100 million Task Force for Dialogue with the Islamic World supports cultural and education projects—exceeding democracy funding several times over. New work in the Middle East from Germany's main political aid budget includes a focus on education that seeks to open up a national-level policy-making process in this sector. Nearly half of French aid to the Middle East similarly goes to education and culture, and Sweden's largest single slice of funding goes to the Swedish cultural institute in Alexandria. Several member states advocate cultural cooperation initiatives—such as the inception of a Euro-Mediterranean Foundation that will support a range of cultural exchanges—as a softer and more palatable alternative to muscular democracy promotion.

The "developmentalist" feel to EU funding is seen in the stress on principles such as communal self-administration and participation. Political aid projects are commonly aimed at enhancing the capacity of the NGO sector to contribute effectively to social development. Some donors, such as Sweden and Italy, work uniquely through NGOs. A particular European focus is the funding of structured dialogues between the state and NGOs on social development. Support for unions in the region targets social rights issues and bargaining techniques rather than political independence. Denmark, for example, supports Danish unions to convene tripartite dialogue in Morocco. Such social dialogue is also a priority of Germany's Stiftungen. Spain classifies its political work as "institutional development, social participation, and good governance"—a category rising to account for 13 percent of Spanish aid generally for 2001–2004.

EU good governance work prioritizes technical and regulatory harmonization with European single-market rules. It is at this level—working on the transparency of procurement procedures, the design of new fiscal systems to replace revenues lost through tariff removal, and microcredit projects aimed at strengthening local-level decision-making capacities—rather than in the headline-grabbing high-politics sphere that European influence is most significant. The central logic of EU policy toward Iran is to try to use negotiations for a trade and cooperation agreement as a stepping-stone to prepare Iran for World Trade Organization (WTO) membership, with all the economic governance reform this would entail. This is similarly now the prominent strand of policy under the EU's new agreement with Saudi Arabia, and initial ideas for aid work in Libya also prioritize economic governance reform as a vehicle for tying the erstwhile "rogue" into the international community. Resources and conditionality in the Palestinian territories primarily target issues such as financial transparency, auditing provisions, pensions restructuring, and the streamlining of public administration.

Aid from the United Kingdom is especially wed to this governance orientation and is most strongly focused on integrating grassroots capacity-building work into support for standard public administration reform programs. In its Arab reform work, the United Kingdom emphasizes support for the chamber of commerce in Saudi Arabia and help for women's involvement in business in Egypt. A stress on local-level cross-ethnic representation in technocratic departments also gives its work in

Iraq a nuanced distinctiveness from U.S. strategy in that country. Germany's most significant new initiative is the creation of two new subregional governance funds for the Maghreb and Mashreq, respectively. Other German projects aim to incorporate governance components into sectoral work on issues such as resource management and the "genderization" of economic policy. European funding in Turkey is allocated mainly for approximation to EU legislative frameworks, as a means of indirectly facilitating change at the political level.

A fifth and crucial element of European caution lies in the paucity of support for moderate Islamist opposition forces. Despite the commitments made by countless ministerial statements and policy documents, in practice little new engagement with Islam has been forthcoming. Donors have proceeded no further than including general discussion on "Islam and democracy" in some civil society forums. A plethora of initiatives aim at "cultural understanding" between Islam and the West, but concrete support is lacking for moderate Islamists to widen political participation within their own societies. The British government in fact stopped talking to a number of the prominent Islamist opposition groups based in London after September 11. Even those states most overtly critical toward incumbent regimes—such as Sweden—eschew support for politically active Islamist groups. The EU's new guidelines on democracy and human rights promotion in the Middle East fail even to mention the Islamist issue. The EU largely avoids working with Islamists even on fairly apolitical issues: for example, declining to work through professional syndicates captured by Islamists. In short, Islamists continue to be the apparent untouchables of the democracy assistance world.

There is much stated official recognition that this is the single most important area in which European approaches must change. One assertion now ritually made by donors themselves is that support must move beyond the traditional range of advocacy and service delivery NGOs that have less local legitimacy than Islamist welfare organizations. And yet, uncertainty continues to paralyze any implementation of such strictures. When delegations in a number of Arab states asked Brussels for a line on whether they should engage with and fund Islamist-oriented social NGOs, no reply was forthcoming. A senior representative of one EU member state admits that the decision of whether to engage with local Islamists has depended almost entirely on the views of the ambassador in the state in question and that the case for a systematic policy on this most crucial of issues "is a battle still to be won" at the ministerial level. Preferences so far remain limited to backing the kind of modest increases in officially sanctioned Islamist representation in still-weak parliaments, rather than seeking any more pervasive support for Islamists as potential agents of genuine democratization. Some observe that the decentralization of many spending decisions to European Commission delegations—relatively small in-country teams bereft of significant political weight—has, in fact, compounded the reluctance to back controversial and openly critical local organizations. European policy makers acknowledge that it is the United States that has gone furthest in trying to identify "moderate" Islamists within local communities—somewhat the reverse of what one might expect from the ritual comparing of European subtleties with American intolerance for local forms.

Self-Definition or Self-Delusion?

In sum, European approaches have exhibited a socioeconomic, techno-governance character, combining relatively innocuous grassroots initiatives with top-down cooperation purporting to "nudge" unthreateningly the outlooks of entrenched elites. It is through a combination of governance initiatives and service delivery NGOs that the EU has sought to walk—what it perceives to be—the thin line left between regimes and radical Islamists. The gradualism of European strategy clearly has much to commend it. It undoubtedly chimes well with the broad consensus that democracy must be generated primarily from within and mesh with concomitant economic and social change.

And yet, a challenge remains for the EU to imbue its policy of democracy promotion with greater tangible thrust without ceding the virtues of locally attuned gradualism. Excelling in holistic conceptual design, European strategies suffer from an unduly tentative and amorphous operationalization of such reasoning in practice. The weaknesses and strengths of European policy are almost inherent in each other. EU policies are imbued with subtlety and balance, but it is of their same essence that a lack of singular clarity and dramatism is born. European democracy policy resembles a man trying to learn to swim without letting go of the riverbank: keen to reach the deep, rewarding waters of political transformation but reluctant to let go of the supportive engagement built up with Middle Eastern regimes.

The sheer extent to which European policy has been defined in contradistinction to U.S. strategy risks clouding judgment. The almost existential venality of such proclaimed "otherness" has diverted attention from more prosaic consideration of what measures might actually have an impact on Middle East political reform. Through its ubiquitous warnings that democracy "cannot be imposed"—especially "from the barrel of a gun"—the EU might have suitably admonished recidivist tendencies in the Bush administration. But these strictures have shed little light on what the EU might indeed consider a more effective approach to Middle East reform.

Notwithstanding genuine aspects of distinctive thinking on political reform, Europe's strategies have, in practice, emerged from strikingly inchoate decision-making processes. Rather than European policy representing a sophisticated and carefully reasoned conceptual approach, arbitrary accidentalism abounds. The urgency injected by the events of September 11 has done little to attenuate the EU's well-known problems of coordination. Within the multilayered European foreign policy machinery, policy is hampered by a labyrinth of poor linkages—between different ministries, between different states, between different institutions within the EU, and between different departments within the same institutions. Much analysis of U.S. policies attests to the same paucity of coordination, but Europe's complexities are many times more bewildering: Germany alone has a dozen, highly dispersed agencies involved in democracy promotion. Coherence is required if Europe's vaunted gradualism is not in practice to equate to little more than ad hoc muddle.

While rightfully aiming to mold the social, economic, and cultural processes that underpin political reform, the EU should not entirely eschew a concern with the tangible institutional attributes of multiparty democracy. Positive changes to underlying process cannot be sustained in institutional thin air; rather, exploration would be apposite of how bottom-up and top-down reform can be mutually reinforcing. European approaches need to redress a general imprecision in how process-oriented initiatives relate to formal institutional reforms. This is requisite to a more comprehensively political approach transcending the scattering of isolated civil society and governance initiatives that has been ineffectual in making any impact on de facto power relations in the Middle East. Such a comprehensive approach would ensure that these individual initiatives serve as building blocks toward identifiable institutional reforms.

This is not to advocate a less process-oriented approach, but rather to suggest that the EU should harness the social and political domains within single cross-cutting projects and initiatives. Concrete purchase is needed, in particular, in effecting a leap from gradual changes in economic governance to the tangible results of political reform. European policy also needs to be less reluctant to respond politically to reform opportunities. The EU's highly formalized and institutionalized partnerships tend to work to their own internal momentum, in a complete vacuum from outside events. Policy aimed at the gradual conveyor belt of underlying change needs to be complemented by more dexterous and nimble political interventions targeting visible change when breakthrough opportunities present themselves. If the EU's rejection of sweeping punitive conditionality has merit, it is difficult to see how its failure to react to democratic backsliding forms part of a "partnership" for reform in places such as Bahrain, Egypt, Jordan, Morocco, and Yemen.

The juncture is clearly one of considerable fluidity. European democracy promotion is now a far more self-reflexive enterprise than ten, even five, years ago. Many of what are now the well-rehearsed pleas for democracy aid to extend itself beyond the narrow circle of "usual suspects" appear fully incorporated into the official mind-set. And yet, it remains to be determined whether will, means, and analytical design combine to generate fundamentally more effective policy. If they do not, Europe's timorous slithering from one riverbed stone to the next is unlikely to take it appreciably closer to the far bank of a politically reformed and stable Middle East.

Notes

This chapter was originally published as Carnegie Paper 45 (June 2004).

1. See chapter 5.

2. Chris Patten, "Special Seminar with NGOs," speech, Brussels, July 14, 2003, available at http://europa.eu.int/comm/external_relations/w29/2.htm.

3. *A Secure Europe in a Better World: European Security Strategy*, adopted by the heads of State and Government at the European Council (Brussels: December 2003), 10, available at http://www.iss-eu.org/solana/solanae.pdf.

4. Joschka Fischer, Speech to the 40th Munich conference on Security Policy, February 7, 2004, available at http://www.security-conference.de.

5. Dominique de Villepin, *Law, Force and Justice*, speech presented at International Institute for Strategic Studies, London, March 27, 2003, available at http://www.ambafrance-us.org/news/statmnts/2003/villepin_iraq032703.asp.

6. Council of the European Union and the European Commission, *Strengthening the EU's Relations with the Arab World* (Brussels: December 2003), available at http://www.medea.be/.les/UE_monde_arabe_12_2003_EN.pdf.

7. Richard N. Haass, "Toward Greater Democracy in the Muslim World," *Washington Quarterly* (Summer 2003): 137–48.

8. Jack Straw, "Launch of the Civility Programme on Middle East Reform," speech presented at the Foreign Policy Centre, London, March 1, 2004, available at http://fpc.org.uk/articles/242.

9. Dominique de Villepin, *Discours au Senat*, June 14, 2003, available at http://www.diplomatie.gouv.fr/atu/article.asp.

10. Interview in *Le Figaro*, February 19, 2004.

11. Department for International Development (DFID), *Regional Action Plan: Middle East and North Africa*, consultation draft (London: June 2003).

12. Seventy percent of 2003 EIDHR funding went to these four human rights categories, leaving only €30 million for "democracy," good governance, and the rule of law. Available at http://europa.eu.int/comm/europeaid/projects/eidhr/projects_2003_en.htm.

Conclusion

13

Getting to the Core

Marina Ottaway and Thomas Carothers

THE JOURNEY TOWARD DEMOCRACY in the Middle East crosses territory that remains largely uncharted. As the chapters in this volume make clear, there are no simple answers to the problem of political transformation in the region. The experience of countries elsewhere in the world that have undergone or attempted democratic transitions in recent years offers valuable lessons but nevertheless only limited indications of what can be expected. The political history and circumstances of the Middle East are distinctive, and the evolution of Arab political systems will inevitably follow its own path.

To have a chance of success, democracy-promotion efforts in the Middle East will require new approaches carefully tailored to the regional circumstances, as well as a willingness to go beyond low-risk indirect approaches to take on the harder, more central challenges of expanding the depth and breadth of political contestation and encouraging real redistributions of power. Duplication of the kinds of democracy-promotion programs carried out in countries where authoritarian regimes had already fallen and the population looked to the West as a political model simply will not be enough. Strategies will need to take into account the complexity of relations between the Arab world and the West, as well as the special problems that make political change in the Middle East unusually difficult, particularly the possibility that the outcome could be considerably worse than the status quo. Without a realistic appreciation of and response to these factors, it is unlikely that the new rhetoric about promoting democracy in the Middle East will bear fruit.

Dealing with Credibility and Conflicting Interests

In attempting to promote democracy in the Middle East, the United States faces a situation in which its role as a prodemocratic actor is highly contested but at the same time clearly central. The political roles of European countries are much less controversial, but their actions, though potentially valuable, do not have the same weight and influence. In the Middle East, the United States is indeed the indispensable country, but it is also the target of much hatred.

As Marina Ottaway points out in chapter nine on the problem of credibility, the United States has no credibility in the Arab world as a prodemocratic actor. The likelihood that it will gain such credibility anytime soon is remote. Arab publics, as innumerable surveys make clear, simply do not believe the U.S. government is sincere when it talks about promoting democracy. Arab governments, while deeply annoyed at the criticism Washington metes out to them with increasing frequency, are not really convinced that in the end those rebukes will have real consequences. They do not believe that Washington will take steps that might destabilize long-standing allies and run the risk of making the Middle East an even more dangerous place than it already is.

A major reason for the skepticism about U.S. intentions by Arab publics is that the United States started pushing the democracy agenda at the same time as it started preparing for the war in Iraq. One of the main arguments used by the George W. Bush administration to convince Americans to support the war in Iraq—that the war would open the way for a democratic regime in Baghdad and that the change would have a demonstration effect on the rest of the region—has been given a sinister interpretation in the Arab world. When the United States talks of promoting democracy, many Arabs have concluded, it is really talking about forcefully removing regimes it does not like and replacing them with ones willing to safeguard U.S. interests. Democracy promotion is perceived as a dark, self-interested conspiracy rather than a generous attempt to improve the lives of Arabs and make the region a better, less dangerous place. Some Arabs do not even believe that the United States is interested in reform, except in the case of anti-American regimes, where it wants their elimination. Despite the new rhetoric, they are convinced, the United States remains quite willing to accept autocratic regimes when it suits its interests. Democracy promotion, in other words, is for many in the region either a dark conspiracy or meaningless rhetoric.

It is nearly impossible for the United States to overcome this distrust in the short run. After all, it is a fact that the United States became concerned about democracy in the Middle East after September 11, at the same time as it started planning war in Afghanistan and Iraq. And it is a fact that members of the Bush administration hinted both during and after the Iraq war that Iraq might not be the only regime they would like to see removed—for example, Syria appeared to be another target. Most important, there is no doubt that U.S. interests in the Middle East are complex and contradictory, of which democracy promotion is only one, and in the day-to-day decision-making process, not the most important.

The contrast with the U.S. Cold War posture toward the Soviet Union and its Eastern European allies is instructive. In that case, U.S. political, economic, and security interests dovetailed tightly. The existing regimes did absolutely nothing for the United States except provide a major security problem and competition for the allegiance of countries around the world. There was little apparent downside for the United States to push for their disappearance. The United States could support reformers and democracy with no significant interference from countervailing economic or security interests. This is not true in the Middle East at present. The autocratic regimes do not threaten U.S. interests directly, and many of them in fact serve significant U.S. security and economic interests quite well. The Saudi regime, for example, continues to keep the oil supplies flowing and to increase them when necessary to stabilize the market. U.S. security agencies count on cooperation from the repressive security forces of a number of Arab countries for vital help in tracking down terrorists.

Not only are U.S. interests in the region mixed and often mutually contradictory, but the underlying logic of the new democracy imperative is not persuasive to many Arab observers. Authoritarian regimes in the Middle East, the current U.S. argument goes, are a threat to the United States because their disastrous economic policies and repressive politics impoverish and frustrate their populations, and this in turn creates fertile ground for the growth of terrorists. In addition, the Wahhabis, who are spreading their intolerant ideology with Saudi support or at least willingness to look the other way, provide an ideological justification for the violence bred by poverty and political repression. But the link between poverty and political repression on the one hand and terrorism on the other is open to question. The very poor are not usually the organizers of terrorist groups, as an analysis of the persons responsible for the September 11 attacks makes evident. And terrorist movements can grow in democratic countries as well—see the Irish Republican Army, the ETA in Spain, the Italian Red Brigades, and the German Baader-Meinhof gang. Most important, it is far from clear whether the present autocratic regimes, if they were to suddenly open up to deep-reaching political change, would be replaced by governments inclined to be friendly or helpful to the United States. U.S. security and democracy interests, in other words, do not neatly coincide in the Arab world at least in the short run— and it is the short run that drives most policy making.

Another major issue that makes it difficult for the United States to be accepted in Arab eyes as a defender of the interests of Arab populations against their autocratic leaders is U.S. policy toward Israel and the Palestinians. This is an issue on which U.S. and Arab views diverge radically, and will continue to do so, even if successful steps are taken toward a solution to the Israeli–Palestinian conflict. From the Arab point of view, the creation of the state of Israel was a manifestation of imperialism and an act of aggression against them; and although most Arabs have come to accept that the situation is irreversible, the sense of injury persists. To the United States, the creation of the state of Israel was an act of justice, and support for Israel has deep roots in U.S. society.

In addition, there is the problem of Israel's occupation of the West Bank and Gaza. That situation is not irreversible—most of the territory may well end up being returned to Palestinians, although the longer negotiations stall, the more likely it becomes that new land will be permanently annexed by Israel. Certainly, a resumption of negotiations on the issue is crucial to ease the tension between the Arab world and the United States. The problem, however, is that at present Arabs do not believe the United States acts as an honest broker. A positive settlement of the Palestinian–Israeli conflict—even something along the lines of the Taba settlement—would certainly reduce tensions between the Arab world and the United States but would probably not eliminate Arabs' strongly held belief that the United States cares much more about Israel than about them.

Neither the problem of credibility nor the related issue of conflicting interests will go away anytime soon. No matter which party is in the

White House, the United States and the Arab world will see the Palestinian–Israeli conflict through different lenses, the United States will remain dependent on Middle East oil, and Washington will look to the security services of many of the autocratic governments of the region for help on counterterrorism operations. These realities do not mean that the United States has no role to play in promoting democracy in the Middle East, but they must be factored into the new wave of U.S. policies and programs focused on supporting positive political change.

This means, for example, that the U.S. government must be willing to allow U.S. democracy-promotion organizations that it funds to have some real operational independence from the U.S. government, both in terms of the counterparts with which they choose to work and the methods they use. It means that U.S. democracy promoters will have to assume that many Arabs will be leery of working directly with U.S. democracy programs and that special efforts will have to be made to win their trust. In this regard, the situation is very much the opposite of postcommunist Eastern Europe. And more broadly it means that U.S. policy makers will have to show that they are capable of keeping their eye on the long-term imperative of democracy promotion and resist trading it off reflexively in the face of the many short-term pressures that will come along to delay or prevent a real effort to support real change.

European countries have been emphasizing the need for political reform and democracy in the Middle East for much longer than the United States, as Richard Youngs analyzes in his chapter. They will undoubtedly continue to do so, through the Barcelona Process and possibly in collaboration with the United States as part of the Broader Middle East and North Africa Initiative approved by the G-8 at their meeting in June 2004. European countries are not as controversial as the United States when they talk about democracy in the Middle East because they carry less baggage in Arab eyes. They have not launched the war in Iraq, and some have refused to support it. They are perceived as more even-handed in their dealing with the Arab–Israeli conflict and more willing to see Palestinians as victims of injustice rather than simply as perpetrators of terrorism. And they have been more soft-spoken in their dealing with Arab countries, thus a bit more credible than the United States when they talk about partnership. At the same time, however, the role of Europe is seen as secondary. Europe is not doing any harm to the Arab world, but it cannot be a central player in the way that the United States can.

Dealing with Arab Reality

In addition to dealing with their own problems of credibility, relevance, and conflicting interests, the United States and other countries concerned about democracy in the Middle East need to tailor their approaches more closely to the reality of the political situations prevailing in the region. In theory, Western policy makers and aid practitioners claim this is what they are doing. In practice, there is little clear evidence suggesting they are making serious efforts to identify the approach best suited to individual countries. Instead, many of them appear to rely on broad, often superficial assumptions. Among the most cherished is the idea that indirect approaches, such as supporting economic reform, civil society, and women's rights, are effective tools to facilitate democratization.

Indirect approaches to democracy promotion appeal as being relatively safe politically, attractive to domestic constituencies in donor countries, and not likely to provoke an immediate negative reaction by even autocratic host country governments, which strong pressure to reform institutions or allow real checks and balances would. Unfortunately, indirect approaches have so far produced few results in terms of stimulating real democratic change and will probably not be more successful in the future.

Various chapters in this volume examine strategies that have been central to U.S. and European efforts to promote democracy abroad in other regions, but that appear likely to have limited impact in the Arab world. Amy Hawthorne discusses the building of civil society and concludes that Western countries expect too much from it. Eva Bellin explores the complex ties between economic and political reform and cautions that economic reform is not a direct avenue to democratic transitions. Marina Ottaway's chapter on women's rights and democracy warns that although the improvement of women's rights is a worthwhile goal in and of itself, it bears little relationship to democracy promotion. A common and ultimately self-defeating tendency in all these strategies is the democracy promoter's preference for relying on individuals who profess their belief in democracy, rather than on organizations capable of building large-scale political constituencies. Constituencies are the missing element in political transitions in the Middle East.

Support for civil society organizations has been an important part of U.S. democracy promotion everywhere, an approach of choice in favorable situations and a solution of last resort when nothing else seems possible. It was a solution of choice in the early days of democracy promotion, particularly in Eastern European countries in the late 1980s and early 1990s. In the permissive environment created by the disappearance of authoritarian regimes, and with populations lacking recent experience with democracy, encouraging civic activism appeared to be a sensible approach. In less permissive environments, with authoritarian governments still firmly in place and often barricaded behind a strong security apparatus, support for civil society appeared to be a way of at least keeping hope alive when all other avenues for democracy promotion were closed. In retrospect, the impact of civil society assistance has been limited even in permissive environments, creating a plethora of small organizations but not necessarily having much impact on government policy or even extending political participation much beyond a small cadre of activists. In the difficult environment of Arab countries, civil society organizations of the type Western donors fund have been especially ineffective and politically isolated, unable to establish a strong presence in a field where government-affiliated organizations, Islamic charities, and politicized Islamist groups dominate. Women's groups have scored some successes in altering legislation, but the most influential of these groups are those sponsored by host governments, often under the protection of the president's wife or women in the royal family.

Arab governments, furthermore, are learning quickly to play the civil society game. They are setting up their own government-funded and thus government-controlled human rights organizations, and allowing, even encouraging, prodemocracy nongovernmental organizations (NGOs) and think tanks to organize domestic and international meetings of intellectuals and to issue statements, thereby helping give a democratic aura to the host government. What is missing, and what governments intend to prevent, are civil society organizations with large memberships. Discussions among individuals are fine, but discussions that involve membership-based organizations become threatening. The much-publicized meeting of civil society activists at the Alexandria Library in Egypt in early 2004 was, by design, a gathering of individuals, not of representatives of organizations.

Like Arab governments talking of reform, foreign democracy promoters want change, but without conflict and without changing the distribution of power sufficiently to threaten the incumbent governments and raise the threat of instability. Democratization from the top is the ideal embraced by Arab governments, a surprising number of Arab intellectuals, and many foreign supporters of democratic change. This approach might work in countries where governments are strongly motivated to introduce change either by popular pressure or by a strong ideological commitment to change. But both of these elements are limited at best in the Arab world. Governments remain strong and are certainly not inclined to share power.

To the extent Arab governments are and feel challenged, it is not by democratic organizations, but by Islamist ones, which have a much broader popular base of support than the secular, elite organizations supported by the United States or Europe. There is a striking contrast in the Arab world today between the broad-based Islamist groups well integrated in their social milieu and the narrowly based organizations foreigners think of as civil society. The weakness of the democratic constituencies, the strength of the Islamist groups, and the continued reluctance of incumbent governments to take more than cautious steps toward reform constitute a formidable challenge to democracy for which the soft, indirect strategies are no match.

Getting to the Core

Significant progress toward democracy in the Middle East will only be achieved if the core features of democracy—giving citizens the ability to choose those who hold the main levers of political power and creating genuine checks and balances through which state institutions share power—are addressed. Unless these elements are achieved, Arab countries can undergo political reform, even significant changes that will make a difference in the lives of their citizens, without making progress toward democracy. As Daniel Brumberg makes clear in his chapter, many Middle East regimes are willing to become more liberal, as long as they can do so without seeing their power seriously challenged. Thus, they allow multiparty elections, a degree of freedom of the press, some limited political space for civil society organizations and political parties, but maintain reserved powers outside the domain of open competition and stunt the development of institutional checks and balances. They become liberalized autocracies rather than democratizing countries. And the difference between even the most liberal of liberalized autocracies and a democratic regime is a qualitative rather than a quantitative one: A little more press freedom or greater space for prodemocracy NGOs will not turn Morocco into a constitutional monarchy, as long as the king is seen as the Commander of the Faithful, with power above that of all institutions because it comes from divine rather than human sources.

The transition from liberalized autocracies to democratizing regimes would require incumbent governments to cede real power both to citizens and to state institutions, such as judiciaries and legislatures, that can challenge their power. In theory, this could happen either because incumbent regimes decide to surrender power voluntarily—historically a rare occurrence—or because of the emergence of large, well-organized constituencies for democratic change capable of challenging those regimes successfully. In practice, this means either the growth of large social movements or of strong, well-organized political parties. These are the organizations that could bring about a redistribution of power, rather than simply a liberalization of existing regimes.

The idea of democracy has not always proven a good rallying point for the development of broad-based social movements and political parties. Marina Ottaway argues in her chapter on constituencies for democracy in the Arab world that abstract and process-oriented democratic ideals have not usually competed successfully with ideologies with an immediate popular appeal, such as nationalism, socialism, or religious ideals. However, democratic breakthrough can take place when parties or movements with a large constituency also accept democracy as a means of gaining access to power. The acceptance of democratic means by socialist parties, initially for purely instrumental reasons rather than out of conviction, was crucial to the democratization of some European countries. So was the rise of Christian Democratic parties in some Catholic countries. Nationalism also helped build constituencies for democracy at times. In the Arab world, the first, albeit very imperfect, steps toward democracy took place in Egypt, when the Wafd party in the 1930s and 1940s combined nationalism and democratic ideals in a successful challenge to the monarchy.

Today in the Middle East, the political organizations and movements with the largest popular constituencies are Islamist. Although many of these organizations, including the extremely influential Muslim Brotherhood, remain very hesitant to embrace democracy, Islamist groups will be crucial to democratic transitions in the Arab world, in view of the present weakness of secular parties of all ideological persuasions and the important following the Islamists have. Unless such broad-based groups buy into the process, democratization will not take place. Unfortunately, at present, as Graham Fuller argues in his chapter, the evolution of Islamist groups toward acceptance of democracy is impeded by their sense of being under siege from the West—and from the United States in particular.

For countries that are seeking to promote democracy in the Middle East, the absence of the kind of broad-based constituencies needed to force autocratic governments to accept curbs on their own power creates serious difficulties. Such constituencies will have to be developed. They cannot be developed by the elite, technocratic civil society organizations with which Western countries can work comfortably. As a result, Western countries face the challenge of learning to deal with the organizations that have sizable constituencies, even if they are suspicious of the West and at best ambivalent about democracy. Attempting to understand such groups better, let alone trying to work with them, immediately pulls the United States and even European countries outside their comfort zone; but it has to be done.

As a complement to the building of constituency-based organizations, the development of institutions and processes that allow and channel political competition is also crucial for the democratic transformation of the Middle East. As Thomas Carothers elaborates in his chapter on democracy-promotion strategies, the broadening of the areas of political contestation is crucial to the transformation of the region. With the exception of Saudi Arabia and the United Arab Emirates, all countries in the Middle East now formally allow some form of elections and have thus introduced some political competition in their political system. However, competition is limited and manipulated to the point of irrelevance in most countries. The head of government is typically protected from competition, either because he is a king, or because, as in Egypt, the president is elected by a tame parliament and approved by popular referendum, without competition. Where multiparty elections for the national leader do take place, as in Algeria, they are carefully bounded or manipulated. Parliamentary elections are also a model of noncompetition in many countries, with a large enough portion of the parliament appointed by the executive to ensure that even a wide margin election victory by the opposition in the contestation for the elected seats will not give it control over the parliament and allow it to challenge the executive.

Reform of the institutions that permit competition is a complement to the development of organizations with broad-based constituencies. Neither is going to be effective without the other. Organizations that can command a popular following will never accept democracy if they do not see it as a means to bring about change, that is to say, if the country does not have genuine processes and institutions allowing open, fair political contestation. There is no good reason why an organization should abandon violent means in order to participate in an election that is meaningless by definition. Conversely, even the best-designed election laws and parliamentary reform would achieve little in the absence of political parties capable of building, and more importantly of sustaining, constituencies that want more than the overthrow of the incumbent regime and will not disintegrate right after the elections.

For democracy to become a reality in the region, major progress—well beyond limited liberalization—has to be made in opening up and improving core processes of political contestation. Three areas of possible change are critical. First, the range of permitted political parties should be broadened in many Arab societies and reforms of political party laws should be encouraged that would facilitate the strengthening of those parties that do exist. Although external aid for parties is no panacea in the effort to strengthen weak parties, it can be helpful. It is noticeable that the extensive world of Western political party aid that is so ubiquitous in Eastern Europe, Latin America, and other regions is only lightly present in the Middle East. Second, what elections are held should be made more free and fair, which requires much greater respect for political and civil rights. The establishment of strong, independent electoral commissions can also help improve elections. So too can allowing independent election monitoring, both by international election observers and nongovernmental domestic monitoring groups. The Arab world is one of the few parts of the world left where international and domestic election monitoring is not accepted as routine. Third, those institutions that are directly elected, such as legislatures and local governments, should be given more power. And the reserved political power kept out of reach of any direct public accountability and public choice should be progressively reduced. The redistribution of basic political powers will require constitutional reforms, and the whole subject of constitutional reform deserves much greater attention than it is currently receiving.

All of these types of change are exceedingly difficult to achieve because they go to the heart of the power structures currently in place. Nevertheless, experience in other regions shows that progress is possible. These are areas in which the democracy-promotion community has extensive useful experience and much to contribute if it receives the necessary support. Unfortunately, Western democracy promoters, particularly in the United States, often feel under great pressure to demonstrate that they are accomplishing rapid results. Consequently, they feel driven to focus on what are often superficial manifestations of political change, such as whether a country holds elections, rather than the actual degree of political competition that the elections truly entail. For example, the decision by several of the small Gulf countries to hold elections has been hailed as a real breakthrough by the United States, although closer analysis suggests that these countries are becoming adept at playing the game perfected by liberalized autocracies and semiauthoritarian regimes: They are learning to open political space without allowing challenges to the status quo and to hold elections the opposition cannot possibly win.

Obviously it is very difficult for external actors to encourage recalcitrant, entrenched governments to open up their political systems to real competition. As Michele Dunne elucidates in her chapter, attempting to do so seriously requires an artful combination of sustained, nuanced diplomatic pressure and strategically designed aid interventions that take advantage of existing small openings and that help create inducements for new ones. As she shows, successful prodemocratic jawboning by the United States or other external actors is not a simple thing. And finding a way to give democracy aid providers enough independence to operate with some flexibility in a politically hypersensitive region, while still benefiting from the backing that diplomatic pressure can provide at key junctures, requires a balancing act that will tax even the most determined and skillful government. Moreover, trying to push a friendly authoritarian regime to allow true competition could lead to the political demise not only of specific leaders, but also of the underlying political system. For each Czech Republic that has moved almost seamlessly to democracy with nothing worse happening than an amicable divorce from

Slovakia, there are many messy, dangerous situations that developed during the 1990s as autocratic regimes fell. As a result, Western governments inevitably feel the temptation not to push for real democratization, or even not necessarily very hard for limited liberalization. Yet real options for getting to the core exist, if the United States and Europe are willing to take some chances and apply themselves seriously to a challenge that they themselves have identified as central to their own security.

Partnership through Differentiation

In most countries around the world where the established democracies are engaged in promoting democracy, the efforts of European and U.S. democracy-promotion actors are very similar on the ground, even though the different intervening countries claim to have a distinctive approach. While each democracy-promoting country tends to favor some types of programs over others, and has, in a manner of speaking, its own foibles and preferences, the differences tend to be fairly minor. Typically, almost all of the Western democracy aid in any particular country reaches a common set of state institutions and civil society organizations, with many of these institutions and organizations receiving support from multiple Western sources. Donor coordination, always invoked and rarely fully achieved, is important in democracy promotion precisely because there is so much similarity, and thus overlap and duplication, in assistance programs.

In the Middle East, particularly at present, the roles of the United States and European countries are not as interchangeable. As noted earlier, the United States and Europe relate to the countries of the Middle East in different ways and are seen by them in a different light. The United States is distrusted, hated, but also seen as the country that holds the key to a solution of the Palestinian–Israeli conflict. European countries are seen as more sympathetic to the Arab view of the Palestinian issue, more willing to engage over the long run, but also as less influential. The United States is inclined to resounding rhetoric, fond of splashy initiatives, but also quick to change course. European countries are more willing to engage over the long run and to toil quietly out of the limelight, but also timid when it comes to pushing Arab governments to reform.

These differences, and the Arabs' contrasting perceptions of the United States and European countries, could turn into an asset if Western democracy promoters accept the idea of allowing the two sides to play to their own strengths. First, however, both sides would need to admit that the differences are real, that they are deep rooted and not just the result of a temporary spat over the war in Iraq, and that they do affect what different countries can and cannot do in terms of democracy promotion. Joint U.S.–EU initiatives in the Middle East do not play to strength of either side but are based on a least-common-denominator approach that, in view of the differences, tends to be feeble. The example of the Broader Middle East and North Africa Initiative launched by the G-8 in June 2004 at the insistence of the Bush administration is a good example of such a flawed approach. Reluctantly accepted by European countries after the United States agreed to dilute the initial concept, it is an unfunded initiative that will likely end up doing little to strengthen the separate efforts of the various formal partners to the agreement.

The strength of the United States is its power and its willingness to use the bully pulpit to castigate Arab regimes and denounce their weaknesses, to talk openly of reform, and, ultimately, to use force when necessary. Whether the United States is likely to use force in other Middle Eastern countries in the foreseeable future—in light of the difficulties encountered in Iraq and the strains on the U.S. military—is certainly open to question. Nevertheless, the perception still exists in the Arab world that it is only a matter of time before the United States overthrows another regime. "Who is next?" is a question asked in Arab countries with disturbing frequency.

This U.S. willingness to speak up and threaten, like it or not, has forced Arab countries to respond. Internal pressure, coupled with the realization by many regimes that the status quo cannot last indefinitely, has led to a flurry of reforms, ranging from the modest to the purely cosmetic, as Amy Hawthorne's chapter on the new reform ferment shows. This is certainly more in terms of political reform than European countries have been able to achieve in ten years through the Euro-Mediterranean initiative.

But there are downsides to this position of strength. First, when the United States implicitly or explicitly relies on the threat of military force to back up its calls for political reform, it becomes very hard or even impossible for Arab reformers to associate themselves in any way with the U.S. agenda. The United States thus ends up losing the chance of close partnership with the people and organizations with which it might most likely be drawn to cooperate. Second, resounding rhetoric and high-profile initiatives cannot be sustained indefinitely. The United States needs to show quickly that pressure produces results. As a consequence, the United States has proven dispiritingly willing to accept timid or even just pro forma cosmetic reforms as genuine steps toward democratization. When Bahrain becomes a poster child of reform, and even Saudi Arabia gets high marks for talking about the possibility of some sort of local election in the indefinite future, it is difficult for Arab countries not to conclude that the United States will be satisfied with little.

Moreover, leaving aside threats of force, even the use of the bully pulpit for only peaceful calls for reform makes it difficult for the United States to truly engage in a dialogue with Arab countries and understand the complexities of the reform process. The bully pulpit lends itself to proclamations about good and evil, right and wrong, not to elaborating on the enormous complexity and the many gray areas of the political reform process. If you add to the mixture the discontinuities in U.S. policy resulting from the four-year election cycle and the partisan politicization of foreign policy, the United States has a hard time engaging consistently over the long term on these issues.

European countries can. They have done so for ten years, and undoubtedly they will continue to do so. The continuity of the European policy is ensured by the fact that engagement, particularly with its Mediterranean rim, is not a matter of choice but of necessity for Europe. The repercussions of the political and economic problems of the Middle East are felt directly by European countries—they are taking place in the immediate neighborhood. There is no military barrier that can make a difference under these conditions. But while European countries have been patiently engaging in unending economic dialogue and cultural exchanges, they have tiptoed cautiously around the crucial political issues. By forcing the issue of political reform into the public debate, the United States may have opened the door to a more effective European policy. It remains to be seen whether European countries will walk through that door.

We are not proposing here that Europe should play good cop to the American bad cop in a carefully orchestrated game where both cooperate to achieve the same results. Europe and the United States do not need to agree on what they ultimately want in the region in order to play to their own strengths but also to take advantage of what the other side does. Europe and the United States are unlikely to truly agree on many crucial issues concerning the Middle East, from the solution of the Palestinian–Israeli conflict to the kind of regimes they would like to see emerge in the Arab world—democratic, to be sure, but what else? Yet the policies Europe and the United States pursue, even if pursued somewhat independently of each other, can have a complementary effect if each side plays to its strengths and recognizes the value of the other doing so.

Calibrating Expectations

No matter how carefully the United States and European countries take into account the special characteristics and conditions of the Arab world, the strengths on which each can draw, and the weaknesses that make it difficult for them to be effective in all areas, a final question remains: What is reasonable to expect from Western efforts to promote democracy in the Middle East?

The answers given to this question have been quite contradictory since policy makers have started focusing on Middle East reform after September 11. At one extreme have been the voices predicting that the war in Iraq would unleash a tsunami of democracy in the Middle East. Underlying this assumption, in addition to clear political motivations, is an image of the Arab world similar to Eastern Europe in the late 1980s, an edifice ready to collapse under its own weight, and needing only a shove to come tumbling down. This euphoric view of reform in the Middle East has been undermined by the difficulties of the war in Iraq and has been replaced widely by a more sober assessment that change will be slow—"a generational task" has become the expression of choice. In some quarters, the old skepticism that the Arab world is really not fit for democracy is resurfacing. Although this is not an idea likely to ever be expressed openly by the U.S. or European governments, it may be manifested in the form of tacit acceptance of friendly autocrats, particularly those that add a liberal veneer to cover the lack of democracy or make helpful gestures on the Palestinian–Israeli conflict.

The expectation that democracy could sweep through the Arab world quickly, even if Iraq turns out well in the end and Western governments fully take up the challenge of promoting democracy in the region, is not supported by anything we know about democratic transitions and the impact of democracy assistance. Even in the former socialist world, where indeed many regimes collapsed suddenly and dramatically, the building of democracy has been a slow, uneven process, with no assurance of success. The troubling political situation in most parts of the former Soviet Union highlights this fact. At the other extreme, the contention that the Arab world is culturally incapable of becoming democratic is belied by the intensity of the discussions about democracy that are taking place in the region, even inside Islamist movements. Debate does not amount to change, but the idea that democracy is too far outside the reaches of Arab culture and society to ever take hold is certainly contradicted by this debate.

It appears therefore that Western officials, aid practitioners, and others committed to supporting democratic change in the Middle East should be prepared for a long, uncertain journey. It is certainly possible that democratic change will spread in the region over the next ten or twenty years. At the same time, however, there is no guarantee that it will happen. Democracy promotion is never easy, but it is especially hard in the Middle East due to a knotty combination of factors, including the deeply entrenched nature of the nondemocratic regimes of the region, the legacy of Western support for these regimes and the continued conflicting mix of Western interests, and a host of special issues such as the existence of political Islam, the difficulties of Arab–Israeli relations, and the presence of a significant share of the world's oil. In this daunting context, outside actors will in most instances not be the primary determinants of change. But they can make positive contributions. And they will do so above all if they translate their newly discovered policy imperative, the urgency of which tempts dramatic and hurried actions, into a sophisticated blend of sustained and subtle measures that reflect the realities of the problems and challenges on the ground rather than the fears and hopes that drive the West to engage.

Bibliography

Democracy and Democracy Promotion in the Middle East

Democracy in the Middle East

Abootalebj, Ali R. "Civil Society, Democracy and the Middle East," *Middle East Review of International Affairs*, vol. 2, no. 3 (September 1998).

Adabi, Jacob. "Middle East and North Africa: Governance, Democratization, and Human Rights," *Journal of Third World Studies*, vol. 17, no. 2 (Fall 2000): 290–93.

Afshar, Haleh. "Competing Interests: Democracy, Islamification and Women Politicians in Iran," *Parliamentary Affairs*, vol. 55, no. 1 (2002): 109–19.

Al Najjar, Ghanim. "The Challenges Facing Kuwaiti Democracy," *Middle East Journal*, vol. 54, no. 2 (Spring 2000): 242–58.

Al-Obaidi, Jabbar. "Communication and the Culture of Democracy: Global Media and Promotion of Democracy in the Middle East," *International Journal of Instructional Media*, vol. 30, no. 1 (2003): 97–111.

Alterman, Jon B. "Egypt: Stable, but for How Long?" *Washington Quarterly*, vol. 23, no. 4 (Autumn 2000): 107–18.

Amuzegar, Jahangir. "Iran's 'Virtual Democracy' at a Turning Point," *SAIS Review*, vol. 20, no. 2 (2000): 93–109.

Anderson, Lisa. "Arab Democracy: Dismal Prospects," *World Policy Journal*, vol. 18, no. 3 (Fall 2001): 53–60.

Ansari, Ali M. "Continuous Regime Change from Within," *Washington Quarterly*, vol. 26, no. 4 (Autumn 2003): 53–67.

_____. *Iran, Islam and Democracy: The Politics of Managing Change*. London: Royal Institute of International Affairs, Middle East Programme, 2000.

Ashraf, Ahmad, et al. "Challenges to Democracy in the Middle East," *Peace Research Abstracts*, vol. 37, no. 5 (2000).

Baker, Raymond. *Islam without Fear: Egypt and the New Islamists*. Cambridge, Mass.: Harvard University Press, 2003.

Baroudi, Sami. "The 2002 Arab Human Development Report: Implications for Democracy," *Middle East Policy*, vol. 11 (Spring 2004): 132–41.

Bellin, Eva. *Stalled Democracy: Capital, Labor, and the Paradox of State-Sponsored Development*. Ithaca, N.Y.: Cornell University Press, 2003.

Berman, Sheri. "Islamism, Revolution, and Civil Society," *PS: Political Science & Politics*, vol. 1, no. 2 (June 2003): 257–72.

Bill, James A. "Political Liberalization and Democratization in the Arab World: Comparative Experiences," *American Political Science Review*, vol. 93, no. 2 (June 1999): 467–69.

Bisharat, George. "Peace and the Political Imperative of Legal Reform in Palestine," *Peace Research Abstracts*, vol. 39, no. 1 (2002): 3–152.

Boroumand, Ladan, and Roya Boroumand. "Terror, Islam and Democracy," *Journal of Democracy*, vol. 13, no. 2 (2002): 5–20.

Browers, Michaelle. "The Civil Society Debate and New Trends on the Arab Left," *Theory & Event*, vol. 7, no. 2 (2004).

Brown, Nathan. *Palestinian Politics after the Oslo Accords: Resuming Arab Palestine*. Berkeley: University of California Press, 2003.

_____. *The Palestinian Reform Agenda*. Washington, D.C.: U.S. Institute of Peace, 2002.

Brumberg, Daniel. "Democratization in the Arab World? The Trap of Liberalized Autocracy," *Journal of Democracy*, vol. 13, no. 4 (October 2002): 56–68.

Byman, Daniel L., and Jerrold D. Green. "The Enigma of Political Stability in the Persian Gulf Monarchies," *Middle East Review of International Affairs*, vol. 3, no. 3 (September 1999).

Carothers, Thomas. "Democracy: Terrorism's Uncertain Antidote," *Current History*, vol. 102, no. 668 (December 2003): 403–06.

Carothers, Thomas, Marina Ottaway, Daniel Brumberg, and Amy Hawthorne. "Democratic Mirage in the Middle East," Policy Brief no. 20. Washington, D.C.: Carnegie Endowment for International Peace, October 2002.

Chaquèri, Cosroe. *Origins of Social Democracy in Modern Iran.* Seattle: University of Washington Press, 2001.

Clark, Janine A. *Islam, Charity, and Activism: Middle Class Networks and Social Welfare in Egypt, Jordan, and Yemen.* Bloomington: Indiana University Press, 2004.

Clark, Janine Astrid, and Jillian Schwedler. "Who Opened the Window? Women's Activism in Islamist Parties," *Comparative Politics,* vol. 35, no. 3 (April 2003): 293–312.

Comparative Politics. Special Edition, "Enduring Authoritarianism: Lessons for the Middle East for Comparative Theory." (January 2004).

Dekmejian, Richard. "The Liberal Impulse in Saudi Arabia," *Middle East Journal,* vol. 57, no. 3 (Summer 2003): 400–13.

Denoeux, Guillan. "The Politics of Morocco's 'Fight against Corruption,'" *Middle East Policy,* vol. 7, no. 2 (February 2000): 165–89.

Diamond, Larry Jay, Marc F. Plattner, and Daniel Brumberg, eds. *Islam and Democracy in the Middle East.* Baltimore, Md.: Johns Hopkins University Press, 2003.

Doran, Michael Scott. "The Saudi Paradox," *Foreign Affairs,* vol. 83, no. 1 (January/February 2004): 35–51.

Dunne, Michele Durocher. *Democracy in Contemporary Egyptian Political Discourse.* Amsterdam: John Benjamins Publishing Co., 2003.

Ehteshami, Anoushiravan. "Is the Middle East Democratizing?" *British Journal of Middle Eastern Studies,* vol. 26, no. 2 (November 1999): 199–217.

Eickelman, Dale F. "The Coming Transformation of the Muslim World," *Middle East Review of International Affairs,* vol. 3, no. 3 (September 1999).

Enhaili, Aziz, and Oumelkheir Adda. "State and Islamism in the Maghreb," *Middle East Review of International Affairs,* vol. 7, no. 1 (March 2003): 66–76.

Esposito, John, and John O. Voll. *Islam and Democracy.* Oxford: Oxford University Press, 1997.

Fairbanks, Stephen C. "Theocracy versus Democracy: Iran Considers Political Parties," *Peace Research Abstracts,* vol. 38, no. 2 (2001).

Finlay-Ansary, Abdou. "Muslims and Democracy," *Journal of Democracy,* vol. 10, no. 3 (July 1999): 18–32.

Fish, Steven M. "Islam and Authoritarianism," *World Politics,* vol. 55, no. 1 (October 2002): 4–37.

Fuller, Graham. *The Future of Political Islam.* New York: Palgrave Macmillan, 2003.

Garnham, David, and Mark A. Tessler. *Democracy, War and Peace in the Middle East.* Bloomington: Indiana University Press, 2000.

Ghadbian, Najib. *Democratization and the Islamist Challenge in the Arab World.* Boulder, Colo.: Westview Press, 1997.

Gheissari, Ali, and Vali Nasr. "Iran's Democracy Debate," *Middle East Policy,* vol. 11, no. 2 (2004): 94–106.

Hamarneh, Mustafa. "Democratization in the Mashreq: The Role of External Factors," *Mediterranean Politics,* vol. 5, no. 1 (Spring 2000): 77–95.

Harris, William. *Challenges to Democracy in the Middle East.* Princeton, N.J.: Markus Wiener Publishers, 1997.

Hassouna, Hussein A. "Arab Democracy: The Hope," *World Policy Journal,* vol. 18, no. 3 (Fall 2001): 49–52.

Haynes, Jeff. *Democracy in the Developing World: Africa, Asia, Latin America, and the Middle East.* Cambridge, U.K.: Polity Press, 2001.

Herb, Michael. "Princes and Parliaments in the Arab World," *Middle East Journal,* vol. 58, no. 3 (Summer 2004): 367–84.

Heydemann, Steven. "Defending the Discipline," *Journal of Democracy,* vol. 13, no. 3 (July 2002): 102–08.

———. "Is the Middle East Different?" *Journal of Democracy,* vol. 7, no. 2 (April 1996): 171–75.

Hourani, Albert. *The Modern Middle East.* London: I. B. Tauris, 2003.

Hudson, Michael C. "The Middle East," *PS: Political Science & Politics,* vol. 34, no. 4 (December 2001): 801–04.

Hudson, Michael C., ed. "The Middle East Dilemma: The Politics and Economics of Arab Integration," *Peace Research Abstracts,* vol. 38, no. 3 (2001).

Ibrahim, Saad Eddin. "Future Visions of the Arab Middle East," *Security Dialogue,* vol. 27, no. 4 (December 1996): 425–36.

———. "An Open Door," *Wilson Quarterly,* vol. 28, no. 2 (Spring 2004): 36–46.

———. "Reviving Middle Eastern Liberalism," *Journal of Democracy,* vol. 14, no. 4 (October 2003): 5–10.

Imad-ad-Dean, Ahmad. *Building Muslim Civil Society from the Bottom Up.* Bethesda, Md.: Minaret of Freedom Institute, 2000.

International Crisis Group. "The Challenge of Political Reform: Egypt after the Gulf War," *ICG Middle East Briefing* (September 30, 2003).

————. "The Challenge of Political Reform: Jordanian Democratization and Regional Instability," *ICG Middle East Briefing* (October 8, 2003).

International IDEA. *Democracy in the Arab World: Challenges, Achievements and Prospects.* Stockholm: International IDEA, 2000.

Jahanbakhsh, Forough. *Islam, Democracy and Religious Modernism in Iran (1953-1997) from Bazargan to Soroush.* Ottawa: National Library of Canada, 2000.

Kamrava, Mehran. "Military Professionalism and Civil-Military Relations in the Middle East," *Political Science Quarterly*, vol. 115, no. 1 (Spring 2000): 67–92.

————. *Democracy in the Balance: Culture and Society in the Middle East.* New York: Chatham House Publishers, 1998.

Kassem, Maye. *Egyptian Politics: The Dynamics of Authoritarian Rule.* Boulder, Colo.: Lynne Rienner, 2004.

Keddie, Nikki R. "A Woman's Place: Democratization in the Middle East," *Current History*, vol. 103, no. 669 (January 2004): 25–30.

Kienle, Eberhard. *A Grand Delusion: Democracy and Economic Reform in Egypt.* London: I. B. Tauris, 2001.

King, Stephen J. *Liberalization against Democracy: The Local Politics of Economic Reform in Tunisia.* Bloomington: Indiana University Press, 2003.

Klein, Menachem. "By Conviction, Not by Infliction: The Internal Debate over Reforming the Palestinian Authority," *Middle East Journal*, vol. 57, no. 2 (Spring 2003): 194–212.

Korany, Bahgat, Rex Brynen, and Paul Noble. *Political Liberalization and Democratization in the Arab World: Volume 2.* Boulder, Colo.: Lynne Rienner, 1998.

Kubba, Laith. "The Awakening of Civil Society," *Journal of Democracy*, vol. 11, no. 3 (July 2000): 84–90.

Kurtz, Stanley. "Democratic Imperialism: A Blueprint," *Policy Review*, (April/May 2003): 3–21.

Langhor, Vickie. "An Exit from Arab Autocracy," *Journal of Democracy*, vol. 13, no. 3 (July 2002): 116–22.

Layachi, Azzedine. *Civil Society and Democratization in Morocco.* Cairo: Ibn Khaldun Center, 1995.

Lewis, Bernard. "Middle East, Westernized Despite Itself," *Middle East Quarterly*, vol. 3, no. 1 (March 1996): 53–61.

———. *What Went Wrong? Western Impact and Middle Eastern Response.* New York: Oxford University Press, 2002.

Lynch, Marc. "Taking Arabs Seriously," *Foreign Affairs*, vol. 82, no. 5 (September/October 2003): 81–94.

Magnarella, Paul J. *Middle East and North Africa: Governance, Democratization, Human Rights.* Aldershot, U.K.: Ashgate, 1999.

Malek-Ahmadi, Farshad. *Trapped by History: 100 Years of Struggle for Constitutionalism and Democracy in Iran.* London: Routledge, 2003.

Marquand, David, and Ronald L. Nettler. *Religion and Democracy.* Oxford: Blackwell, 2000.

Mohammadi, Ali. *Iran Encountering Globalization: Problems and Prospects.* London: RoutledgeCurzon, 2003.

Momayezi, Nasser. "The Struggle for Democracy in the Middle East," *International Studies*, vol. 34, no. 1 (January-March 1997): 24–38.

Niblock, Tim. "Democratization: A Theoretical and Practical Debate," *British Journal of Middle Eastern Studies*, vol. 25, no. 2 (June 1999): 221–34.

O'Sullivan, John. "Debating Democracy," *National Review*, vol. 55, no. 24 (December 22, 2003): 35–37.

Owen, Roger. *State, Power and Politics in the Making of a Modern Middle East.* New York: Routledge, 2004.

Pahlavi, Reza. *Winds of Change: The Future of Democracy in Iran.* Washington, D.C.: Regnery Publications, 2002.

Paidar, Parvin. *Gender of Democracy: The Encounter between Feminism and Reformism in Contemporary Iran.* Geneva: United Nations, Research Institute for Social Development, 2001.

Perthes, Volker. *Arab Elites: Negotiating the Politics of Change.* Boulder, Colo.: Lynne Rienner, 2004.

Peterson, J. E. "Oman: Three and a Half Decades of Change and Development," *Middle East Policy*, vol. 11, no. 2 (Summer 2004): 107–24.

Pollack, Kenneth M., with Daniel L. Byman. *Democracy in the Middle East: Democracy as Realism.* London: Prospect, 2003.

Quandt, William. "The Middle East on the Brink: Prospects of Change in the 21st Century," *Middle East Journal*, vol. 50, no. 1 (Winter 1996): 9–17.

Rimanelli, Marco. *Comparative Democratization and Peaceful Change in Single-Party Dominated Countries.* New York: St. Martin's Press, 1999.

Robinson, Glenn E. "Defensive Democratization in Jordan," *International Journal of Middle East Studies*, vol. 30, no. 3 (August 1998): 387–411.

Ross, Michael Lewin. "Does Oil Hinder Democracy?" *World Politics*, vol. 53, no. 3 (April 2001): 325–61.

Roy, Sara. "Hamas and the Transformation(s) of Political Islam in Palestine," *Current History*, vol. 102, no. 660 (January 2003): 13–20.

Rubin, Barry, ed. *Revolutionaries and Reformers: Contemporary Islamist Movements in the Middle East*. Albany: State University of New York Press, 2003.

Ryan, Curtis R., and Jillian Schwedler. "Return to Democratization or New Hybrid Regime? The 2003 Elections in Jordan," *Middle East Policy*, vol. 11, no. 2 (Summer 2004): 138–51.

Sachedina, Abdulaziz. *The Islamic Roots of Democratic Pluralism*. Oxford: Oxford University Press, 2001.

Sadiki, Larbi. "Popular Uprisings and Arab Democratization," *International Journal of Middle East Studies*, vol. 32, no. 1 (February 2000): 71–95.

————. *Islamist Democracy: (Re)visions of Polity and Society in the Middle East*. London: Hurst, 2002.

————. *The Search for Arab Democracy: Discourses and Counter-Discourses*. London: Hurst, 2004.

Sadowski, James Y. "Prospects for Democracy in the Middle East: The Case of Kuwait," *Peace Research Abstracts*, vol. 37, no. 3 (2000).

Saikal, Amin, and Albrecht Schnabel, eds. *Democratization in the Middle East: Experiences, Struggles, Challenges*. Tokyo: United Nations University Press, 2003.

Salamé, Ghassan, ed. *Democracy without Democrats? The Renewal of Politics in the Muslim World*. London: I. B. Tauris, 1994.

Samii, A. William. "Iran's Guardian Council as an Obstacle to Democracy," *Middle East Journal*, vol. 55, no. 4 (Autumn 2001): 643–62.

Schenker, David. *Palestinian Democracy and Governance: An Appraisal of the Legislative Council*. Washington, D.C.: Washington Institute for Near East Policy, 2000.

Schlumberger, Oliver. "The Middle East and the Question of Democratization: Some Critical Remarks," *Democratization*, vol. 7, no. 4 (Winter 2000): 104–32.

Sivan, Emmanuel. "The Clash within Islam," *Survival*, vol. 45, no. 1 (Spring 2003): 25–44.

Smock, David. *Islam and Democracy*. Washington, D.C.: U.S. Institute of Peace, 2002.

Souresrafil, Omid. *Revolution in Iran: The Transition to Democracy*. London: Pluto, 2001.

Stepan, Alfred C., with Graeme B. Robertson. "An 'Arab' More than a 'Muslim' Democracy Gap," *Journal of Democracy*, vol. 14, no. 3 (July 2003): 30–44.

Takeyh, Ray. "Faith Based Initiatives: Can Islam Bring Democracy to the Middle East?" *Foreign Policy* (November/December 2001): 68–70.

————. "The Lineaments of Islamic Democracy," *World Policy Journal*, vol. 18, no. 4 (Winter 2001/2002): 59–67.

Talbi, Mohamed. "A Record of Failure," *Journal of Democracy*, vol. 11, no. 3 (July 2000): 58–68.

Tamimi, Azzam. "Middle East Democracy: Forbidden Fruit," *World Today*, vol. 59, no. 1 (2003): 4–6.

Tessler, Mark. "Islam and Democracy in the Middle East: The Impact of Religious Orientations on Attitudes toward Democracy in Four Arab Countries," *Comparative Politics*, vol. 34, no. 3 (2002): 337–55.

Tetreault, Mary Ann. "Patterns of Culture and Democratization in Kuwait," *Washington Report on Middle East Affairs*, vol. 30, no. 2 (Summer 1995): 26–46.

————. *Politics and Society in Contemporary Kuwait*. New York: Columbia University Press, 2000.

Walsh, John. "Egypt's Muslim Brotherhood: Understanding Centrist Islam," *Harvard International Review*, vol. 24, no. 4 (Winter 2003): 32–36.

Wickham, Carrie Rosefsky. "The Path to Moderation: Strategy and Learning in the Formation of Egypt's Wasat Party," *Comparative Politics*, vol. 36, no. 2 (January 2004): 205–28.

Wiktorowicz, Quintan. "The Limits of Democracy in the Middle East: The Case of Jordan," *Middle East Journal*, vol. 53, no. 4 (Autumn 1999): 606–20.

Wiktorowicz, Quintan, ed. *Islamic Activism: A Social Movement Theory Approach*. Bloomington: Indiana University Press, 2004.

World Bank. *Better Governance for Development in the Middle East and North Africa*. Washington, D.C.: September 2003.

Xuejiang, Li. "Democracy and the Middle East," *World Press Review*, vol. 50, no. 7 (2003): 7–9.

Yetiv, Steve. "Kuwait's Democratic Experiment in Its Broader International Context," *Middle East Journal*, vol. 56, no. 2 (Spring 2002): 257–71.

Democracy Promotion in the Middle East

Afkhami, Mahnaz. "Promoting Women's Rights in the Muslim World," *Journal of Democracy*, vol. 8, no. 1 (January 1997): 157–66.

Alterman, Jon B. "The False Promise of Arab Liberals," *Policy Review*, no. 125 (June and July 2004): 77–86.

Blinken, Antony J. "Winning the War of Ideas," *Washington Quarterly*, vol. 25, no. 2 (Spring 2002): 101–14.

Brumberg, Daniel. "Beyond Liberalism?" *Wilson Quarterly*, vol. 28, no. 2 (Spring 2004): 47–55.

Carothers, Thomas. "The Clinton Record on Democracy Promotion," Carnegie Working Paper no. 16. Washington, D.C.: Carnegie Endowment for International Peace, 2000.

Carpacio, Sheila. "Foreign Aid for Promoting Democracy in the Middle East," *Middle East Journal*. vol. 56, no. 3 (Summer 2002): 379–96.

Daguzun, Jean-Francois. "France, Democratization and North Africa," *Democratization*, vol. 9, no. 1 (Spring 2002): 135–48.

Dillman, Bradford. "Round Up the Unusual Suspects: U.S. Policy towards Algeria and Its Islamists," *Middle East Policy*, vol. 8, no. 3 (September 2001): 126–44.

Feldman, Noah. *After Jihad: America and the Struggle for Islamic Democracy*. New York: Farrar, Straus and Giroux, 2003.

Freedman, Robert O. "U.S. Policy towards the Middle East in Clinton's Second Term," *Middle East Review of International Affairs*, vol. 3, no. 1 (March 1999).

Gerges, Fawaz. *America and Political Islam: Clash of Cultures or Clash of Interests?* Cambridge, U.K.: Cambridge University Press, 1999.

Haass, Richard. "Towards Greater Democracy in the Muslim World," *Washington Quarterly*, vol. 26, no. 3 (Summer 2003): 137–48.

Haddad, Yvonne Yazbeck, and John L. Esposito. *Muslims on the Americanization Path?* New York: New York University Press, 2000.

Halabi, Yakub. "Orientalism and US Democratization Policy in the Middle East," *International Studies*, vol. 36, no. 4 (October-December 1999): 375–92.

Hawthorne, Amy. "Can the United States Promote Democracy in the Middle East?" *Current History*, vol. 102, no. 660 (January 2003): 21–26.

Hibbard, Scott W., and David Little. *Islamic Activism and U.S. Foreign Policy*. Washington, D.C.: U.S. Institute of Peace, 1997.

Hoffman, David. "Beyond Public Diplomacy," *Foreign Affairs*, vol. 81, no. 2 (March/April 2002): 83–95.

Hudson, Michael C. "To Play the Hegemon: Fifty Years of U.S. Policy toward the Middle East," *Middle East Journal*, vol. 50, no. 3 (Summer 1996): 329–44.

———. "U.S.-Arab Relations: Imperial Headaches: Managing Unruly Regions in an Age of Globalization," *Middle East Policy*, vol. 9, no. 4 (2002): 61–74.

International Crisis Group. "The Broader Middle East Initiative: Imperiled at Birth," *ICG Middle East Briefing* (June 7, 2004).

Junemann, Annette. *Euro-Mediterranean Relations after September 11: International, Regional, and Domestic Dynamics*. Portland, Ore.: Frank Cass, 2003.

Khalidi, Rashid. *Resurrecting Empire: America and the Western Adventure in the Middle East*. Boston: Beacon Press, 2004.

Khan, M. A. Muqtedar. "Prospects for Muslim Democracy: The Role of U.S. Policy," *Middle East Policy*, vol. 10, no. 3 (Fall 2003): 79–89.

———. *Beyond Jihad and Crusade: A New Framework for U.S. Policy in the Islamic World*. Washington, D.C.: Brookings Institution Press, forthcoming.

Kibble, David G. "Monarchs, Mosques, and Military Hardware: A Pragmatic Approach to the Promotion of Human Rights and Democracy in the Middle East," *Comparative Strategy*, vol. 17, no. 4 (October 1998): 381–91.

Lesch, David W., ed. *The Middle East and the U.S.: A Historical and Political Reassessment*. Boulder, Colo.: Westview, 1999.

Lewis, Bernard. *The United States and the Middle East*. New York: Council on Foreign Relations, 2002.

Liotta, P. H., and James F. Miskel. "Dangerous Democracy? American Internationalism and the Greater Near East," *Orbis*, vol. 48, no. 3 (Summer 2004): 437–49.

Muravchik, Joshua. "Bringing Democracy to the Arab World," *Current History*, vol. 103, no. 669 (January 2004): 8–10.

Neep, Daniel. "Dilemmas of Democratization in the Middle East: The 'Forward Strategy of Freedom,'" *Middle East Policy*, vol. 11, no. 3 (Fall 2004): 73–84.

Ottaway, Marina, and Thomas Carothers. *Funding Virtue: Civil Society Aid and Democracy Promotion.* Washington, D.C.: Carnegie Endowment for International Peace, 2000.

Perthes, Völker. "America's 'Greater Middle East' and Europe: Key Issues for Dialogue," *Middle East Policy*, vol. 11, no. 3 (Fall 2004): 85–97.

Pinto, Maria do Céu. *Political Islam and the United States: A Study of U.S. Policy towards Islamist Movements in the Middle East.* Reading, U.K.: Ithaca Press, 1999.

Rose, James J. "The United States and the Challenge of Democratization in the Arab World/Islam, the West, and Jerusalem," *Australian Journal of International Affairs*, vol. 52, no. 3 (July 1998): 204–06.

Roy, Sara. "Role of Donor Aid," *Journal of Palestinian Studies*, Columbia International Affairs Online, 2001.

Rubin, Barry M. "What Is Right in U.S. Interests," *Washington Quarterly*, vol. 24, no. 3 (Summer 2001): 127–34.

Russillo, Victor L. *Reassessing U.S. Policy toward Iran.* Carlisle Barracks, Pa.: U.S. Army War College, 2003.

Takeyh, Ray. "Uncle Sam in the Arab Street," *National Interest*, no. 27 (Spring 2004): 45–51.

Takeyh, Ray, and Nikolas K. Gvosdev. "Democratic Impulses versus Imperial Interests: America's New Mid-East Conundrum," *Orbis*, vol. 47, no. 5 (Summer 2003): 415–31.

Walker, Martin. "The Democratic Mosaic," *Wilson Quarterly*, vol. 28, no. 2 (Spring 2004): 28–35.

Windsor, Jennifer L. "Promoting Democracy Can Combat Terrorism," *Washington Quarterly*, vol. 26, no. 3 (Summer 2003): 43–58.

Wittes, Tamara Cofman. "Arab Democracy, American Ambivalence: Will Bush's Rhetoric about Transforming the Middle East Be Matched by American Deeds?" *Weekly Standard*, vol. 9, no. 23 (February 23, 2004): 34–37.

_____. "The New U.S. Proposal for a Greater Middle East Initiative: An Evaluation," Middle East Memo no. 2. Washington, D.C.: Saban Center for Middle East Policy at the Brookings Institution, May 10, 2004.

————. "The Promise of Arab Liberalism," *Policy Review*, no. 125 (June and July 2004): 61–76.

Wood, Pia Christina. "French Foreign Policy and Tunisia: Do Human Rights Matter?" *Middle East Policy*, vol. 9, no. 2 (June 2002): 92–110.

Youngs, Richard. "European Approaches to Democracy Assistance: Learning the Right Lessons?" *Third World Quarterly*, vol. 24, no. 1 (2003): 127–38.

————. *The European Union and Democracy Promotion: The Case of North Africa*. With Richard Gillespie. London: Frank Cass, 2002.

————. "European Approaches to Security in the Mediterranean," *Middle East Journal*, vol. 57, no. 3 (Summer 2003): 414–31.

Zonis, Marvin, and Salman Farmanfarmaian. "All in the Timing: U.S.-Iran Relations," *Peace Research Abstracts*, vol. 38, no. 3 (2001).

Zoubir, Yahia H. "Algeria and U.S. Interests: Containing Radical Islamism and Promoting Democracy," *Middle East Policy*, vol. 9, no. 1 (March 2002): 64–81.

Democracy and Democracy Promotion in Iraq

Alterman, Jon B. "Not in My Backyard: Iraq's Neighbors' Interests," *Washington Quarterly*, vol. 26, no. 3 (Summer 2003): 149–60.

Barton, Frederick D., and Bathsheba Crocker. "Winning the Peace in Iraq," *Washington Quarterly*, vol. 26, no. 2 (Spring 2003): 7–22.

Benomar, Jamal. "Constitution-Making After Conflict: Lessons for Iraq," *Journal of Democracy*, vol. 15, no. 2 (April 2004): 81–95.

Brancati, Dawn. "Can Federalism Stabilize Iraq?" *Washington Quarterly*, vol. 27, no. 2 (Spring 2004): 7–21.

Byman, Daniel. "Constructing a Democratic Iraq: Challenges and Opportunities," *International Security*, vol. 28, no. 1 (Summer 2003): 47–78.

Byman, Daniel L., and Kenneth M. Pollack. "Democracy in Iraq?" *Washington Quarterly*, vol. 26, no. 3 (Summer 2003): 119–36.

Clawson, Patrick, ed. *How to Build a New Iraq after Saddam*. Washington, D.C.: Brookings Institution Press, 2002.

Danchev, Alex, and John McMillian. *The Iraq War and Democratic Politics*. New York: Routledge, 2004.

Dawisha, Adeed. "Iraq: Setbacks, Advances, Prospects," *Journal of Democracy*, vol. 15, no. 1 (January 2004): 5–20.

Dawisha, Adeed, and Karen Dawisha. "How to Build a Democratic Iraq," *Foreign Affairs*, vol. 82, no. 3 (May/June 2003): 36–50.

Diamond, Larry. "What Went Wrong in Iraq," *Foreign Affairs*, vol. 83, no. 5 (September/October 2004): 34–56.

Dobbins, James F. "America's Role in Nation Building from Germany to Iraq," *Survival*, vol. 45, no. 4 (Winter 2003): 87–109.

Dodge, Toby. "US Intervention and Possible Iraqi Futures," *Survival*, vol. 45, no. 3 (September 1, 2003): 103–22.

———. *Inventing Iraq: The Failure of Nation-Building and a History Denied*. New York: Columbia University Press, 2003.

Dodge, Toby, and Steven Simon, eds. "Iraq at the Crossroads: State and Society in the Shadow of Regime Change," Adelphi Paper no. 354. London: International Institute for Strategic Studies, 2003.

Ehteshami, Anoushiravan. "Iran-Iraq Relations after Saddam," *Washington Quarterly*, vol. 26, no. 4 (Autumn 2003): 115–29.

Esposito, John L. "Political Islam and the West," *Military Technology*, vol. 25, no. 2 (February 2001): 89–97.

Hashim, Ahmed. "The Sunni Insurgency in Iraq," *Perspective*, Middle East Institute (August 15, 2003): 1–37.

Hollis, Rosemary. "Getting Out of the Iraq Trap," *International Affairs*, vol. 79, no. 1 (2003): 23–35.

International Crisis Group. "Governing Iraq," *ICG Middle East Report*, no. 27 (August 25, 2003).

———. "Iraq's Kurds: Toward an Historic Compromise?" *ICG Middle East Report*, no. 26 (April 8, 2004).

———. "Iraq's Transition: On a Knife Edge," *ICG Middle East Report*, no. 27 (April 27, 2004).

Kemp, Geoffrey. "Losing the Peace?" *National Interest*, vol. 76 (Summer 2004): 46–48.

Makiya, Kanan. "A Model for Post-Saddam Iraq," *Journal of Democracy*, vol. 14, no. 3 (July 2003): 5.

Miller, Debra. *Iraq*. San Diego, Calif.: Greenhaven Press, 2004.

Nader, Laura. "Iraq and Democracy," *Anthropological Quarterly*, vol. 76, no. 3 (Summer 2003): 479–83.

Nasr, Vali. "Regional Implications of Shia Revival in Iraq," *Washington Quarterly*, vol. 27, no. 3 (Summer 2004): 7–24.

Ottaway, Marina, and Thomas Carothers. "The Right Road to Sovereignty in Iraq," Policy Brief no. 27. Washington, D.C.: Carnegie Endowment for International Peace, October 2003.

Pollack, Kenneth M. "After Saddam: Assessing the Reconstruction of Iraq," Saban Center Analysis Paper no. 1. Washington, D.C.: Brookings Institution, January 7, 2004.

————. *The Threatening Storm: The Case for Invading Iraq*. New York: Random House, 2002.

Ricciardone, Francis J., Jr. "Supporting a Transition to Democracy in Iraq," *Middle East Policy*, vol. 7, no. 4 (October 2000): 141–44.

Salmoni, Barak. "America's Iraq Strategy: Democratic Chimeras, Regional Realities," *Current History*, vol. 103, no. 669 (January 2004): 17–20.

Satloff, Robert, John L. Esposito, and Shibley Telhami. "Foreign Policy Debate: Propaganda, the Satans, and Other Misunderstandings," *SAIS Review*, vol. 21, no. 2 (Summer 2001): 139–54.

Vesely, Milan. "Debunking the Domino Theory," *Middle East*, no. 334 (May 2003): 20–21.

Vinjamuri, Leslie. "Order and Justice in Iraq," *Survival*, vol. 45, no. 4 (Winter 2003–2004): 135–52.

von Hippel, Karin. "Forgotten Lessons in Iraq." Madrid: Foundation for International Relations and External Dialogue (FRIDE), May 2004.

Walker, Martin, Saad Eddin Ibrahim, Daniel Brumberg, et al. "Ready for Democracy?" *Wilson Quarterly*, vol. 28, no. 2 (2004): 27–64.

Wimmer, Andreas. "Democracy and Ethno-Religious Conflict in Iraq," *Survival*, vol. 45, no. 4 (Winter 2003–2004): 111–34.

Yaphe, Judith. "War and Occupation in Iraq: What Went Right? What Could Go Wrong?" *Middle East Journal*, vol. 57, no. 3 (Summer 2003): 381–99.

Index

Contributors

Eva Bellin is associate professor in the Department of Political Science at Hunter College/City University of New York. An expert on the political economy of the Arab world, she is the author of *Stalled Democracy: Capital, Labor, and the Paradox of State-Sponsored Development* (Ithaca: Cornell University Press, 2002). She was previously associate professor in the Department of Government at Harvard University.

Daniel Brumberg is associate professor in the Department of Government at Georgetown University. From 2002 to 2004 he was visiting scholar and then senior associate in the Carnegie Endowment's Democracy and Rule of Law Project. He is the author of *Reinventing Khomeini: The Struggle for Reform in Iran* (University of Chicago, 2001), as well as many articles on political and social change in the Middle East and wider Islamic world.

Thomas Carothers directs the Democracy and Rule of Law Project at the Carnegie Endowment for International Peace. He has worked on democracy promotion programs with many U.S. and European organizations and written extensively on the subject, including *Aiding Democracy Abroad: The Learning Curve* (Carnegie Endowment, 1999) and *Critical Mission: Essays on Democracy Promotion* (Carnegie Endowment, 2004).

Michele Dunne is editor of the Carnegie Endowment's *Arab Reform Bulletin* and visiting assistant professor in the Department of Arabic Language at Georgetown University. She previously served for many years in the Department of State with assignments at the National Security

Council staff, the Secretary of State's Policy Planning Staff, the U.S. Embassy in Cairo, and the U.S. Consulate General in Jerusalem.

Graham Fuller is a former vice-chair of the National Intelligence Council at the U.S. Central Intelligence Agency, a former senior political scientist at RAND, and currently an independent writer and analyst. He is the author of many books and articles on the Muslim world. His latest book is *The Future of Political Islam* (New York: Palgrave, 2003).

Amy Hawthorne, a specialist in Arab politics and democracy promotion, was previously an associate in the Democracy and Rule of Law Project at the Carnegie Endowment for International Peace and editor of the Carnegie Endowment's *Arab Reform Bulletin*. She has also served as senior program officer for the Middle East at the International Foundation for Election Systems.

Marina Ottaway is a senior associate in the Carnegie Endowment's Democracy and Rule of Law Project and adjunct professor at the Johns Hopkins School of Advanced International Studies. She has written widely on African politics, democracy promotion, Middle East politics, and state reconstruction. Her most recent book is *Democracy Challenged: The Rise of Semi-Authoritarianism* (Carnegie Endowment, 2003).

Richard Youngs is a researcher at the Fundacion para las Relaciones Internacionales y el Dialogo Exterior (FRIDE) in Madrid, and lecturer in the Department for Politics and International Studies, University of Warwick, U.K. He has previously worked in the British Foreign and Commonwealth Office and coordinated an EU project on democracy promotion. He is author of *The European Union and the Promotion of Democracy* (Oxford University Press, 2001) and *International Democracy and the West* (Oxford University Press, 2004).